D0490048

THE MEREHURST BOOK OF

Needlework

THE MEREHURST BOOK OF

Needlework

with contributions from

JULIA BARTON, PAT EARNSHAW, BARBARA AND ROY HIRST,
ANNE ANDREW, JUNE LINSLEY, PEGGY FIELD,
GAIL HARKER, DOROTHY OSLER, PAULINE BROWN, ENID MASON
AND DIANA BRINTON

Published in 1993 by Merehurst Limited
Ferry House, 51–57 Lacy Road, Putney, London SW15 1PR

ISBN 1-85391-109-7

A catalogue record for this book is available from the British Library.

Edited by Diana Brinton
Designed by Bill Mason
Photography by Stewart Grant, unless specified to the contrary.
Diagrams by Lindsay Blow and Kate Simunek

Typesetting by Rowland Phototypesetting Limited
Bury St Edmunds, Suffolk

Colour separation by Scantrans, Singapore

Printed in Hong Kong by Leefung-Asco Printers Ltd

CONTENTS

The Wizard of Oz *was designed and made by Alison Bramley. Size: 240cm (96in) in diameter.*

Introduction

Over the past few decades an amazing transformation has taken place in the textile crafts, which have become one of the most active, rapidly developing and exciting fields of contemporary art. In the past regarded often with a considerable degree of condescension as 'women's work', hand and machine embroidery, quilting, patchwork and appliqué have now come into their own as vehicles for conveying not only the visual impact of things but also the essential feel of them. Amateurs and artists, the highly skilled and complete beginners, all have benefited from this new look at traditional skills.

An essential part of this reappraisal of the value of textile arts has been a willingness to experiment. The contemporary embroiderer or quilt designer is not satisfied merely with copying traditional patterns in the time-honoured way, or even devising new designs in the traditional style. New fabrics, new threads, new dyes and colouring media that can be used at home – all these have proved a source of inspiration and at the same time have spurred people on to develop techniques to cope with these materials or to adapt old techniques to different uses.

Three-dimensional butterflies and moths were worked by hand. Couched gold threads were used to support the applied details.

This book contains a comprehensive survey of contemporary skills of embroidery, by hand and machine, and also of patchwork, appliqué and quilting. Stitches, methods and techniques are all clearly demonstrated with step-by-step photographs or artworks. The skills include the simple and basic techniques that a beginner must acquire before moving on to more complex work as well as approaches and techniques that will be of value to the more experienced needlewoman.

Few people have a complete mastery of all the crafts shown here, yet one of the chief aspects of contemporary work is that it incorporates different forms of needlework wherever and whenever the need arises. The same finished piece may therefore include both hand and machine embroidery, and perhaps some pieces of applied smocking as well as touches of quilting. One of the aims of this book, therefore, is to enable users to augment their palette of skills.

Many of the techniques shown have a long history, and the basic method of working remains the same even though a new approach may create an end result that looks far from traditional. In one of her stitch demonstrations, for example, Julia Barton shows how fly stitch, which is one of the oldest and simplest of stitches, can be used to create an embroidered picture simply by altering the sizes of the stitches, inverting some, and using a wide range of threads and textures. Similarly, Peggy Field and June Linsley demonstrate the versatility of canvas embroidery, and the attractive effects that even complete beginners can achieve if they approach this traditional form of embroidery with a fresh eye.

The value of experiment is seen in Anne Andrew's smocking samples, in which the gathering method and stitches are first shown in the traditional manner and then the work is reversed and the stitches are unseen, being used for their effect on the gathering lines, or the further examples in which the gathering lines are themselves deliberately distorted.

The attitude towards machine embroidery has also changed radically. Once seen chiefly as a speedy way of imitating hand embroidery and quilting effects, it has now come to fruition as an art form. Gail Harker shows how to achieve mastery of a whole range of both automatic and machine embroidery techniques, so that these can be used either to create finished embroideries or as an adjunct to other forms of needlecraft.

In the fields of patchwork, appliqué and quilting there is arguably a greater continuity between today's needlewomen and those of the past than between embroiderers past and present. The finest of the quilts made in the last century show a

Paddy Killer designed her Little Mermaid *cushion to match a counterpane. Sympathetic design elements are carried over to the cushion. The sun and hair are painted on with permanent paints.*

free and innovative approach to the use of form and colour which makes them appear at times startlingly contemporary. Nevertheless, techniques have changed and are still changing as new tools and materials become available. Dorothy Osler demonstrates both traditional and modern skills of patchwork and quilting, while Pauline Brown displays a wide range of appliqué techniques, and Enid Mason shows how contemporary artists successfully combine several of these techniques together with handmade papers and felts, as well as hand and machine embroidery.

There is much that we can learn from the embroiderers and quiltmakers of the past, particularly those who, in their day, combined a high degree of technical skill with a willingness to be adventurous and experimental in their approach. Their work remains to be treasured, respected and enjoyed, and it is hoped that this book will help users to achieve a technical mastery which will enable them to experiment and to create works of art for the delight of future generations.

Influenced by North American Indian and Peruvian imagery, Hilary Bower's Hunting Panel *features horses of dyed handmade paper on a background of dyed felt. Hand and machine stitchery in cotton and silks are also used to give variation to the surface. Embroidery was also worked on cold-water-soluble fabric, and the pieces were then stitched to the main panel. Gold dye and fabric paints embellish and pronounce certain areas.*

CHAPTER ONE

Hand Embroidery

Over the last couple of decades, the art of embroidery has changed dramatically, and today hand embroidery, transformed and revitalized, has become an invaluable tool of textile artists and designers. Combining traditional stitchery techniques with the wealth of new fabrics, threads and dyes that are now available, contemporary embroiderers convey colour, texture, and life in all its forms, from the delicacy of a flower in bloom to the humour of people observed in a crowd.

Many of the stitches favoured by contemporary embroiderers, and demonstrated here, are the same stitches that were used in the past for traditional styles, but with a new-found freedom and a willingness to innovate to create the desired effect, the end results can be totally different. Cross stitch, for example, is one of the earliest embroidery stitches and is still used in a wide range of ethnic and traditional styles, but it is also adapted by artists who use it randomly, combining it with other stitches and techniques to create effects far removed from the stylized counted-thread patterns.

The stitches shown here have been grouped under several individual headings, but a finished work of art might well contain surface embroidery, canvaswork, smocking and scraps of needlelace, as well as appliqué and quilting. The key to success is experiment – take a subject, such as a butterfly wing or a lichen-covered stone, and express it in different fabrics, dye techniques, threads and stitches. Another starting point is to select any stitch that appeals and vary it in as many ways as possible.

MATERIALS AND EQUIPMENT

A modern embroidery may incorporate many unusual objects – even, as in Ros Hills' *Summer in India*, on page 45, sweet wrappings – but specialist fabrics, needles and threads still have a major role to play.

Fabrics

Almost any fabric is potentially useful for embroidery. In fact, one of the most exciting aspects of embroidery today is the enormous range of fabrics available and the ingenious uses modern embroiderers find for them. Once you begin designing your own embroidery you will find yourself collecting and hoarding all sorts of materials, from old nylon stockings to upholstery fabric.

Broadly speaking, fabrics for embroidery can be divided into the following categories, depending upon their uses:

- background fabrics
- fabrics for appliqué
- evenweave fabrics.

Background fabrics

The most important consideration in choosing a background fabric is that it must be suitable for the type of embroidery that you are going to do.

For large panels and hangings, hessian (burlap) and heavy-duty furnishing fabrics are suitable. They will take the weight of whatever is applied to them; and some are sufficiently loosely woven to allow thick threads to be used.

For small panels, in which finer threads might be used, a lighter, more closely woven furnishing fabric or a plain-weave embroidery linen would be suitable.

Backgrounds for machine embroidery are typically closely woven fabrics, such as cotton poplin or calico (unbleached muslin).

Another fabric well suited to stitchery is felt. This is usually available from craft shops in a selection of colours, but it can also be obtained in white, specially prepared for dyeing, from some mail-order firms. It has a soft quality which is suitable for both hand and machine stitching.

Fabrics for appliqué

This category includes any fabric that can be applied to the background, either to add a different texture or, in the case of transparent fabrics, to create veiled or subtle relief effects. Almost any fabric can be used for appliqué, the only limitation being the weight of the background fabric, which must be firm enough to support the fabric applied to it.

Transparent fabrics, such as chiffon, net, voile and organza, can all be used to provide sheer layers in a design. They can be ruched and gathered before being sewn to the background, or they can be applied in flat layers to give shadowy effects. Slightly thicker fabrics, such as fine linen scrim, cotton scrim and medical gauze, can be pulled into holes before being applied over other layers of fabric.

Opaque fabrics are also very useful for appliqué, especially where specific textures are required. For instance, a piece of green satin or velvet might be chosen because it suggests the texture of a particular leaf; or a piece of thin, worn-looking leather might be suitable for interpreting part of a stone wall. The choice of fabric will depend on the texture required and on the use of the finished embroidery. Consideration must be given to the washability and general care of the fabric, particularly in the case of clothing or of household objects such as cushions and bed-covers.

Evenweave fabrics

This kind of fabric has the same number of threads per centimetre (or inch) in both directions – that is, in both warp and weft. It comes in various weights, from 14 to 36 threads per 2.5 cm (1 inch) and is usually of cotton or linen. Evenweave fabrics are used mainly for counted-thread techniques, in which it is important not only that the threads can be easily counted but also that they form a square grid, so that the patterns created by the stitches will not be distorted.

Single thread evenweave can be used for any counted-thread embroidery, and is especially suitable for drawn-thread work, pulled work and pattern darning. Double thread evenweave, such as the relatively coarse Aida cloth, is often used for cross-stitch and blackwork embroidery. A finer double evenweave fabric, called Hardanger fabric, is designed especially for the traditional Norwegian embroidery of that name.

This technique and the other counted-thread styles of embroidery lie outside the scope of this book; however, you may sometimes find evenweave fabrics useful as backgrounds for free stitchery or as materials for appliqué.

Threads

Almost any kind of thread can be used for embroidery today. The only restriction in choosing threads for working is that they should be suitable for the fabric and for the type of embroidery. It is worthwhile collecting together as many different threads as possible. Knitting yarn shops often have a basket containing ends of lines, which are usually a fraction of the original price. A friend who knits may also have some leftover yarn to spare. Some of the metallic yarns used in crochet and knitwear, depending on the fashion, can enliven the surface of your embroidery – as can the fine metallic threads intended for machine work.

Aim for the greatest possible variety: thick and thin, matt and shiny. If you store them according to colour, you will find them much more convenient to use than if stored according to type. Clear containers will make it easier to see what you've got. The big plastic jars used in sweet shops in Britain are ideal; see if the shopkeeper will let you have his empty ones.

You may not be fortunate enough to have a good specialist embroidery shop near you, but there are many mail-order companies, whose addresses are to be found in embroidery and craft magazines.

Wool threads

Tapestry wool This is a thick, matt thread traditionally used for canvas embroidery (needlepoint).
Crewel wool This strong, fine wool thread was traditionally used for crewel work. It can be used in several strands for canvas embroidery (needlepoint), but when used for surface stitchery, it gives a better effect when used singly.
Persian wool This consists of three easily separated strands of yarn, somewhat thicker than crewel and thinner than tapestry. It is used for both canvas and surface embroidery.

Cotton threads

Perlé cotton Also called *coton perlé* or pearl cotton, this thick, twisted, lustrous thread is lovely to use. It is available in three thicknesses, numbers 3, 5 and 8 (the finest). No. 5 is the most popular and comes in the greatest variety of colours.
Coton à broder This is a single thickness, smooth, lustrous thread which is particularly suitable for counted-thread work.
Stranded cotton (embroidery floss) This consists of six strands, which can be used singly or combined as required.
Soft (matte) embroidery cotton This is almost the only matt thread

Some of the many threads that can be used for embroidery. From upper left downwards: extra-fine ribbon, two reels of machine embroidery thread and one of silk thread, two skeins of perlé cotton, two skeins each of soft embroidery cotton and French crewel wool. From upper right downwards: two skeins of stranded cotton floss and one of stranded rayon thread, a skein of linen thread, two skeins of coton à broder, metallic embroidery thread, and one skein each of crewel wool, soft embroidery cotton, silk knitting yarn, Persian wool and tapestry wool.

in the cotton range. It is very thick and most effective for large-scale work.

Machine embroidery threads These are widely available in two thicknesses, sizes 30 and 50. No. 30 is the thicker of the two and easier to use.

Linen threads

Usually available from lacemakers' suppliers, these threads are traditionally used on evenweave linen for counted-thread work. The colour range is limited, but threads are easy to dye.

Silk threads

Silk buttonhole twist Unfortunately, this is almost impossible to find anymore, but if you have some left over from dressmaking, you might consider using it to add a bit of lustre.

Silk sewing thread This can be found in haberdashery (notions) departments. It is often used in machinery embroidery. A much larger range of silk threads in wonderful colours can be obtained from some mail-order suppliers.

Rayon threads

Hand embroidery threads These highly lustrous threads, some stranded and lightly spun and some single-filament, are available from some embroidery shops and mail-order companies.

Machine embroidery threads are also very shiny. These come in a large colour range, usually from a mail-order supplier.

Metal threads

A wide range of metal or metallic-looking threads can be used in embroidery. Some – though these tend to be rather expensive – are made from real silver or gold; some contain a proportion of one of these; some are made from alloys, and others are made from synthetics to imitate metals.

When looking for affordable metallic-looking threads, bear in mind knitting and crochet yarns, which frequently can be used to good effect, and tend to be much cheaper than embroidery threads. The finest metal embroidery threads can be stitched in the normal way, but others require special sewing techniques (see page 43). Traditionally, these threads were much used in ecclesiastical embroidery, but they are readily adapted to contemporary work.

Chinese or Japanese gold do not tarnish, being made from real gold leaf on paper, wrapped around a silk core (the Chinese is made from finer paper strips); cheaper substitutes are available.
Cords and twists are made from several threads twisted together, each ply being a metal spun around a silk core. They are used for outlining and in traditional ceremonial embroidery.
Crinkle comes in various thicknesses, its crinkled surface reflecting light at varied angles.
Passing is a strong thread, available in various thicknesses, with either a smooth or wavy finish.
Plate is a wide flat thread, with a smooth shiny surface.
Synthetic metal threads, which include lurex threads, can generally be used for stitching, though the heavier types, and knitting and crochet yarns, may need to be couched; they have the advantage of being washable.
Tambour is a fine metal thread that can be used for stitching.

Purls are another category of metal thread. These are made from wire coiled into a spring shape. Some can be couched in place; in other cases lengths are cut and then stitched down like beads.

Check is made from wire spun to give a sparkling effect; the type known as wire check is made from a heavier wire and is a deep yellow.
Bullion is the largest size of purl.
Pearl purl, also called bead purl, looks like a tiny row of beads.
Rough purl is made from round wire and has a matt surface.
Smooth purl is very shiny, being made from flat wire.

Majesty, *by Barbara and Roy Hirst, incorporates a wide range of raised work, metal thread and needlelace techniques.*

Sewing equipment

Scissors

Three pairs of scissors are essential: one large pair for cutting fabrics, one small, fine-pointed pair for cutting threads, and an old pair for cutting paper.

Needles

Crewel A sharp needle with a long eye, available in many sizes, suitable for a variety of threads.
Chenille A needle with a relatively large eye which (in the larger sizes) will take very thick threads. Also called a heavy embroidery needle.
Tapestry A needle with a blunt point, available in different thicknesses; used mainly in counted-thread work and canvas embroidery (needlepoint), but also for some free embroidery stitches.
Sharp A fine needle for use with sewing threads.
Between Similar to sharp, but comparatively short; often used for hand quilting.
Beading A very fine, long needle, used mainly for stitching on beads.
Rug A very large needle with a blunt point, for use on rug canvas.

Pins

Steel dressmakers' pins are the best to use. Glass-headed pins are longer and are very useful for thick fabrics and for quilting.

Fabric markers

Water-erasable marker Often called a 'quilters' pen', this can be used to mark the design directly onto the fabric. After the embroidery is worked, the marks are removed by sponging with water. Another type of pen, whose mark fades in the air, is better for delicate fabrics. In any case, these pens should be tested on the fabric before use.
Embroidery transfer pencil This is used for drawing the design onto paper; the design is then ironed off onto the fabric. Some of these pencils tend to smudge, and the mark is not always easy to remove; so this method must be used with caution.
Tailor's chalk This is an old-fashioned method of marking fabric, but it is still very useful today, since the mark is easy to remove. It is normally used only for temporary marking before a more permanent mark, such as basting is made.

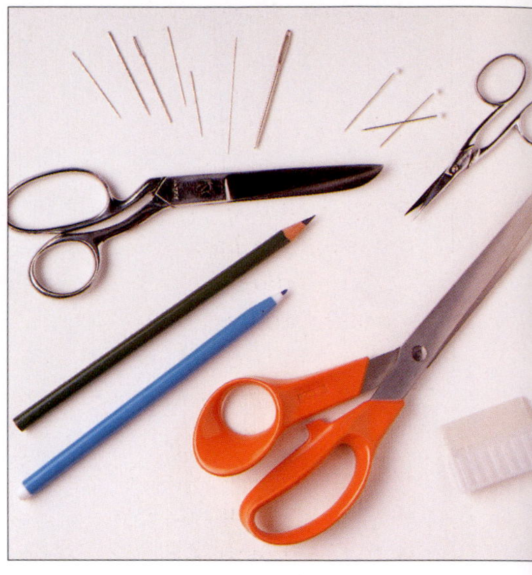

A selection of sewing equipment including needles (from left, crewel, chenille, tapestry, sharp, between, beading and rug), an embroidery transfer pencil, a water-erasable marker and tailor's chalk.

Using frames

For most types of embroidery, you will need to use a frame, in order to hold the fabric taut. Frames vary considerably in size, type and price; the choice of frame in a particular case will depend on the type of embroidery being worked. It is advisable, in hand embroidery, to choose a frame that will accommodate the whole area to be embroidered. This enables work to progress on the whole piece at once and prevents the work from becoming marked or creased by the frame.

Hoop or tambour frames are particularly useful for machine embroidery and small pieces of hand stitching. The traditional tambour frame consists of two wooden rings, the outer ring having a tightening screw to enable the fabric to be gripped tightly. Some tambour frames are equipped with a clamp which is attached to a table, leaving both hands free for working. Another type has a flat base on which the embroiderer sits. Standing tambour frames are also available.

Stretcher frames These consist of four strips of wood joined to form a rectangle. The simplest type can be made from four strips of fairly soft wood, such as pine, measuring about 2.5 by 1.5 cm (1 by ½ in) in section. These are joined with wood glue and held rigid by four flat right-angle brackets. A slightly more sophisticated version has mitred corners, which are glued and nailed together like a picture frame. In art supply shops you can buy canvas stretchers with mitred corners, which are slotted together. Alternatively, an old picture frame can be used.

Slate frames, also called *scroll frames*, are adjustable wooden frames. They vary slightly in their construction, but a common type consists of two rollers with webbing attached and two strips or laths which hold the rollers at the chosen distance. Although the work cannot be wider than the length of the webbing strips, it can be longer than the side strips; the excess is rolled over the rollers and then unrolled as required. Some slate frames can be attached to a table or floor stand. The method of mounting the fabric (see page 21) allows it to be re-tautened if necessary.

The three basic types of embroidery frame: an adjustable slate frame, a rectangular frame made from canvas stretchers, and a ring frame with an adjustable screw.

Hoop frames

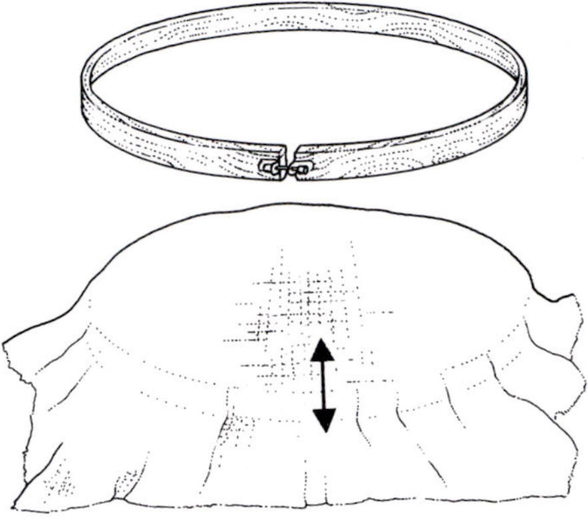

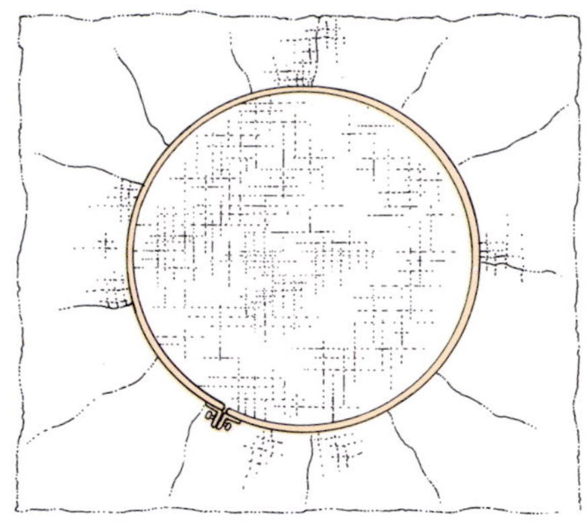

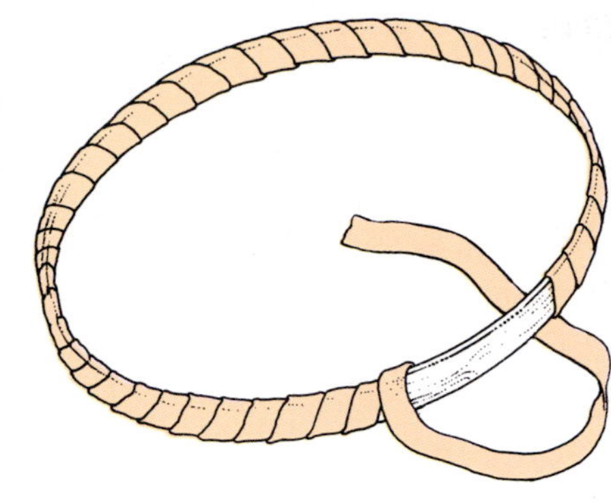

1 To dress a hoop frame – in other words, put the backing or background fabric in the frame – first adjust the screw of the outer frame so that it fits loosely over the inner ring. Lay the inner ring on a flat surface and cover it with the fabric, face up.

2 Press the outer ring over the fabric and the inner ring, ensuring that the warp and weft are at right angles. If not, repeat the process. (It is not advisable to pull the fabric once it has been mounted.) Tighten the screw to secure the fabric.

3 To protect delicate fabrics, the inner ring should be bound diagonally with bias seam binding along its entire length. The ring must be completely covered and the two ends of seam binding stitched firmly together.

Stretcher frames

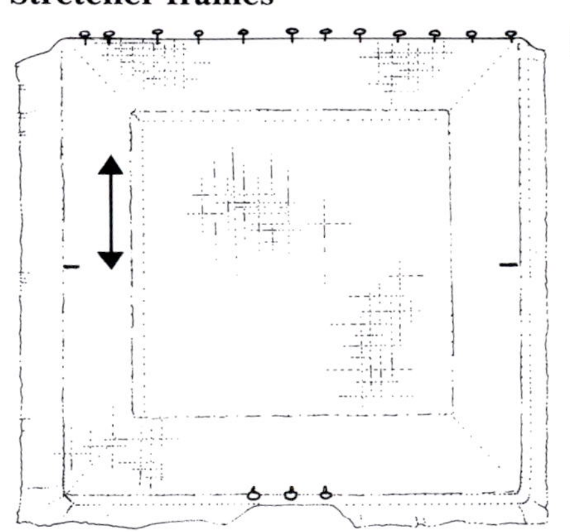

1 To dress a stretcher frame, the fabric to be stretched should be cut on the straight grain and should be slightly larger than the frame. Mark the centre point at each side of the frame and make corresponding marks on the fabric. Starting at the top edge, align the centre marks and secure the fabric to the frame with a drawing pin. Continue fastening with drawing pins at 12mm (½in) intervals, working out to the sides.

Turn the frame and fasten the fabric to the opposite edge in the same way, stretching the fabric taut.

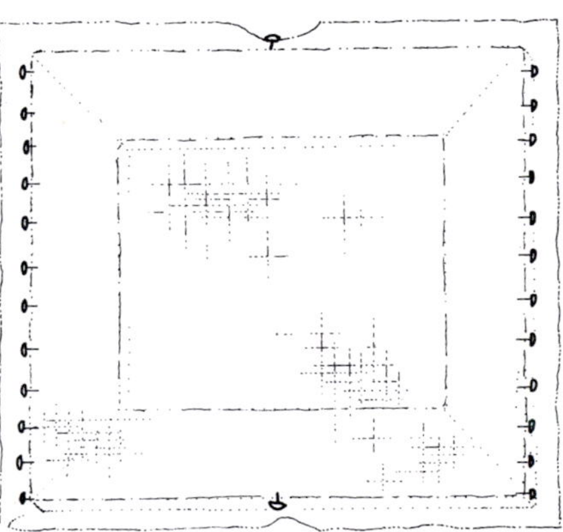

2 Secure the centre points at each side with drawing pins and continue working out towards the edges, pinning first one side and then the other. Check that the warp and weft threads are at right angles and that the fabric is stretched taut.

Slate frames

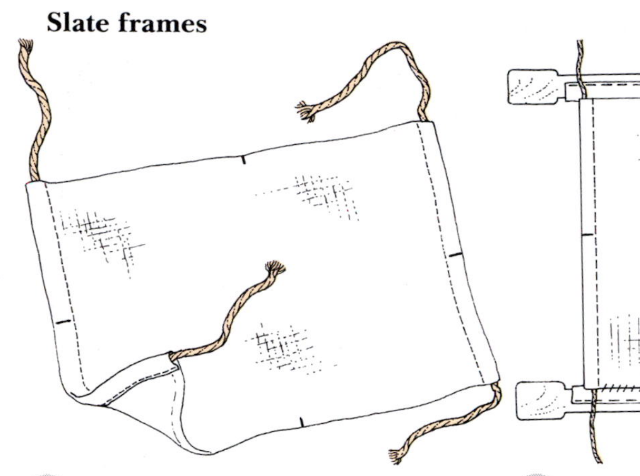

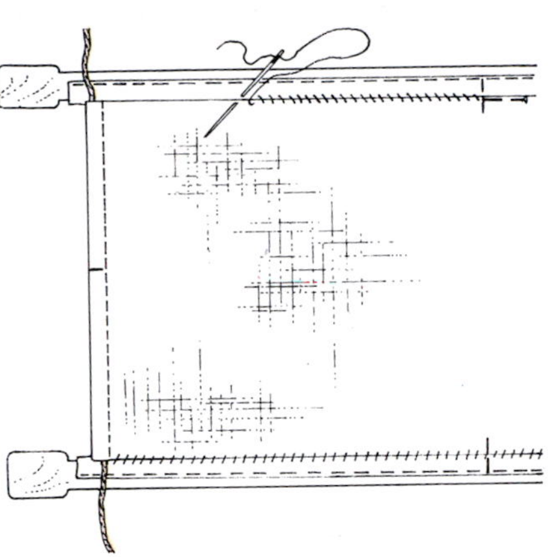

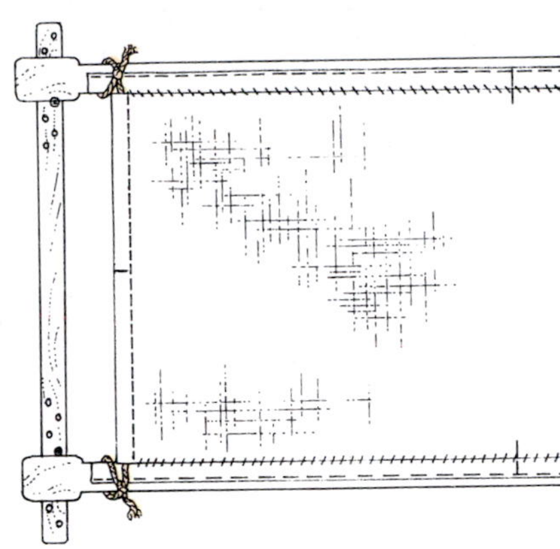

1. Mark the centre point at each side of the backing or background fabric, and press a 12mm (½in) hem on the top and bottom edges, then a 2.5cm (1in) hem on the side edges. Cut two lengths of string at least 50cm (20in) longer than the sides; place these inside the side hems and machine stitch a casing over each string.

2. With wrong sides together, align the centre points on the top and bottom edges of the fabric with those on the roller tape. Pin each edge in position and then firmly overcast fabric and tape together, using linen or doubled buttonhole twist.

3. Insert the side battens through the rollers and secure them with the pegs, stretching the fabric fairly taught. Tie the ends of the string to the rollers.

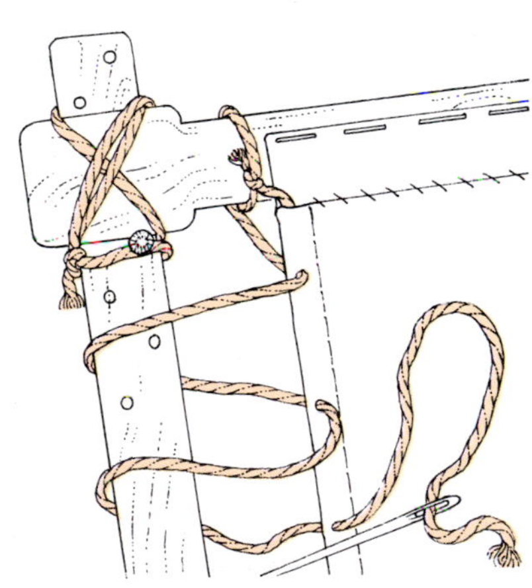

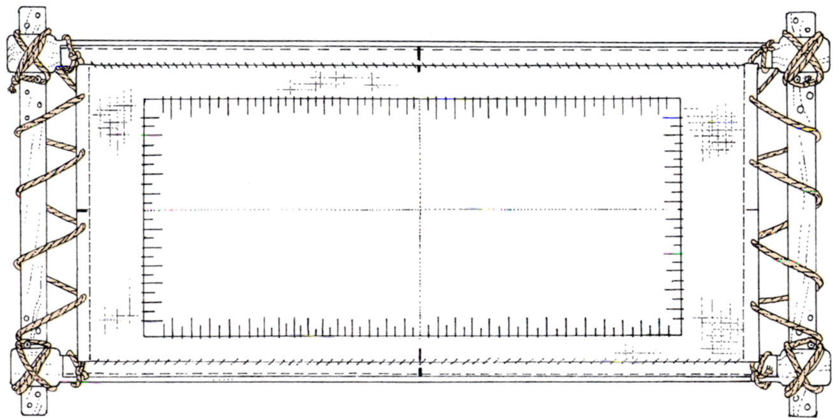

4. With a large-eyed needle, threaded with string, lace the sides of the fabric to the side battens, taking the lacing over the side and around the reinforcing strings. Pull the strings to tighten the fabric so that the sides are perpendicular to the top and bottom. Tie the string ends around the batten ends and the rollers.

5. To attach the embroidery background fabric to the stretched backing, slightly loosen the tension of the backing fabric and place the background fabric centrally on this, pinning at intervals. Overcast the raw edges with alternate long and short stitches to distribute the tension. Re-stretch, so that the fabric is taut.

EMBROIDERY STITCHES

As embroidery develops a freestyle and innovative approach it becomes increasingly difficult to classify and define stitches; in the hands of a contemporary textile artist, cross stitch may easily blend into long stitch or herringbone, for example, and the endlessly complex and confused attempts by the Victorians to identify and name every possible variation of the basic stitches have been thankfully abandoned. What is shown here are the simple stitches on which the variations are based, together with some of those variations, plus several embroidery techniques.

All of the above are used by contemporary embroiderers, though often in unusual ways and with non-traditional results. Buttonhole bars, for example, which are used to very delicate effect in traditional broderie anglaise or Richelieu embroidery, may be worked in chunky threads to suggest lichen-covered rocks (see page 35).

For convenience, the stitches and techniques demonstrated here have been grouped under various headings – basic embroidery stitches, needlelace, smocking and canvas embroidery. When practising individual stitches, however, remember that many can be adapted to a range of techniques, even in traditional embroidery. Cross stitch, for example, can be a canvaswork stitch, but is used in many ethnic embroideries the world over and can be worked freestyle. Feather stitch is shown here under smocking, but is a common embroidery stitch.

In any case, contemporary embroiderers mix techniques, stitches and needlework skills as the need arises, so if you are practising a particular stitch, experiment to see if it can be adapted to a different genre. French knots are commonly thought of as surface embroidery stitches, but they blend beautifully either with canvaswork, where they can often soften a harsh division between colours and add surface texture and a sense of depth, or with smocking, where they can be used for delicate highlights or points of interest. Elements of needlelace may well be combined with surface stitchery, machine embroidery, and painting and dyeing techniques in a single finished work.

Always try out the same stitch in a wide range of threads – the effect may change dramatically with different thread thicknesses, and the use of a range of threads can often add a three-dimensional quality to an embroidery.

Independent View, *by Rosemary Campbell, captures the mood of the unspoilt country around Arbroath and expresses the freedom felt when the individual is at one with his or her surroundings. The panel is composed of two small landscapes within a greater viewpoint of windswept sand dunes. It has two layers, the lower one using handmade felt, machine embroidery, appliqué and collage, and the upper employing collage, handmade paper, silk painting, freehand stitching and shadow work. Long straight stitches create the feeling of rough grass on the dunes.*

Linear stitches

Linear stitches are important in giving a sense of movement and rhythm to a piece of embroidery. They can achieve different effects by the direction in which they are used. Vertical lines tend to suggest a thrusting, upward movement, as in the growth of plants in early spring. Horizontal lines give a feeling of calm and repose, which can be employed effectively in seascapes and in landscapes featuring farmland, for example. The shape of the lines is important: curved lines can suggest undulating waves or rolling hills; straight lines have a harder,

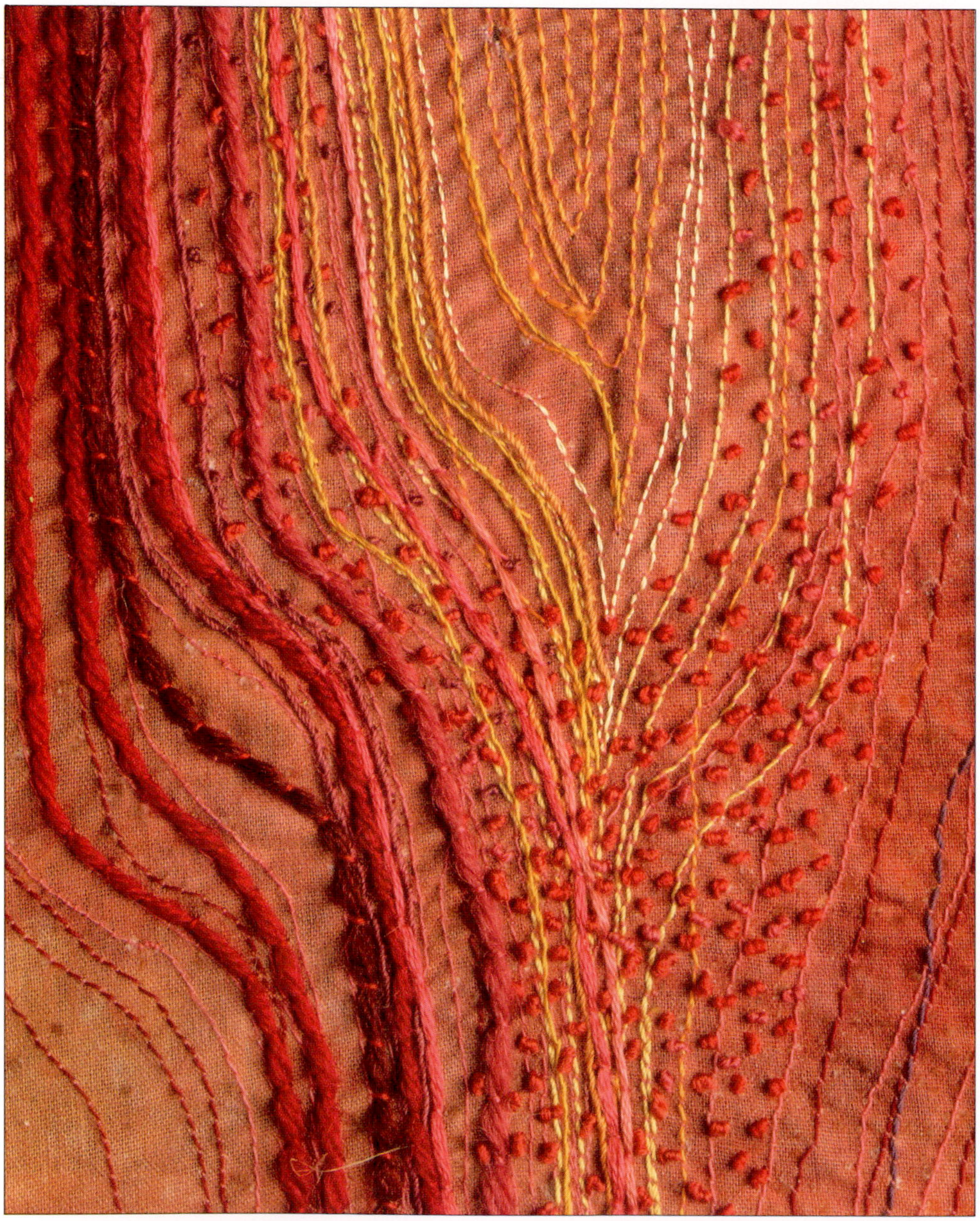

Running stitch

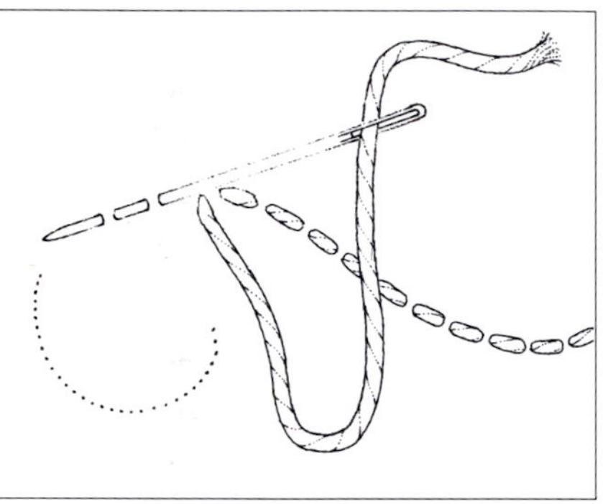

Perhaps the simplest stitch of all – but still one of the most frequently used, it consists simply of short stitches of equal length, with only a few threads of the background fabric picked up between stitches. It is often used to outline shapes, giving definition, and in various styles of embroidery, such as broderie anglaise, it is used to surround motifs before they are buttonholed and cut away.

spiky feeling, reminiscent of icicles or streaks of lighting. The spacing of lines also needs careful consideration. They will look best if some are grouped close together and others spaced farther apart. The use of different threads, such as knitting yarns, ribbons and strips of fabric, as well as fine embroidery threads, can all help to give the work the necessary variety and textural interest.

The simplest of all stitches is running stitch, but even with this it is possible to achieve subtle effects, by altering the length and spacing of stitches on adjacent rows, for example.

Double running stitch

Also known as Holbein stitch, this is worked over counted threads on evenweave fabric and is much used in cross stitch designs and in blackwork, which was a very popular embroidery style in Elizabethan times.

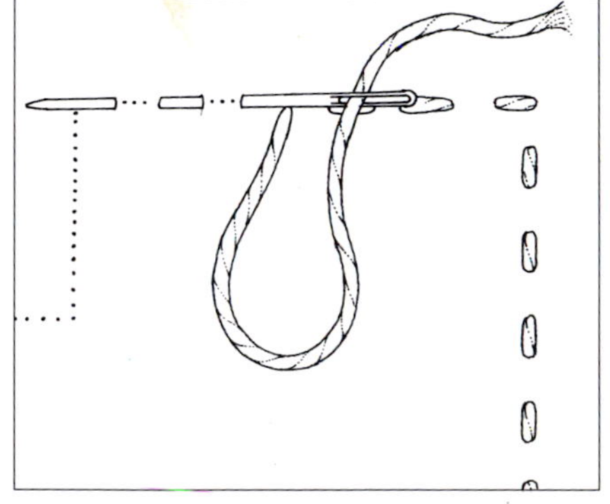

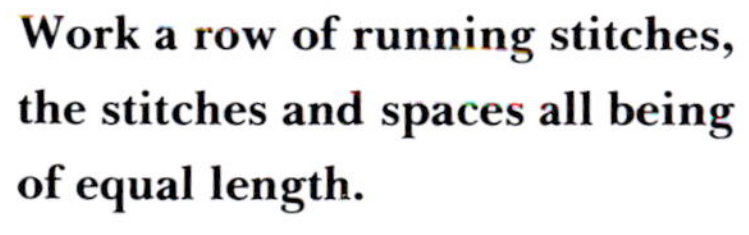

1 **Work a row of running stitches, the stitches and spaces all being of equal length.**

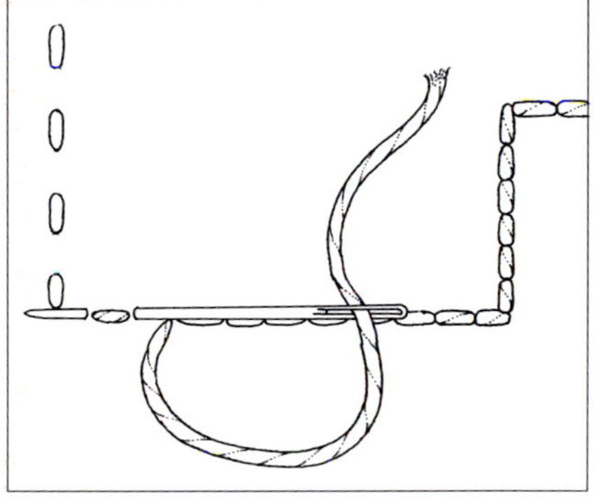

2 **When the first line is completed, return along the row, filling in the spaces.**

Back stitch

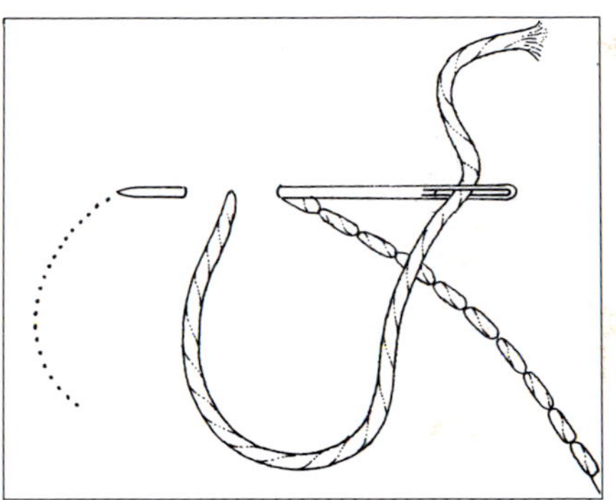

Bring the needle up a short distance from the beginning of the stitching line. Insert it again at the beginning of the line, bringing it out beyond the starting point. You can vary the length of the stitches; another variation is to work from the wrong side of the fabric, so that the stitches overlap slightly on the front.

Stem stitch

Especially useful, as the name implies, for representing stems, this has an attractive rope-like quality.

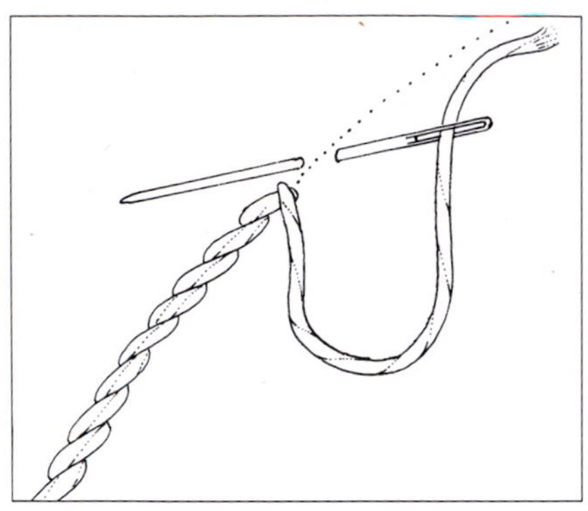

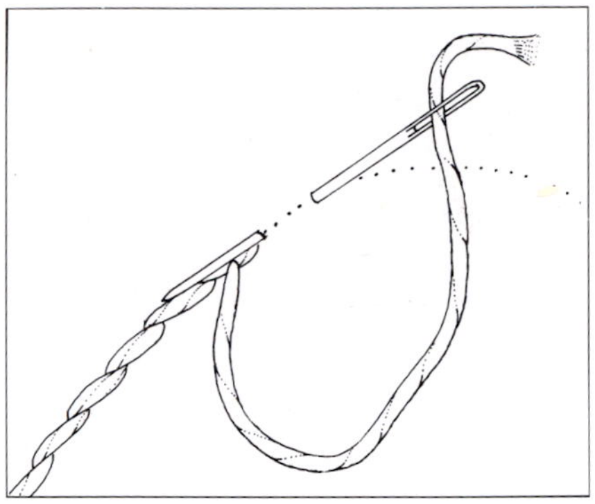

1 **For a broad stem, bring the needle up at the start of the line; take it forward and insert it slightly to the right of the line, keeping the thread to the right side of the needle. Bring it up slightly to the left of the marked line, halfway along the first stitch.**

2 **For a narrower effect, take the needle up and down directly on the line.**

Although normally thought of as a linear stitch, stem stitch can also be used as a filling stitch, creating a solid, woven effect.

Split stitch

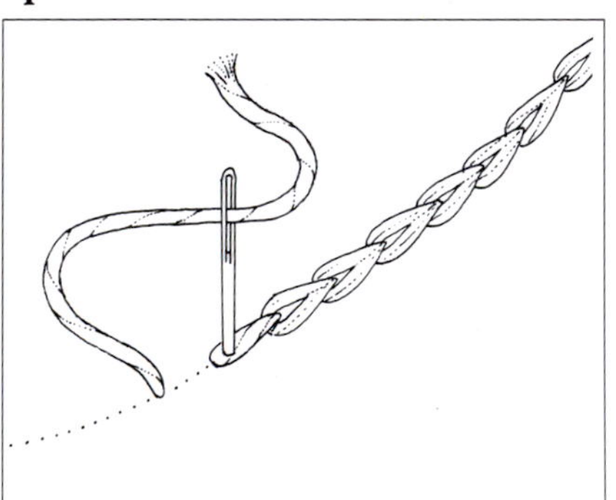

This can also be used either as an outline or as a filling stitch. It is similar to stem stitch, but the needle splits the thread of the previous stitch as it comes up through the fabric, creating the effect of a narrow chain stitch.

Outline stitch

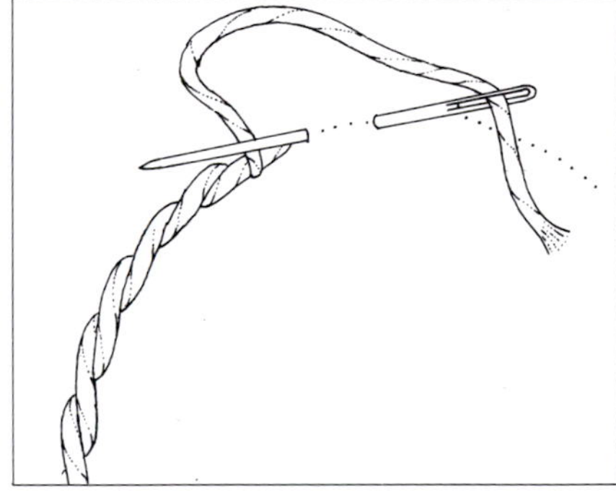

This is similar to stem stitch, but the thread is kept above the needle, and the stitches slant in the opposite direction to stem stitching.

Herringbone stitch

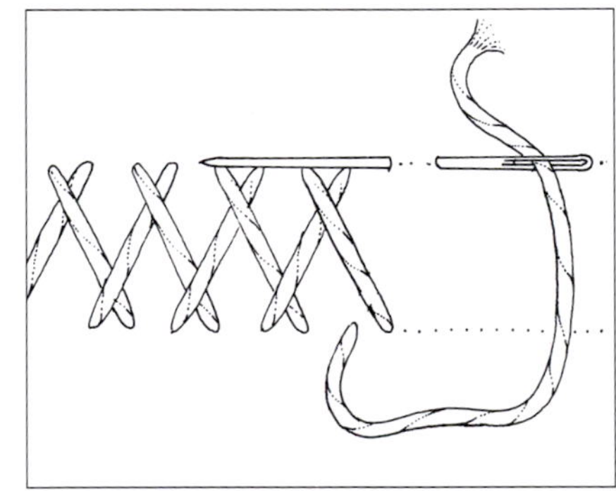

Bring the thread up on the lower line, then back through on the upper line, a little to the right. Take a short stitch to the left, then take the needle back down to the lower line, a little to the right, and again take a short stitch to the left. One variation is to make small couching stitches in a contrast colour at each intersection.

Chain stitches

Chain stitch is a perfect example of the versatility of simple stitches. Normally a linear stitch, it has so many variations, even in traditional embroidery, that it is only possible to include a few of them. Contemporary embroiderers achieve an enormous range of textures and effects with the basic chain stitch simply by varying the sizes of the loops and the threads, and by overlapping lengths of chain.

Chain stitch

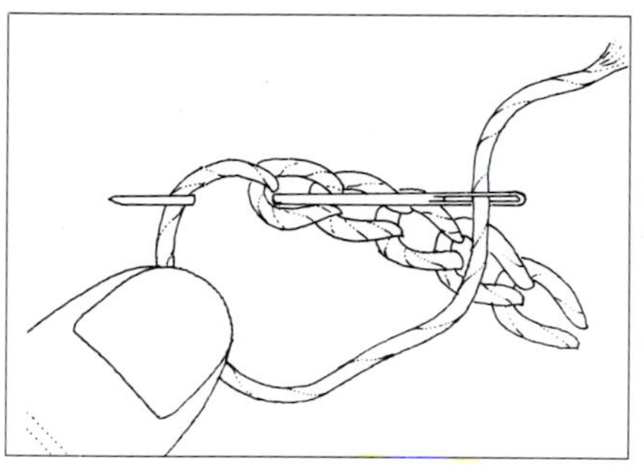

Bring the needle out at the beginning of the line to be worked. Reinsert it at exactly the same point, holding the thread down with your thumb to form the loop. Bring the needle up just inside the loop, and pull the thread through to form the first link.

Open chain stitch

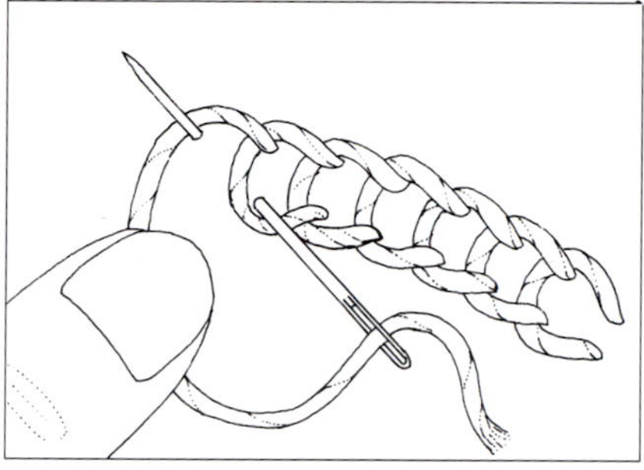

For a broader line, bring the needle out at one side of the loop and reinsert it at the opposite side, level with the exit point. Secure the last loop with tiny stitches at each side.

Two colour chain

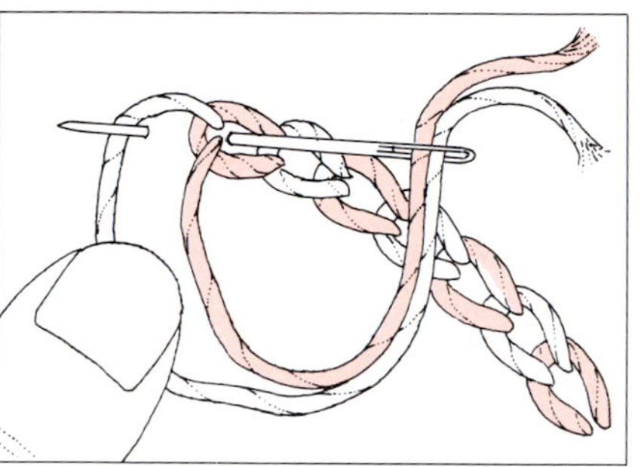

To make a chain of alternating colours, thread two colours through the needle and work as ordinary chain stitch, but bring the needle out over the chosen thread for that link only. The unwanted thread will slip back to the wrong side as the threads are pulled through; pull gently to ensure that it disappears completely. Make the next stitch in the same way, this time taking the needle out over the second colour.

Wheatear

Bring the needle out at the centre top of the embroidery line and make a short stitch to the left. Pass horizontally under the fabric; bring the needle out to the right of the line and reinsert it at the starting point, forming a V. Bring the needle out directly below this point. Take the needle from right to left, under the straight stitches. Insert it back into the fabric at the point where it emerged, completing the chain link. Bring it out to the left, ready for the next two straight stitches.

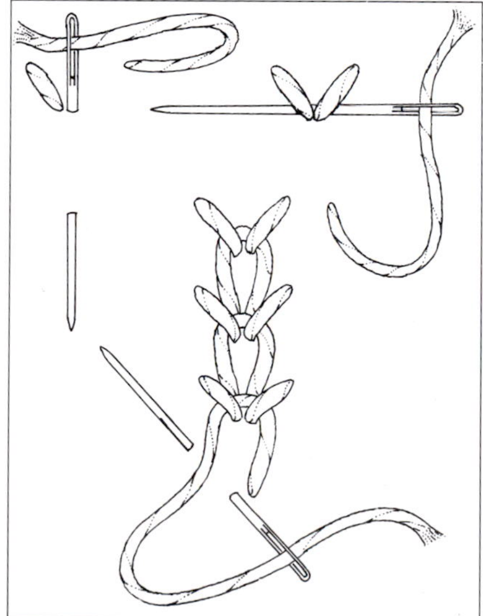

Using linear stitches

Once you have mastered a few linear stitches, it is a good idea to employ one or two of them in a small piece of work, so that you can begin to get a feeling for their expressive potential. Choose a subject with an intrinsically linear quality. It might be something quite simple, such as some rushes growing at the edge of a pond or cloud patterns in the sky; or you might like to try something slightly more complex, such as these graceful fuchsia blossoms.

To provide a framework and background for the stitchery, apply the basic shape(s) to the fabric with fabric paints. The fuchsia blossoms and leaves were painted onto the fabric with a brush; a sponge was used for the background. The sample should be fairly small, so it would be preferable to use fine threads. The ones chosen for this sample are perlé cotton, coton à broder, soft embroidery cotton and crewel wool.

Don't try to incorporate too many stitches in the work; otherwise it can look untidy. Here, chain stitch and stem stitch were used for a contrast of thickness. If your shapes are more solid, you may wish to couch some thick threads onto the work.

It is important to choose a focal area, or one part of the sample which is to be more prominent than the rest. This will need to be worked more densely, possibly with thicker threads, so that it contrasts with smooth, less densely worked areas. One advantage of the painted background is that it does not have to be entirely covered with stitchery. The unstitched parts of the design will complement and set off the stitched areas.

These fuchsias are a good subject for embroidery and also for drawing exercises. The blossoms have a sculptural quality and gracefully curving lines, and the leaves have strong, simple shapes.

Sketches in a variety of drawing and painting media, based on the fuchsias; some emphasize the linear qualities of the flowers, while others show the tonal values.

This little embroidery by Julia Barton is based on a photograph. The image was first applied with fabric paints, then the dominant lines were established (above) using the two chosen stitches, chain and stem. In the completed embroidery (right) the shapes are further enhanced with more lines of stitching which contrast effectively with the sponged, painted background.

Filling stitches

All the following, with the exception of voiding, which is a technique used to emphasize filled areas, are designed to fill large or small areas. Although commonly used for flat embroidery, they can also cover raised shapes, or they may be worked on separate pieces of fabric and then applied to the main embroidery.

Other filling stitches include stem stitch and split stitch, both of which are shown as linear stitches, but can equally well be worked in closely set lines to fill a given area.

Satin stitch

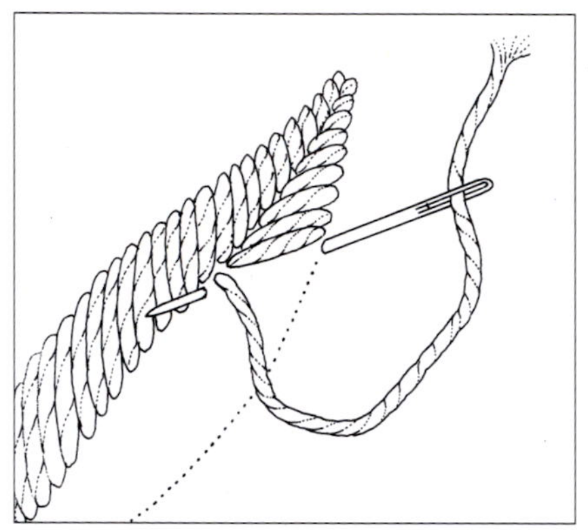

Bring the needle up at one edge of the area that is to be filled; carry the thread to the opposite edge; return under the fabric, and bring it out close to the starting point. Continue, making sure no fabric shows between stitches. To cover a large area, work several stitches across rather than one long stitch.

Long and short stitch

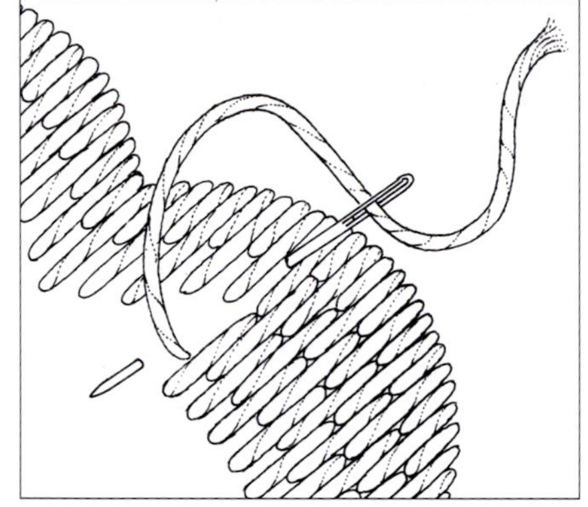

This is similar to satin stitch, but the stitches are staggered. Working from the outer edge of the marked shape, and keeping the stitching line at the edge even, make a row of alternating long and short stitches. The stitches of the next row are all the same length, fitting into the spaces of the previous row. Continue, finishing with an even edge. The irregular effect of the rows makes it easier to blend in subtle gradations of colour.

Voiding

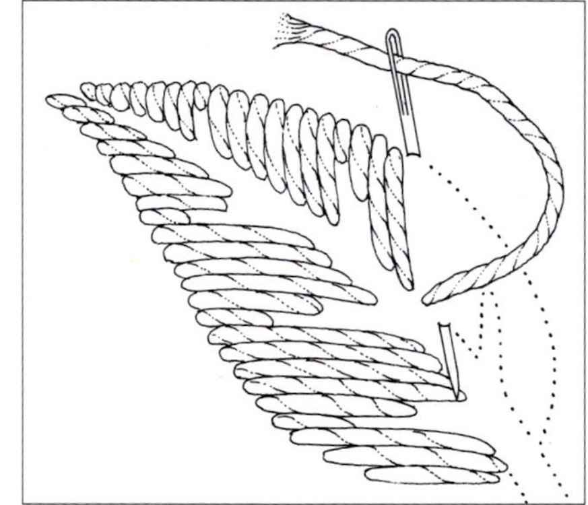

Detail can be provided, particularly in satin stitched shapes, by leaving some areas unworked so that the background shows through. Petals can be embroidered individually, for example, or the veins of leaves remain unstitched.

Brick stitch

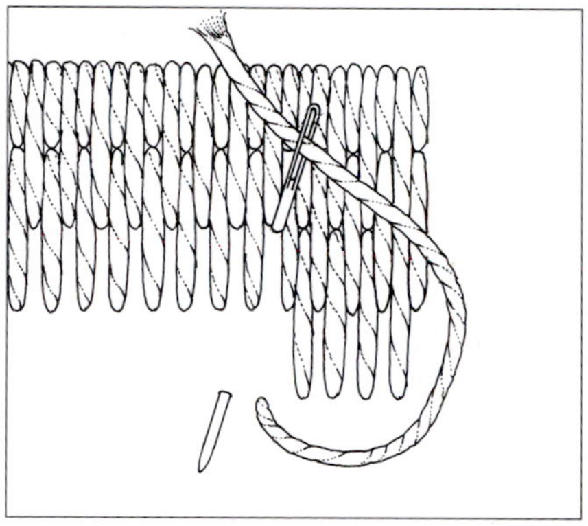

This is stitched in alternate rows – left to right, right to left. The starting row is of long and short stitch, but subsequent stitches are of equal length. All rows are parallel, set close to resemble brick work. It can be used as a shading stitch.

Freely worked encroaching straight stitches, formed with a variety of threads, have been used by Kay Swancutt to suggest a summer meadow.

Burden stitch

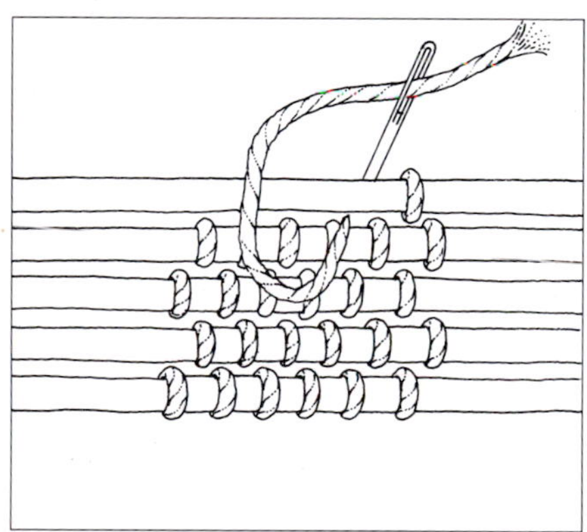

1 The laid threads are visible if couched singly. Pattern may be introduced by using threads of different colours for laying and couching.

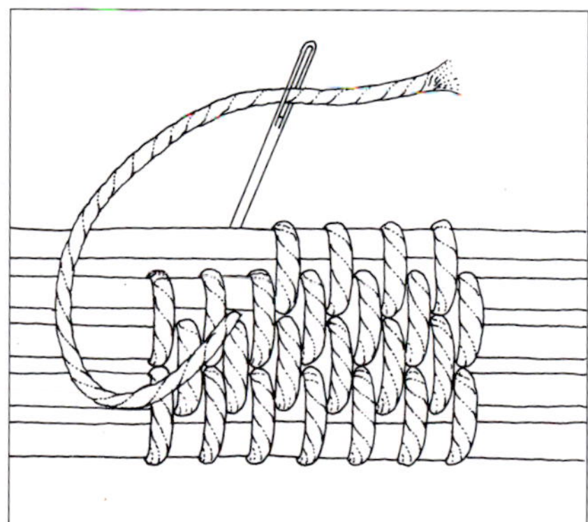

2 When the couching stitch overlays two laid threads, the laid threads are hidden from view. It is still possible to create patterns by changing the colour of the couching thread from time to time.

Pattern stitches

These are essentially allover stitches, which can be used to fill areas of pattern, as in traditional cross stitch and Assisi work. They can also be used where a design has a large area of background which needs some discreet stitchery in matching threads to blend in with the main stitchery of the design. Still another function of pattern stitches is to link areas together to lead the eye from one part of the design to another.

Fly stitch has been included, but it is really a much more versatile stitch than even this general heading would imply. It can be worked in straight lines or freely, as here.

This small piece of stitchery, inspired by rosebay willowherb, is worked entirely in fly stitch, using several threads. Some stitches are elongated, and others have been inverted.

Fly stitch

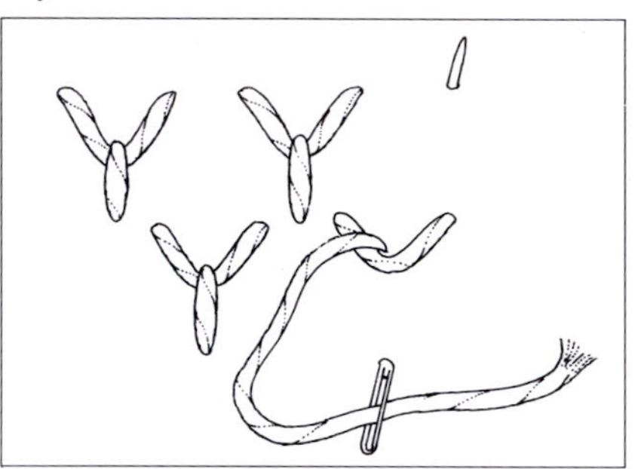

This simple stitch consists of an open loop held down by a vertical stitch, forming a 'Y' shape. It is one of the most versatile stitches. Bring the needle up at the top left corner of the Y. Keeping the thread under the needle, to form a loop, insert the needle at the top right corner of the Y and bring it out at the centre, as shown. Take it down to form the tail of the Y and then bring it up at the top left of the next stitch.

When you have mastered the basic stitch, try altering the shape of the stitches, making them short and fat, then long and thin. Fly stitch is very versatile; the length of the tail can be altered, as well as the shape of the body of the stitch.

Detached chain

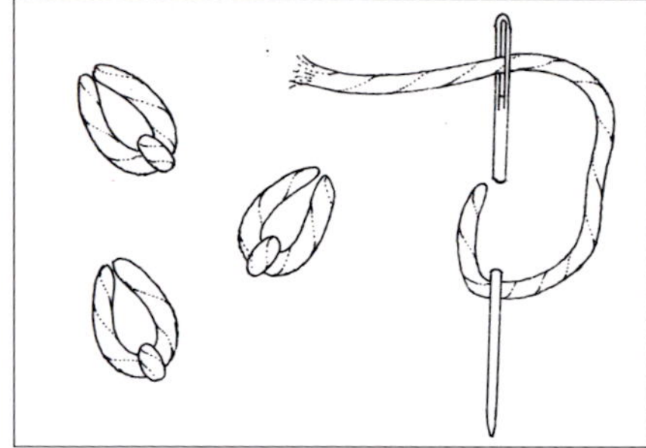

Often known as laisy daisy, this is a useful stitch for filling in areas of pattern. The stitches are formed in the same way as linear chain stitch (see page 27), but the loops are scattered at random, and each is held down by a small stitch, worked as shown.

Ox head

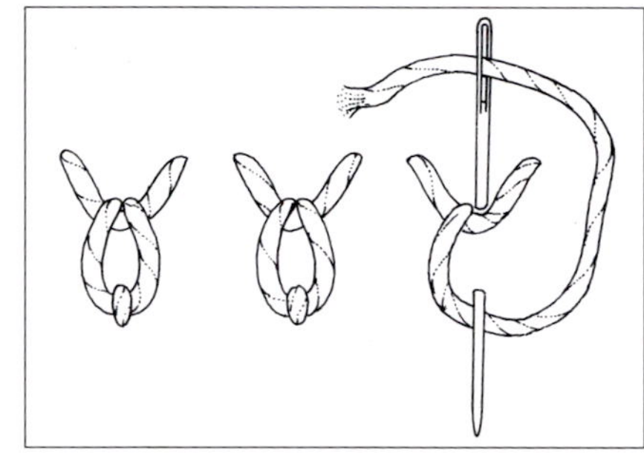

Another useful stitch, which can either be scattered or worked in a regular pattern, this begins with the first stage of fly stitch, but finishes with a single chain stitch in place of the stem of the Y.

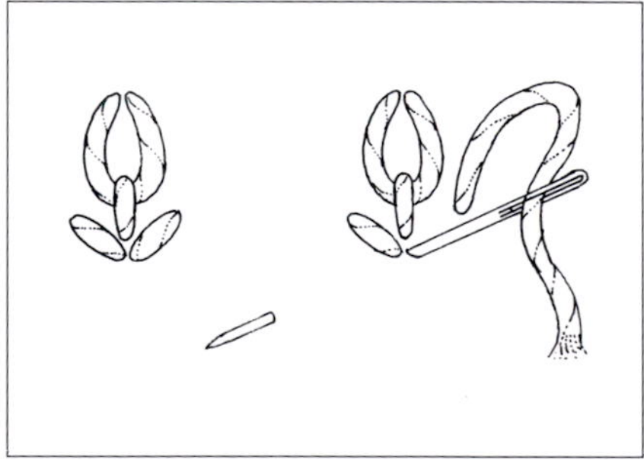

Alternatively, begin with a detached chain, fastened down with a straight stitch, then bring the needle out to the left and make a V shape with two stitches.

Star filling

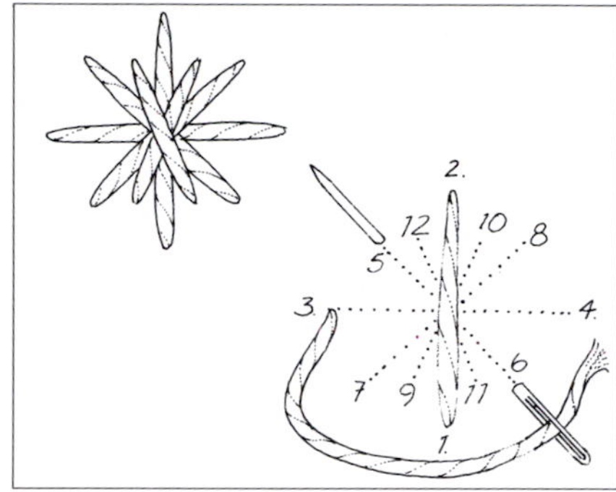

These can be worked closely together or scattered at random. If a thick thread is used, the effect can be highly embossed. As with ermine stitches, start with a vertical stitch, bringing the needle out at 1 and back in at 2, continuing through the numbers, as shown.

Seeding

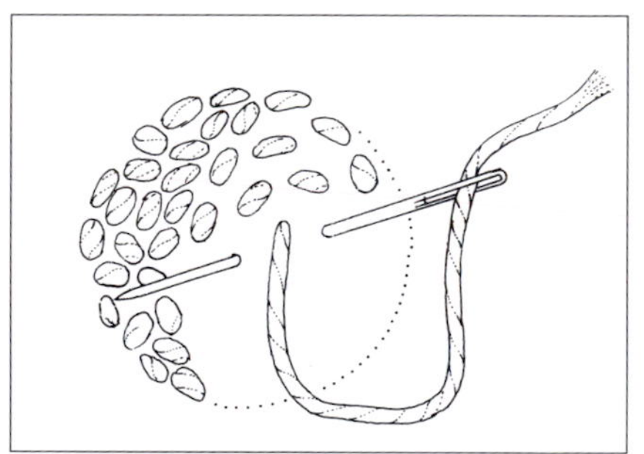

Seeding stitches are simply small, individual straight stitches, worked in all directions. Try varying the density of the stitching to suggest shading or modelling.

Eyelets

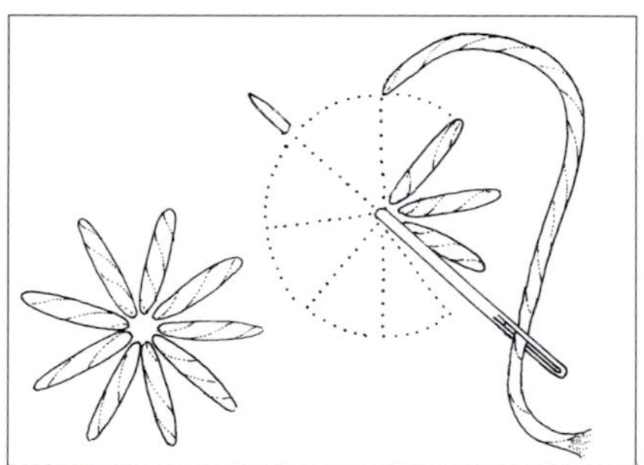

These are useful for stylized, flat floral areas. Open the centre hole slightly with the needle, and always take the needle down into the hole, not up.

Ermine stitch

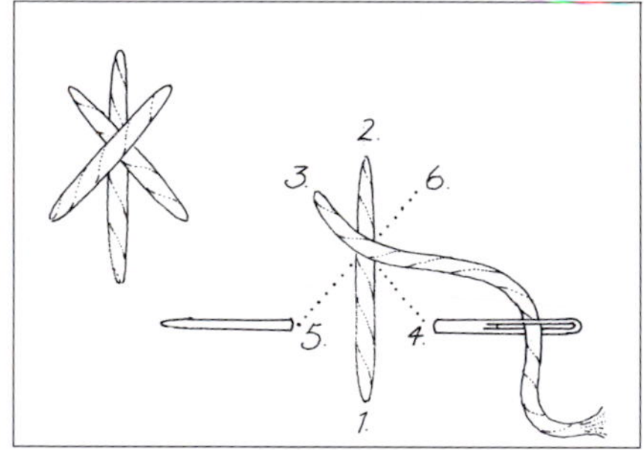

For this simple variation of cross stitch, start with a vertical stitch, taking the needle out at 1 and back in at 2, continuing until you have completed the stitch.

Textural stitches

These stitches are ideal for interpreting textured surfaces in embroidery. Interesting textures can be found in many natural objects, such as the ridged surface of bark, the strata of rock formations or moss growing on a wall, and also in man-made objects, such as bricks or tiled roofs. Stitchery is the perfect medium in which to explore these qualities and to experiment with some of the wonderfully varied threads in your work basket.

Many different stitches can be used for suggesting texture; some will become three-dimensional by being overlapped and built up in layers. Here is a selection of textural stitches, to be tried with a variety of threads.

Other textural stitches include velvet stitch (see page 89).

French knots

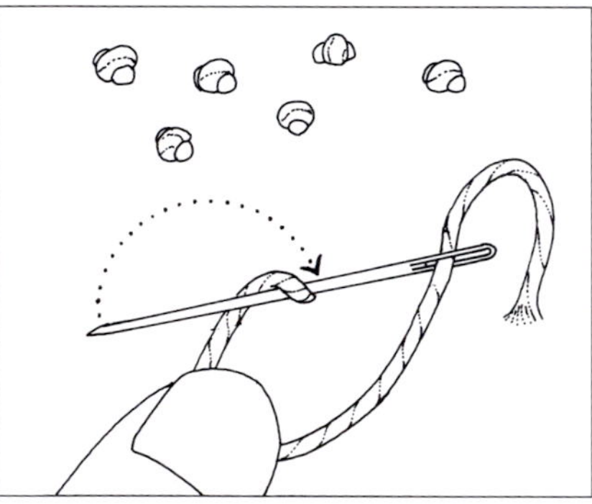

These have a delightfully tactile quality. Some people wrap the thread twice around the needle, but for best results it need be wrapped only once. Use different thicknesses of thread to vary the size of the knots. Bring the thread out at the required position and hold it down to one side with the (left) thumb. Twist the thread twice around the needle, then put the needle back into the fabric, close to the starting point. Pull the thread through to the back and tighten the knot, then bring the needle up at the starting point of the next knot.

Bullion knots

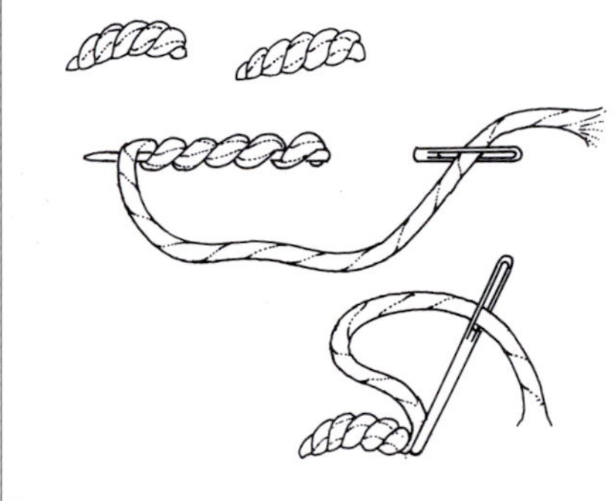

Similar to French knots, these have a slightly directional quality. The effect is well worth the practice they require.

Bring the thread to the surface, and take the needle down a short distance away. Bring it up where the thread emerges, and wind the thread several times around the needle. Pull the thread through the loops, and take the needle down again where it was inserted.

Buttonhole wheels

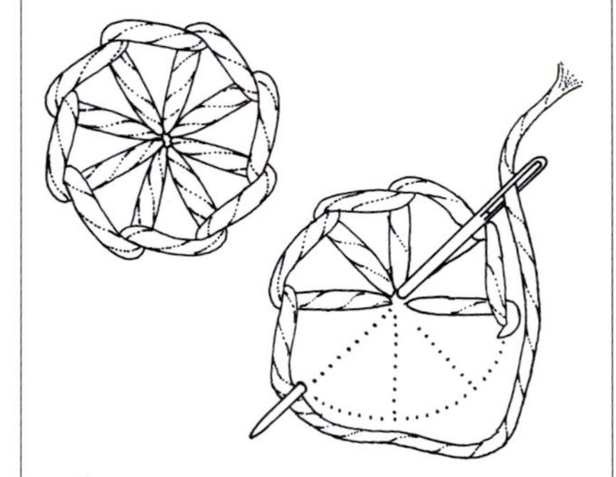

Work the buttonhole stitch (see page 36) in circles, radiating around a central point. Portions of wheels will prevent the effect from looking mechanical, as will varying the spacing of the stitches and varying their length, which produces a spiky effect. Wheels can also be worked with the bars at the centre, producing a star-like pattern that can be used to suggest blossoms, rock formations or coral.

In this embroidery by Julia Barton, inspired by lichen on a rock, a dense texture has been built up with layers of buttonhole wheels, French knots and pieces of detached buttonhole.

Couching

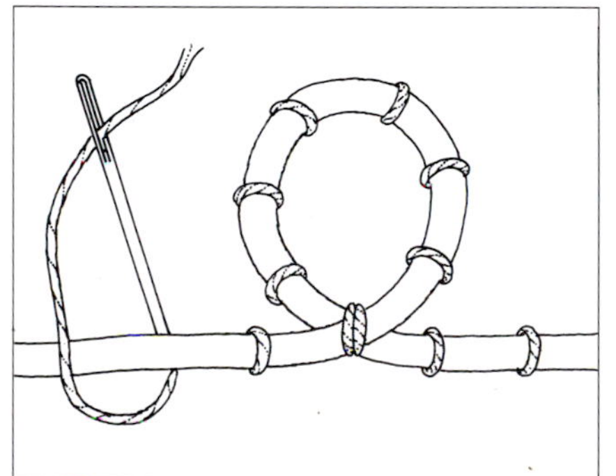

Another common way of adding texture is through couched threads and cords. Lay the thread to be couched along the fabric, then with a second, finer thread, secure it in place with small stitches, set diagonally across the laid thread. The ends of the couched thread are generally taken through the fabric with a chenille needle, but if a thick, stiff thread, such as a wrapped wire, is to be couched, it may be necessary to pierce the fabric with a stiletto or a leather awl. The ends can then be secured on the underside.

This is shown under canvas embroidery, but is frequently used in other forms of stitchery.

For a sample piece of stitchery suggesting texture, select a subject with strong textural appeal, such as a crumbling stone wall or a bit of shoreline strewn with pebbles, shells and seaweed. The design shown here was inspired by a photograph of lichen on a rock in Cornwall. Transfer paints were used to provide a background for the stitchery. Paints in suitable colours were simply sponged onto the paper and the colours were transferred onto a piece of furnishing fabric. The threads used for the embroidery were crewel wood, perlé cotton, soft (matt) embroidery cotton, thick knitting yarn and knitting tape. The stitches chosen are French knots, buttonhole wheels – including partially worked wheels – and detached buttonhole bars.

Buttonhole stitch

Buttonhole is one of the most familiar of all stitches. It is sometimes used, worked widely spaced, on the edges of blankets – hence it other name, blanket stitch. Small, closely worked buttonhole stitches are used on the edges and bars of cutwork embroidery. Like fly stitch, buttonhole consists basically of a loop, but in this case each loop is held in place by the next stitch.

Traditional buttonhole stitch

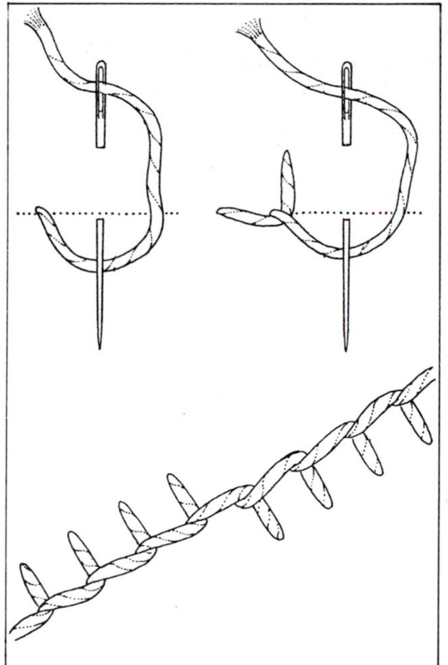

Detached buttonhole stitch

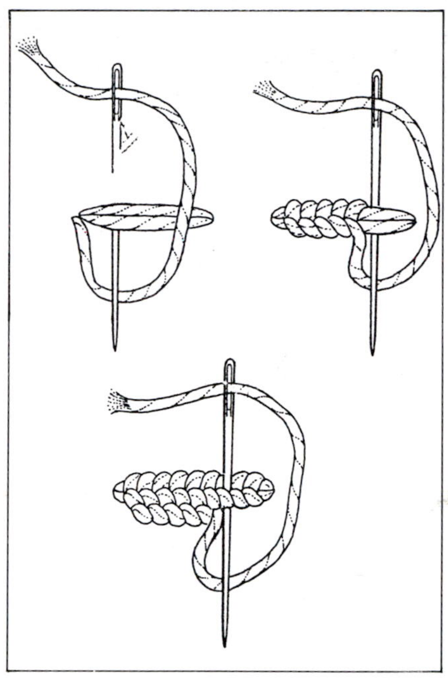

Various forms of buttonhole stitch, including regularly worked, overlapping rows and some detached buttonhole, have been used to suggest rock formations.

To work the stitch in the traditional manner, begin by bringing the needle up on the line (first marked on the fabric if you like). Take it down a short distance to the right, above the line, and bring it up directly below, keeping the loop under the needle. Pull the thread through, and move the needle to the right to form the next stitch. Continue, forming a row of evenly worked stitches.

The effect can be varied by altering the shape and direction. Keeping the vertical stitches upright, alter the spaces between them, and also vary the length, so altering the angle of the horizontal lines.

Next, try inverting the rows, so that some of the stitches point downwards. Superimpose the rows, and see what effects are created by different threads.

Buttonhole stitch can also be worked independently of the fabric, over a foundation bar of threads. To make the bar, take the needle back and forth two or three times across the required length. Cover the bar with buttonhole stitches, without taking the needle through the fabric. For subsequent rows, work into the stitches of the previous row. For a scallop shape, work one stitch less in each row. Try working a number of pieces of detached buttonhole, varying the thread and the direction as shown. The pieces can be overlapped to form a dense texture.

Threaded stitches

Many basic embroidery stitches can be given added texture and colour simply by threading another thickness or colour of thread through them. Contemporary embroiderers often incorporate handmade papers into their designs, and threading can be a useful way of adding surface texture without making too many stitches through the paper.

Threaded running stitch

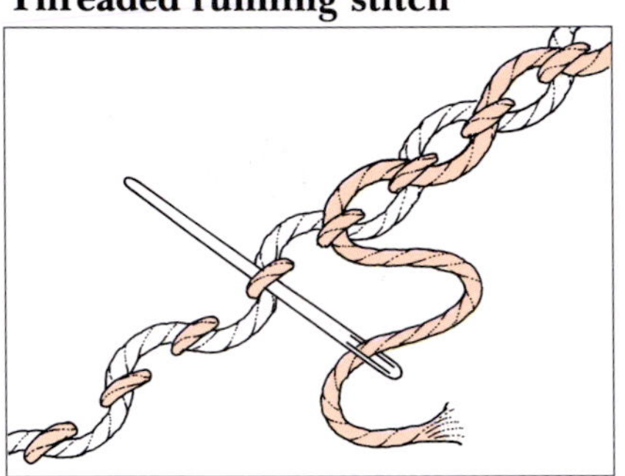

Make a line of running stitch and then, using a blunt-ended needle, pass a second thread in a wave pattern down through one stitch and up through the next. You can make a return journey in a third colour, this time placing the loops on the alternating side, for a two-colour circle effect.

Pekinese stitch

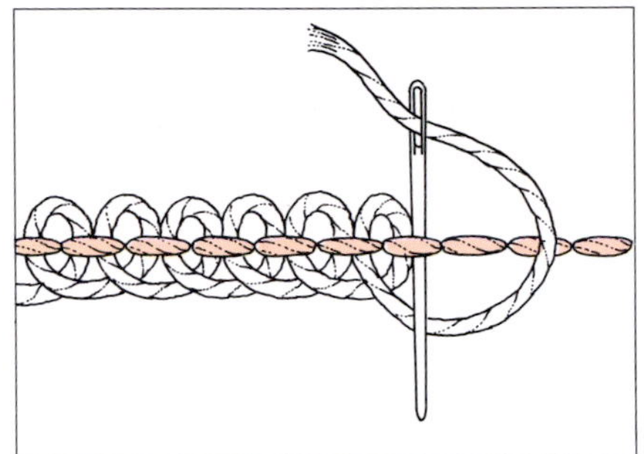

Start with a line of large backstitches, and then, using a contrasting thread, make loops through the backstitches, as shown.

Whipped stem stitch

This creates a very strong outline. Make a row of stem stitch and then, working in the same direction, whip the stem stitches at regular intervals by threading the needle under the stitches without piercing the fabric.

Raised chain stitch band

A useful border stitch, this is worked over a foundation of evenly spaced horizontal stitches. Bring the needle out above the first straight stitch, down over it and then up under the straight stitch, to the left of the thread. Take it to the right of the central stitch, down under the straight stitch and over the resulting loop. Repeat until the band is complete.

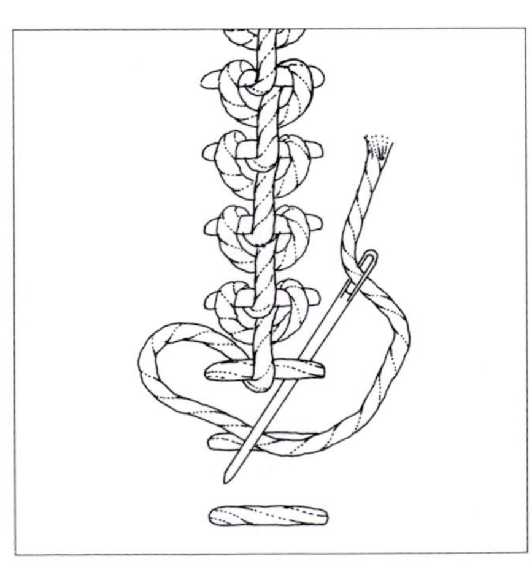

Beadwork

Beads come in many forms – they may be of glass, plastic, china or wood and they range in size from tiny seed pearls to large wooden varieties. Some are faceted and round, others smooth and long, pendant or lozenge-shaped. Sequins and spangles, too, are available in many colours and shapes. The most usual are the small round cup or disc type with a central hole. Specialist shops also stock sequins in the form of flowers, leaves, and stars as well as geometric shapes. Embroidery stones are different from beads in that they have a flat underside; some have holes for thread while others may need to be mounted, glued or sewn with covering stitches. Shisha (or mirror) glass requires a special method of application and makes an interesting addition to a design.

The most successful beadwork designs are those in which the beads or sequins are massed together, perhaps forming the focal point of a piece of work, or gradually diminishing in number from a cluster to a scattering. Because beads and sequins are inherently eyecatching and reflect the light, they will dominate a design as well as producing texture and pattern. For this reason, they tend to form a natural focal point of a design and should be used with care – if the intended focal point is elsewhere, a group of beads may weaken the effect.

If formal patterns are made, the beads should be sewn close together over an area, with attention paid to the direction in which they are laid; a design can look very weak if they are sparsely scattered.

Attaching beads

Background fabrics for beadwork should be firmly woven, and it is essential that the fabric is mounted in a frame. If lightweight fabric, such as chiffon or organza, is used, it may be necessary to back the work with a slightly more substantial supporting material, such as fine lawn. This is cut away when the beading is finished.

Professional beadworkers use vanishing muslin as a supporting fabric. On completion of the design, a hot iron is applied to the back of the work; this causes the vanishing muslin to disintegrate and it can then be brushed away.

In some cases, you will find that your beads are already on a string. This can simply be couched in position, but in most cases it is preferable to transfer the beads to a strong cotton thread. Tie a loose knot at the end of the string, put the cotton thread through the loop and tighten it, then slide the beads

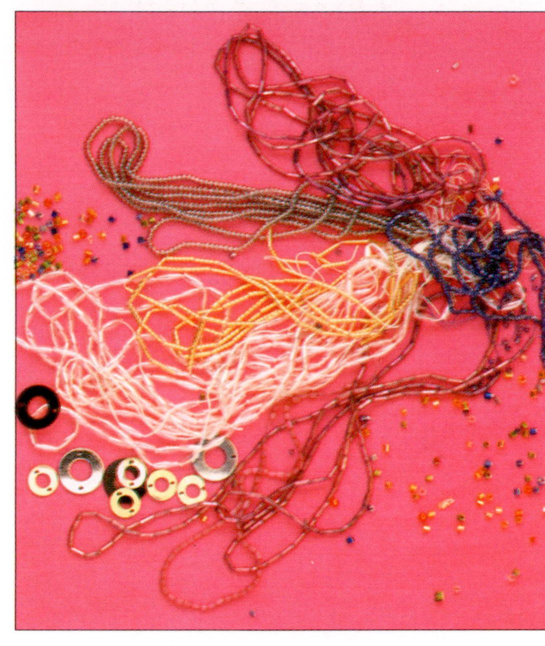

Beads can be bought either loose or threaded on strings, as used for tambourwork. They can add lustre and richness to a design, but should be used with discretion, or they may overwhelm it.

Attaching beads

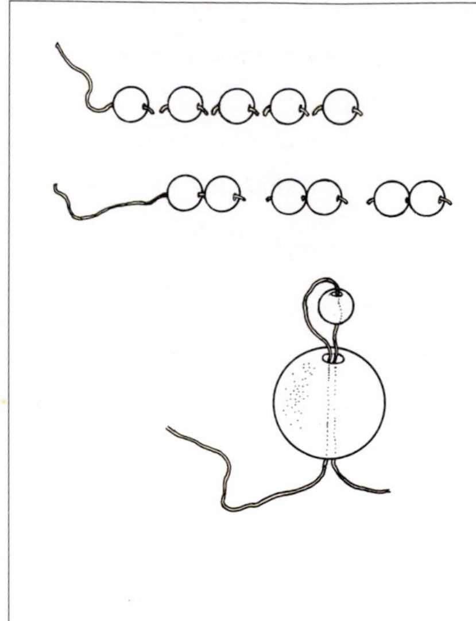

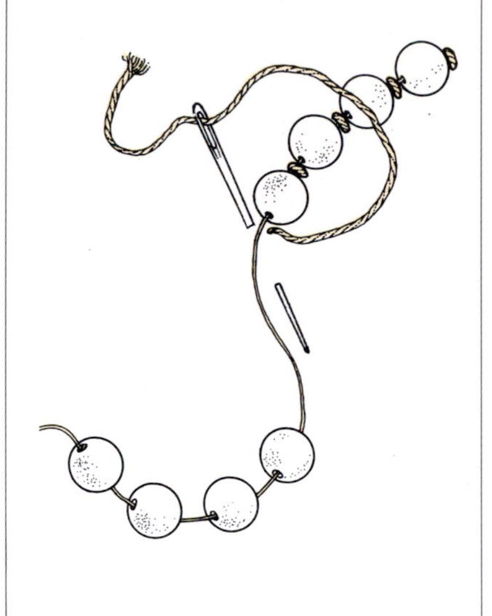

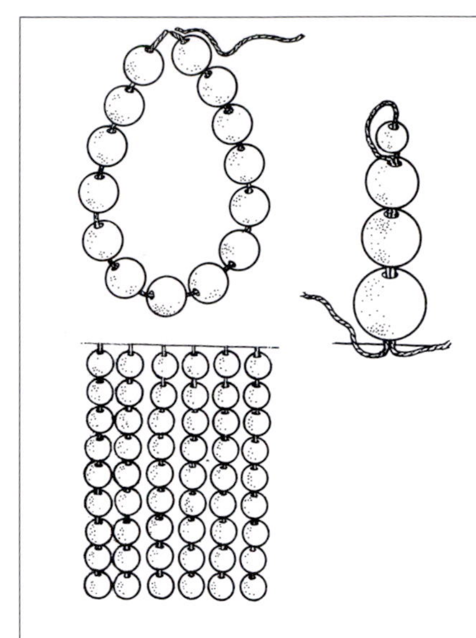

1 **To attach beads singly, secure with a single stitch through the hole; to attach them in twos, secure with a single stitch through both beads. A large bead can be secured by using a smaller one to prevent the thread from pulling through.**

2 **To couch beads in rows, thread the required number on sewing thread and lay them on the line of the design. Using a second needle and thread, take a tiny stitch across the row of beads, between every bead or every two or three beads, depending on the size of the bead, the strength of the fabric and the desired effect.**

3 **To sew a bead loop, pick up several beads (preferably an odd number) on the thread and re-insert the needle into almost the same spot on the fabric. If this process is reproduced many times a thickly encrusted texture will evolve.**

Stalks can be made by threading three or four beads and taking the needle back into the same hole, passing again through all except the top bead.

Bead fringes or hanging tassels may be made in a similar fashion, using a greater number of beads.

from the original string onto the cotton thread.

If they are loose, you will require a beading needle for tiny beads; others can be attached using any needle fine enough to pass through the hole. There are many ways of sewing beads to a fabric – either singly, in twos or threes, in rows, or in loops or fringes. Choose thread that tones with either the background or the overall colour of the beads. Draw it through a block of beeswax before you begin beading: this will smooth the thread and help it to retain its strength.

Sequins

Sequins can be incorporated very successfully into embroidery and appliqué designs. They may be either cup-shaped or flat, in which case the reverse side will feel slightly rough, where the hole was punched through. Take care when attaching sequins to work from the bottom of the design upwards, so that the row will lie smoothly.

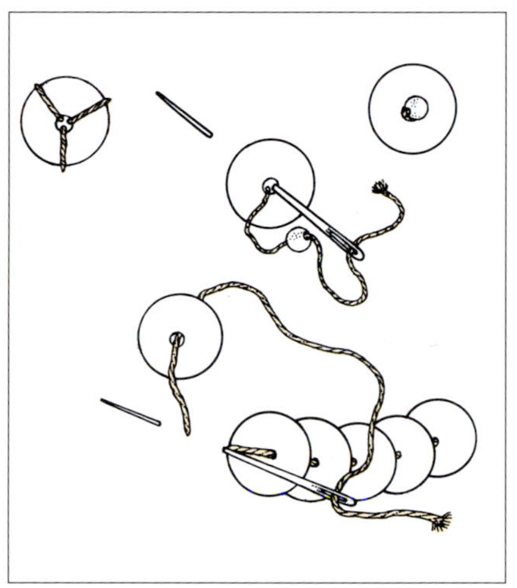

Individual sequins may be attached with two or three straight stitches, taken across and through the central hole, or they can be held in place by a bead or a French knot, stitched over the hole. To attach a line of sequins, secure each with a back stitch, positioning the next sequin to cover the stitch. When stitching rows side by side, the sequins of the second row should overlap the first up to the holes.

Attaching jewels and stones

Some jewels, including imitation and semi-precious stones, already have holes drilled through them to facilitate their attachment. In this case, they may be sewn in place with a beading needle and strong thread. Those without holes need different treatment: they may be glued to the surface with a rubber-based adhesive, or held in place by one of the methods shown here.

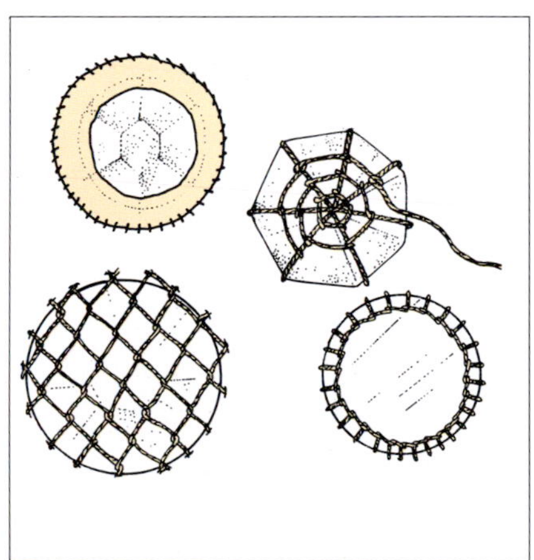

One way of attaching a jewel or stone is to cut a ring of leather, suede, felt, or painted, non-woven interfacing, place this around the stone, covering the edges, and stitch it down to hold the stone in place. Alternatively, the stone can be stitched in place with a spider's web or woven wheel, or with buttonhole stitch.

Decorative objects can also be held in place with pieces of net or mesh, cut to size and stitched in place around the edges.

Shisha glass

Shisha (or mirror) glass embroidery involves the stitching of small pieces of mica to a background. This technique comes originally from India, Pakistan and Baluchistan, where it is used in combination with embroidery stitches for clothes and for decorative purposes on occasions such as festivals and weddings. As with other types of bead embroidery, the background fabric should be firm and closely woven in order to support the weight of the glass, particularly if a large number of pieces is being used. The small circles of silvered glass do not have holes in them, and may be attached in the same way as jewels and stones. The traditional method, however, involves a type of buttonhole stitch worked over glass.

Pieces of shisha glass are incorporated with reverse appliqué in this experimental piece by Judy Hope.

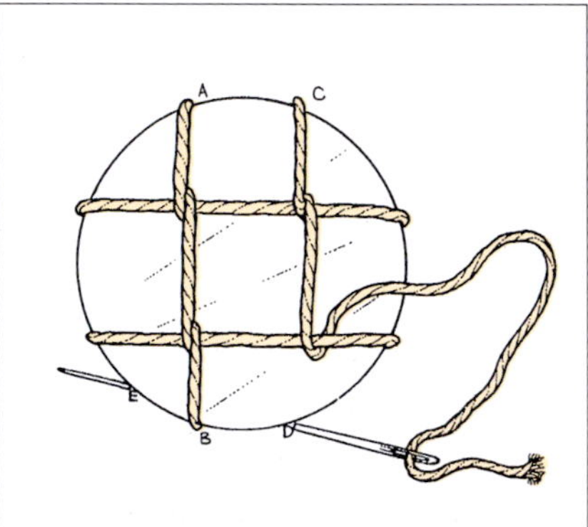

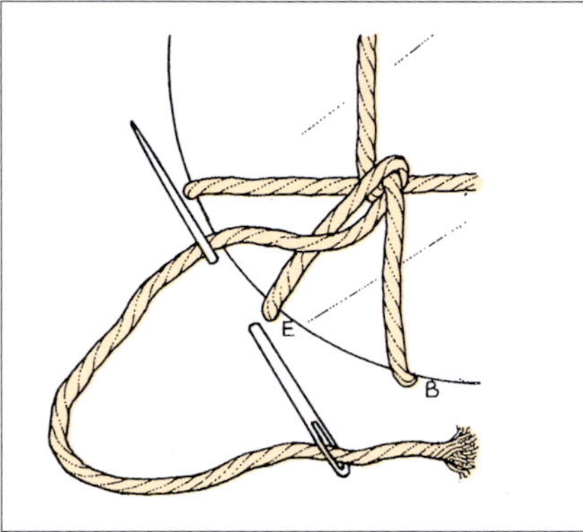

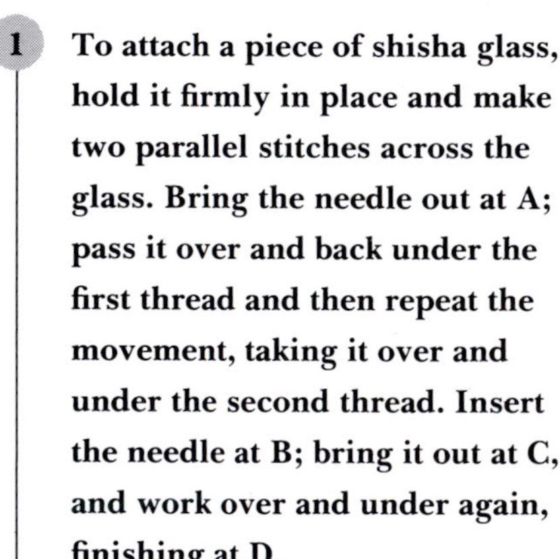

1 **To attach a piece of shisha glass, hold it firmly in place and make two parallel stitches across the glass. Bring the needle out at A; pass it over and back under the first thread and then repeat the movement, taking it over and under the second thread. Insert the needle at B; bring it out at C, and work over and under again, finishing at D.**

2 **Bring the needle out at E and take it over the intersecting threads, as shown.**

Make a small stitch close to the edge of the glass, keeping the thread below the needle.

Repeat, taking the thread over the central framework and gradually working in a clockwise direction around the edge of the glass.

Incorporating other decorative items

Besides the conventional decoration of fabric with beads, jewels and shisha glass, there are many other items which can be applied to an embroidered or appliqué piece. These may range from shells, pebbles, driftwood, feathers and seeds to machine-made components, such as washers, nuts and curtain rings. As most of these do not have holes, they may be attached either with adhesive or by one of the methods described.

Metal threads

Apart from the finer threads, which can be used like normal embroidery threads, these are mainly either couched in position or attached like beads (see page 42).

Couching metal threads

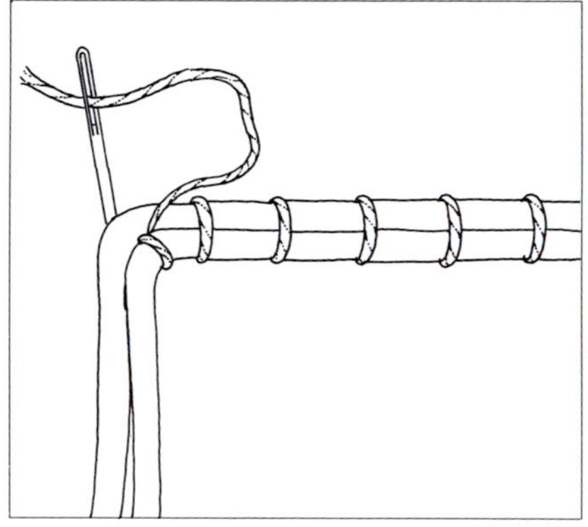

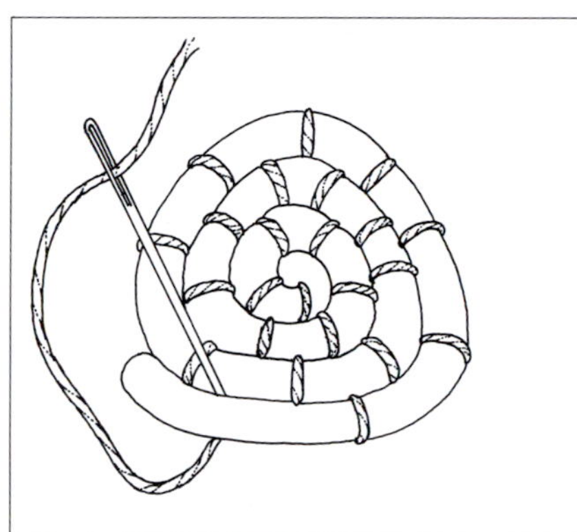

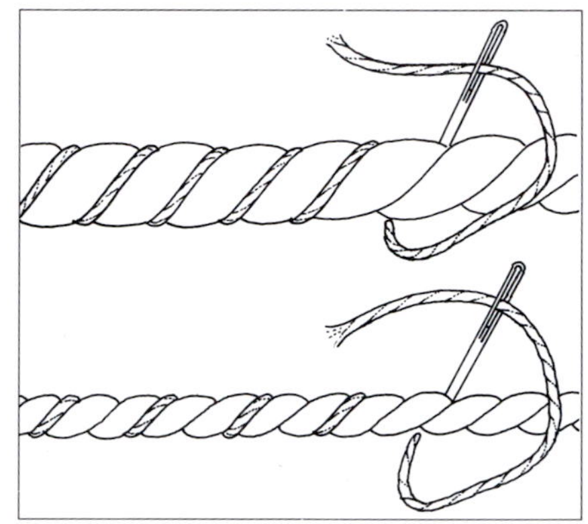

1 **Threads and cords can be folded in two, and the couching stitches set about 6mm (¼in) apart and taken over the doubled length. Use a chenille needle to bring ends through to the back and finish off when the embroidery is complete.**

At corners, make a separate couching stitch over each thread.

2 **When filling in a motif or area with laid threads, alternate couching stitches as in brickwork, varying the distance between couching stitches to maintain this effect when following curves or shaping.**

3 **When couching pearl purl or twist, set the couching thread at the angle of the twist. The thicker varieties will need a couching stitch at each twist; for finer types, couch alternate twists.**

Purl lengths

Bullion and other purl threads can be cut into short lengths and attached like beads, each length being stitched in place individually.

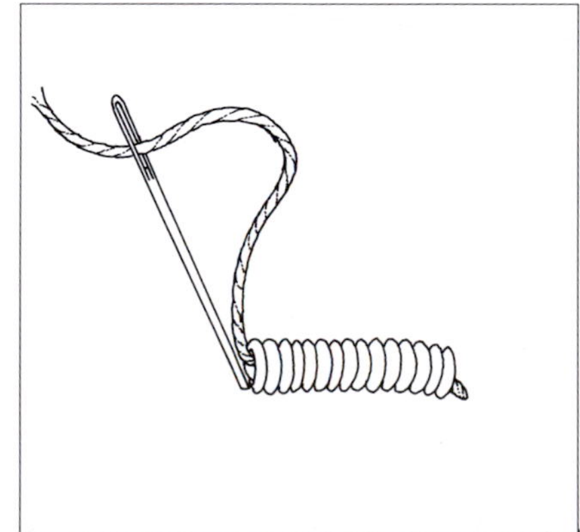

NEEDLELACE

Needlelace is a form of embroidery with the cloth taken away, the needle and thread making loops in the air, and the stitches passing through nothing except themselves. The basic looping, which is simplicity itself, is called detached (or corded) buttonhole stitch, and was used at least 6,000 years ago. In the 17th, 18th and 19th centuries, successive styles of needlelace evolved in Italy, France and Belgium, rivalling bobbin laces in their delicacy and complexity.

Today, many embroiderers are making innovative use of this technique, either creating pictures entirely in needlelace, or incorporating it into raised embroideries, where it is often used for clothing. In the latter case, a completed figure may be 'clothed' in several layers of needlelace, each shape being drawn and worked separately, to create a three-dimensional illusion.

The edge of the lace is formed by a double, continuous thread. This thread has various names, including tracing thread, outlining thread, contour thread, and foundation cord, but the majority of contemporary makers of needlelace refer to it as the cordonnet, a term which originally referred to raised sections of the outline. Each piece of lace is formed on a temporary foundation fabric with a shiny upper surface. The only stitches that penetrate the foundation fabric are the (also temporary) couching stitches that anchor the double cordonnet thread in the desired position. The lace can be made to almost any shape, including one with holes in the centre. When possible, use threads of the same colour for the cordonnet, couching thread and buttonholing.

A fine rust-proof wire, such as a fine beading wire (similar to 5amp fuse wire), can be couched with the cordonnet if the finished piece of lace is to be only freely attached to the embroidery. This permits the lace to be shaped and manipulated, and to fly freely above the surface of the embroidery. Hide the wire by buttonholing over the cordonnet when the shape has been filled but before it has been removed from the foundation fabric.

During the working process, the temporary foundation fabric is held in one hand, leaving the other free to make the needlelace stitches. If preferred, the foundation fabric can be attached to a drum, or needlelace pillow, leaving both hands free to stitch and control thread tension.

The hot colours of Summer in India *were chosen by Ros Hills to evoke the razzle dazzle and excitement of an Indian market. Metallic papers, vivid silk threads and sequins, mounted on a paper collage, were incorporated into the work along with the needlelace.*

Materials

Needles

Sharps are needed for couching down the outlining thread, since the needle has to be pushed through both the pattern and its support. A blunt-tipped needle, either ball point or tapestry, is used for working the stitches; its rounded tip cannot accidentally split the threads.

Threads

Several thicknesses of thread are often used in one piece of lace. Traditional needlelace was worked with extremely fine threads. Some of these were finer than the finest machine embroidery threads now available. Today, cotton threads are available in various forms – crochet, cordonnet special, perlé, à broder, brilliant, and fil à dentelles, each in varying thicknesses. The first two give a crisp firm finish, while softer effects can be achieved with coton à broder. Broder 16 and perlé 3, 5 and 8 all offer an excellent choice of colours, in DMC. Silks of increasing fineness – 30/3, 40/3, 110/3 and 130/3 – blend well together and can be lustrous and colourful, while bright rayon (art silk) machine embroidery threads provide spectacular highlights.

Snarling

Threads tend to untwist or overtwist as you work. This is inevitable because the spiralling movement of the stitches will either loosen or reinforce the twist (ply) of the thread. Overtwisting can be corrected by letting the needle hang and twirl at fairly frequent intervals; untwisting by rotating the needle to tighten the thread. The effect is less bothersome if short lengths of thread are used.

A pattern

Traditionally, lace begins as a *design*, which shows not only the main outlines of the motifs but the appearance of the fillings to be used in each distinct area. The design itself is kept for reference, but its outline is copied or traced, and used as the *pattern*. In the past, the pattern was mounted on parchment, and passed from one lacemaker to another. Today, paper patterns are used, the design being traced or photocopied.

Ordinary paper is far too flexible to stand alone. The pattern could be backed with stiff brown paper, felt, or several layers of cloth. Here, a pattern drawn on tracing paper is backstitched to felt. Various types of thread and needles are also shown, as is a piece of architect's linen and, above it, some acetate film (contact paper). Either of the latter can be used to cover the pattern and attach it to the support. The pricker, in the centre, consists of a sharply-pointed pin fixed into a metal (or wood) handle.

DMC

Supporting and protecting the pattern

If only small needlelace shapes are required, perhaps for items of clothing on a raised embroidery, the individual pattern outlines can be transferred to a shiny PVC or oilcloth as shown (see page 50, Laying a cordonnet).

For a more complex needlelace design, the paper pattern must be retained, and the whole must be supported by a lace pillow or similar device. Whatever method is chosen, contact between lacemaker and lace will always be close, separated as they are from each other only by a short length of thread, and linked by the need for the needle to pass unerringly at every stitch through one particular loop.

In addition to being supported, the paper pattern must be protected from the constant scratching of the needle. Much the simplest shield is tinted self-adhesive acetate (contact paper), or vinyl, film. Cut the size required to cover the pattern; peel off the back; hold the film firmly, sticky side down, over the support, and static attraction will cause the pattern to leap

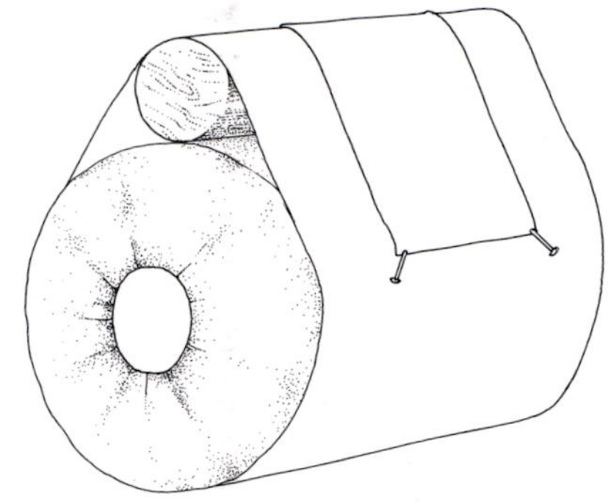

Once the paper pattern has been backed, the layers may in turn be wrapped around a firm pad, small enough to hold in the hand, or be stitched flat to an embroidery frame or, as in the lace-making island of Burano, fixed by pins to a specially designed pillow that can rest on the knees.

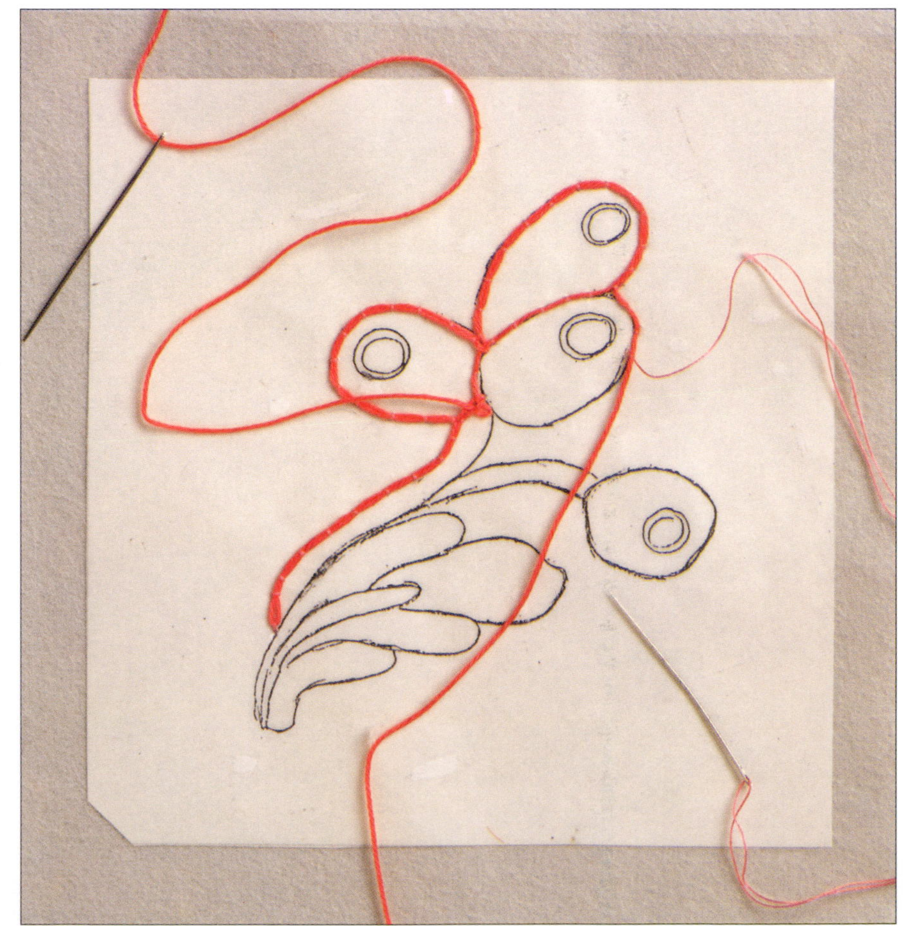

On a complex pattern, cordonnets may also outline the enclosures containing different needlelace fillings. Separate the two strands of the cordonnet and couch one around the enclosure until it joins up again with the double strand. Remember to interlock the cordonnets at every junction so that they cannot separate when the couching stitches are removed. Here, the pattern is held to felt by self-adhesive transparent shelving film.

Architect's linen protects the pattern as effectively as acetate film, but it has no adhesive power and must be stitched down to the support. Here, a sample of the acetate film is being peeled from its backing, ready for use. In the background, a white lace motif is shown, worked over blue-tinted acetate.

upwards towards you. If you are nervous of misattachments – and these are quite irrevocable – first catch the pattern down to the support, using strips of two-sided adhesive tape.

Choose a tint of acetate that will contrast with the threads you intend to use. For economy, clear, matt self-adhesive book covering, available from stationers, can be substituted, in which case it is sensible to draw the pattern on tinted paper.

As well as protecting the pattern on larger works, the stitches must be guarded from secretions from the hands and dirt from the air; cover the lace with a plastic sheet with a small central opening exposing the working area.

The cordonnet

A firm outline of thread is essential for all needlelaces, both to define the shape of the design and to provide an anchorage for the rows of stitches which will pass forwards and back between them. As has already been explained, this has several names, but is here referred to as the cordonnet. It is secured tightly to the pattern by horizontal couching stitches worked along the drawn outline. The couching threads are the only ones to pass through the pattern; all other threads rest on top. Once the lace is off the pattern, only the continuity of the cordonnet and the unfailing attachment of stitch rows to it, will prevent the whole thing falling apart.

It is a wise precaution to make the cordonnet at least twice as long as the actual outline by taking it all around and back again. Double the thread over, and use the loop as the starting point, since this will be easy to secure. If you have a highly convoluted outline, the length needed will be difficult to assess. If the thread runs out, a new one can be joined on by buttonholing the overlapped ends tightly together with the couching thread. Alternatively, they can simply be run through the couching stitches, in either direction.

It is usual to match the colour of the cordonnet with the sewing thread. It may also be advantageous for the colour of the couching thread to match that of the lace. The cordonnet must be quite taut or it will sag as the rows of stitches pull against it. Secure it beneath the left thumb as you make each couching stitch, to prevent slippage. At sharp angles, the couching thread may be knotted tightly at the back of the work.

Laying a cordonnet

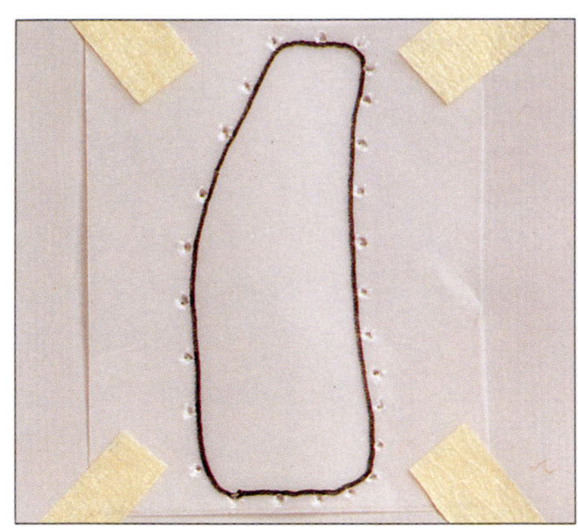

1 Begin by basting the temporary foundation fabric to two layers of cotton backing fabric – 15cm (6in) squares are a convenient size. Trace the required needlelace shapes from the design drawing; this example forms part of a farmer's duffle coat. Use either crewel needles or betweens for couching, and fine tapestry needles or ball point needles to make the needlelace.

2 Place the tracing over the foundation fabric, with a pad beneath, and, using a stiletto, pierce small holes through the pvc around the edges of the traced shape. If the finished lace is to fit over a padded area, make the holes just outside the traced outline. These pinholes mark the line followed by the cordonnet. Remove and discard the tracing paper.

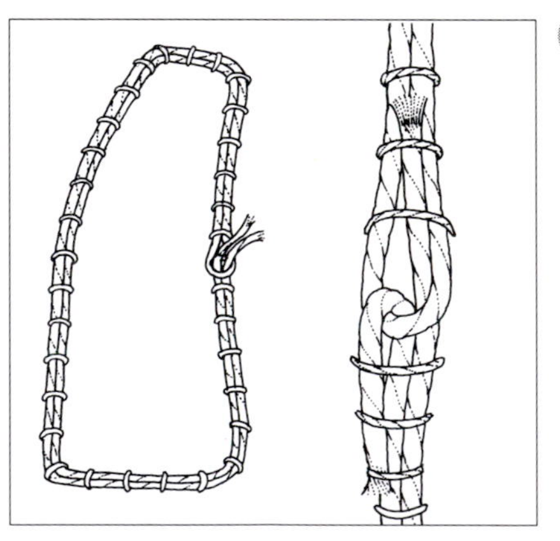

3 Couch the double cordonnet thread over the line of pinholes. Knot the end of the couching thread; bring the needle up through the foundation fabric, and make the first couching stitch in the loop of the double cordonnet thread. Finish by threading and couching the ends of the cordonnet as shown. Couch thin beading wire with the double thread if the lace is to fly 'in the air'.

Wilcke Smith's picture, worked in 1980, features the legendary Fibonacci, whose Book of Counting *was published in 1202. He is wrapped in needlelace stitches and brandishes a golden whip, its tip curled around a tiny square concealing the magic decimal* phi. *Within the curve of the whip huddle generations of rabbits, their ultra-suede bodies revealed by scalpel-slashed cuts in the amate paper ground. These creatures represent Fibonacci's insight into the geometric progression of numbers, first observed in the multiplication of a single pair of rabbits.*

A needlelace starter stitch

The essence of excellent needlelace is an even tension, and in *corded buttonhole stitch*, the long cord stitch that passes across the lace between each row of buttonhole stitches will help you to achieve this. Remember to pass the thread over and around the cordonnet at the beginning and end of each row, and also ensure that the buttonhole stitches along the finishing edge loop over the cordonnet. This total interlinking of stitches and cordonnet provides a kind of selvedge, adding strength to the needlelace. The starting and finishing ends of the working thread must be neatly worked into, and among, other threads of the cordonnet.

Corded buttonhole stitch

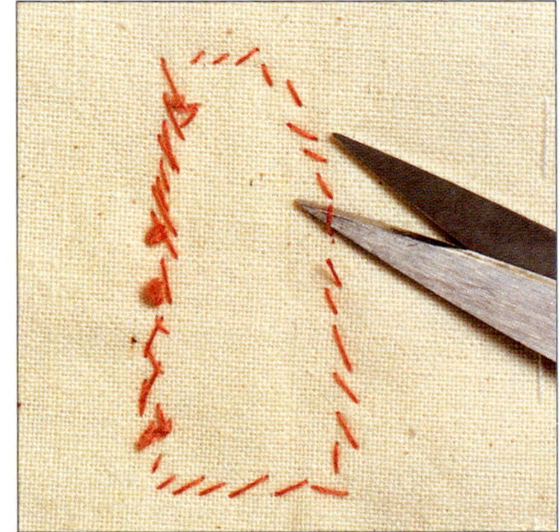

Having prepared the cordonnet, begin stitching at S. Fill the shape with corded buttonhole stitch, as shown in the diagram. The stitches can be worked across or down the shape; attention to this design consideration will enhance the pictorial quality of the finished work. When the shape is filled with lace, buttonhole over the cordonnet around the perimeter of the needlelace for an extra firm, neat finish. Only the couching stitches that anchor the cordonnet are allowed to pass through the foundation fabric.

When the lace is complete, it is removed from the foundation fabric: turn the fabric over and cut the couching stitches on the back. Still working from the back, remove the extraneous pieces of couching thread, using small pliers if necessary. Obstinate fragments of thread can often be dislodged if you cut the basting stitches that hold the pvc to the cotton fabrics and peel these layers apart.

Corded buttonhole variation

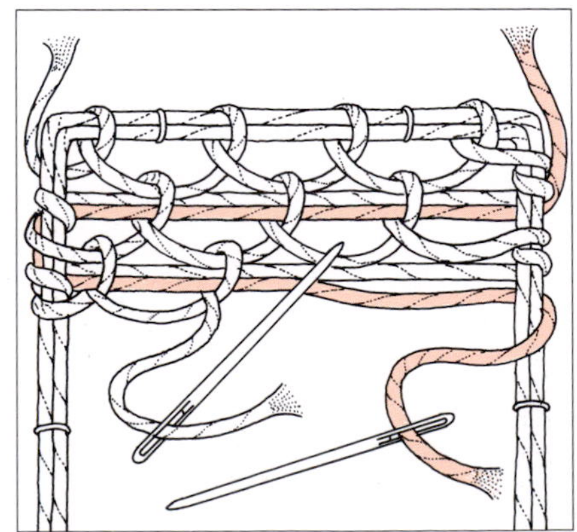

Helpful hints

- If the working thread is three or four times as long as the row, you will have sufficient thread to complete the row with enough thread left over to work it into the cordonnet to conceal the end.
- The type or colour of thread may be changed, but for simplicity this should occur at the beginning of a new row of stitches. When the rows are of varying colours, it may be necessary to select one of the colours to buttonhole the finished lace edge, giving it a neat and uniform appearance.
- Any buttonholing, picots or cordonnette on the edge of the lace, or other additional buttonhole trimmings, should be worked onto the lace before it is removed from the temporary foundation fabric.
- Regularly untwist the working thread to avoid knots and snarls.

More needlelace stitches

The four needlelace stitches given below might well prove sufficient for any raised embroidery, but they represent only a fraction of those that can be attempted. The *corded buttonhole variation* differs from corded buttonhole by the introduction of a second cord thread (using a second needle), which offers a means of introducing a second colour into the lace, with a resulting tweed-like effect. All these stitches are so straightforward that they require no explanation other than the stitch diagram, but you should note that the appearance can vary according to whether the stitches have been worked tightly or loosely, giving a lacy effect. By taking advantage of this, you will extend the range of application of each stitch.

Single Brussels

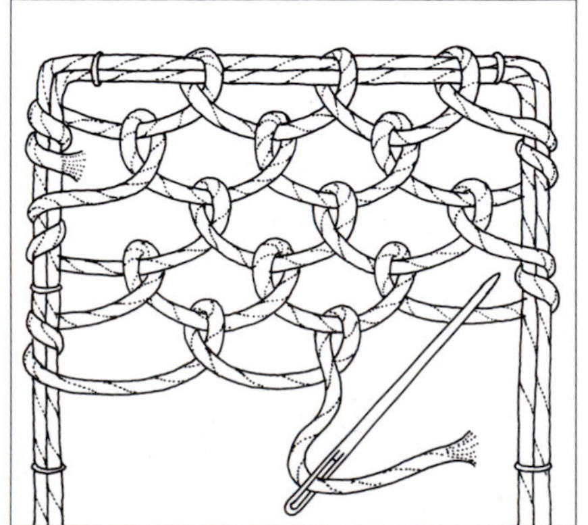

Double Brussels

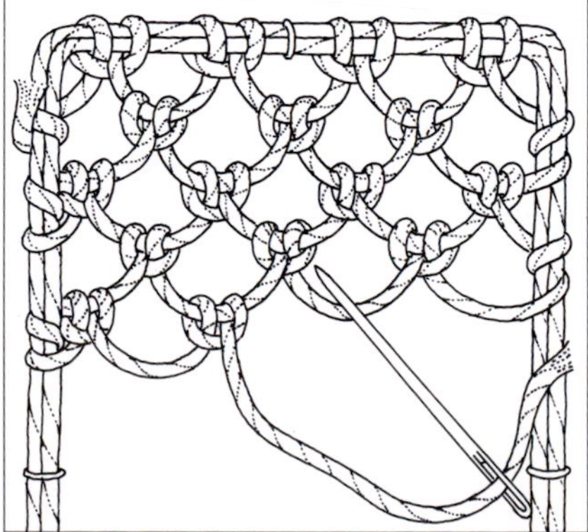

Treble Brussels

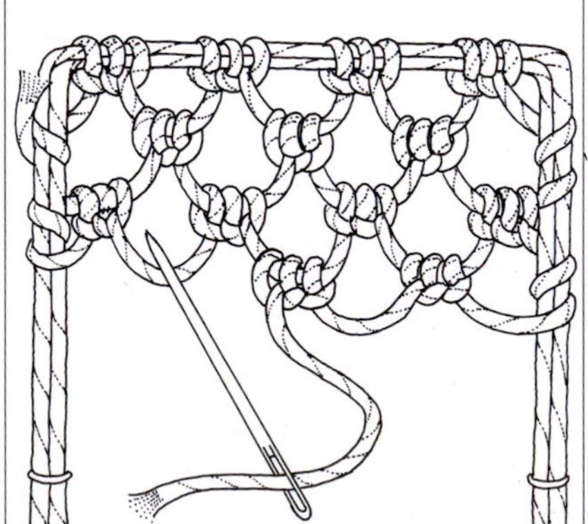

Pin and loop picots

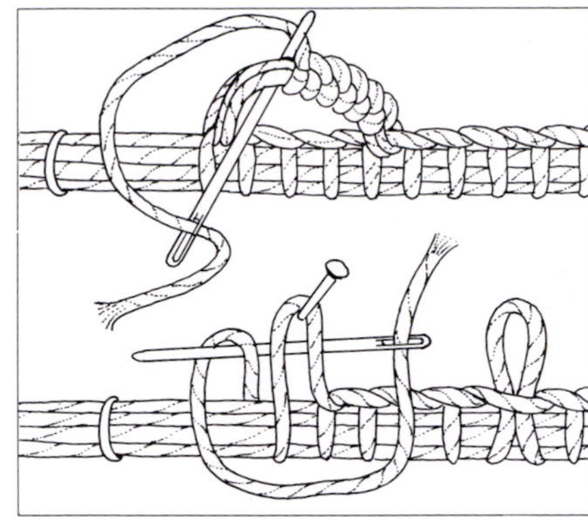

Picots are formed on the edge of the finished lace. For pin picots, use a pin at regular intervals to form projecting decorative loops. Make a regular number of buttonhole stitches along the edge of the lace before working a picot stitch as illustrated. With the loop picot, the loops are formed by bringing the working thread back to an earlier buttonhole stitch, repeating this several times to create a bundle of threads, and then buttonholing over the bundle of looped threads.

Plain and spiral cordonnette

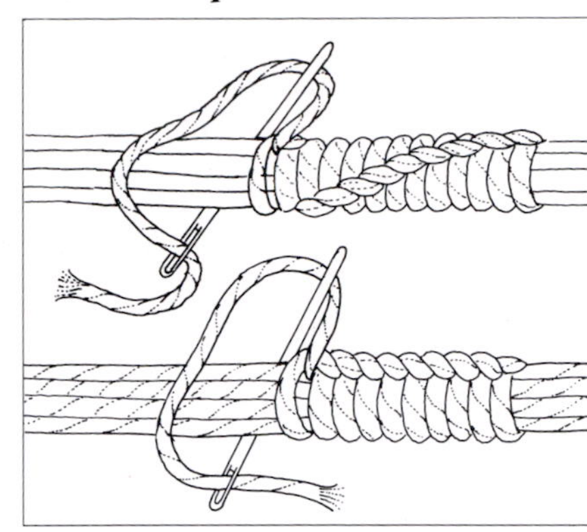

A cordonnette is really a bundle of threads, of any thickness, buttonhole stitched to the cordonnet. Start by anchoring the bundle to the cordonnet with a few stitches and then keep it taut while buttonhole stitching. The spiral effect is created when the knot on each successive stitch is set higher than the last, so that they move from the bottom to the top of the cordonnette. Having reached the top, pass the needle behind the bundle and start again at the bottom. A cordonnette can be worked directly on the ground fabric (start by couching down a bundle of threads).

This simple child study, Edwardian Children, *provides numerous stitch opportunities. Lacy treble brussels stitch on the girl's skirt contrasts with corded brussels; minute scraps of needlelace form a nosegay of flowers; a three-dimensional hat is composed of single brussels stitch and buttonhole stitching over card; and additional needlelace and embellishments include pin picots and loop picots. Size: 21cm × 16cm (8in × 6in)*

Buttonhole trimmings

Each of the trimmings illustrated and described makes use of the simple buttonhole stitch. Although intended as appendages to lace, they can often be divorced from it and are used by raised-work embroiderers in unorthodox ways to decorate and embellish the embroidery.

Buttonhole over card

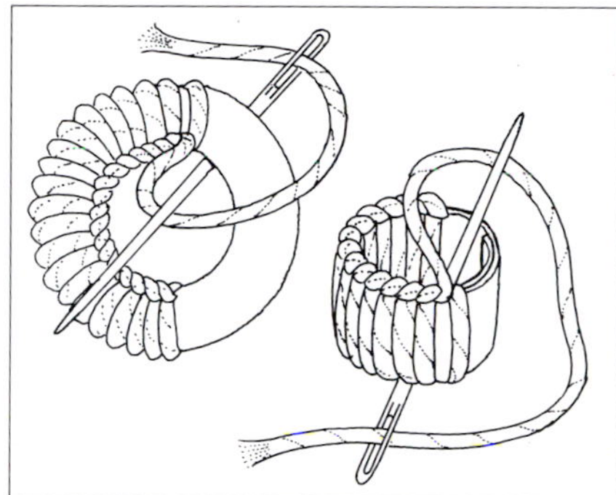

Here, buttonhole stitch is worked over flat and tabular cardboard shapes, which are then assembled to form a hat. Used imaginatively, the technique can be developed to create small pliable relief images. With tubular forms, the end can be closed by continuing the stitches around until the space is filled.

Minute lace fragments

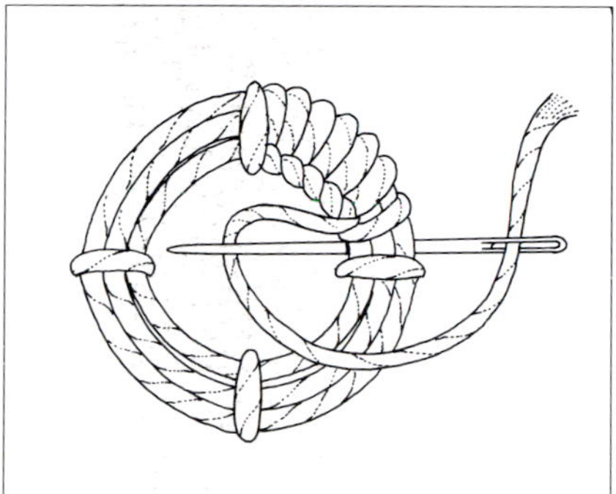

Start by working four couching stitches through a (temporary) foundation fabric, as shown. Pass two or three threads beneath the couching stitches, then buttonhole over the threads, keeping the knot of each buttonhole stitch on the inside of the ring. Stitch around until the space within the ring is filled. If the knots are on the outer edge of the ring, a buttonhole ring can be created.

Couronne

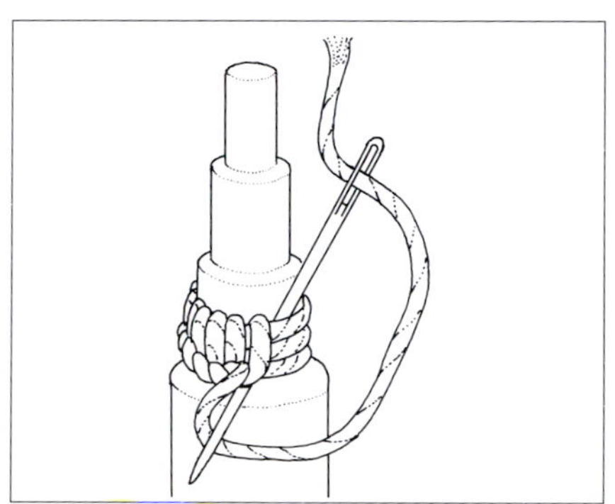

A well-formed couronne, or buttonhole ring, is worked on a ring stick, as shown above. These are available from specialist needlelace stockists, but any dowel-like object will suffice. Wrap the thread around the ring stick for two or three turns, and then continue buttonholing over the wrapped threads. Work the final stitch into the first one. When using the ring stick, the threads are wrapped around a thick part of the stick, but are then slipped onto a thinner part to facilitate buttonholing.

SMOCKING

Traditionally, smocking was used to decorate clothing, but the gathering techniques and smocking stitches shown here can be adapted in many ways, and incorporated into other forms of embroidery.

Materials

Although the vast choice of fabrics available today can be quite bewildering, it is also very exciting. New fabrics are constantly being created, and the colours, textures, richness and delicacy are an inspiration to dressmakers and embroiderers alike.

The traditional natural fabrics for smocking are still available, and cottons, linens, wools and silks will always be popular. However, mixtures of these with man-made fibres combine the practicality of easy care and crease resistance with the properties of the natural fibres. For instance, polyester/cotton mixtures are ideal for children's clothes, because they wear well and wash easily. Cotton, cotton lawn, wool/cotton mixtures and fine denim also smock well.

Care needs to be taken when choosing fabrics to smock for adult clothes. As well as being suitable for the style, a fabric must hang and drape well, to avoid too much bulk. Polyester cottons, pure cottons, silks, wool crêpe, challis and fine jersey all smock beautifully. Chiffon, crêpe de chine, georgette, velvet and loose knitted fabrics are more difficult to handle, but will give lovely results for the more experienced smocker.

Whichever fabric you choose, make sure it is of good quality. There is a temptation, when starting out, to buy a cheap fabric so as not to waste money. This is always a false economy – you will be disappointed with the result, because a poor fabric does not show your smocking to advantage and will not do justice to the time and effort you have spent on it. Good quality fabric does not need to be expensive, and there are plenty of cottons, as well as mixtures of polyester with either cotton or wool, all of which are suitable for smocking. The fabric should be evenly woven and have enough weight to hang well, and when gathered, the folds should have a rounded shape, providing a good base for your smocking stitches.

Smocked and padded shapes are used in this detail from a three-dimensional panel by Sian Burgess to suggest a variety of bracket fungi and toadstools in a woodland setting. The shapes are stitched to a ruched background and surrounded with leaves and ferns.

Gathering threads

These are used to gather the fabric and pull it up into pleats, ready for smocking. Good quality cotton thread or polyester/ cotton No. 40 are suitable for most fabrics, but if you are smocking a heavy-weight fabric you may need to use buttonhole twist or quilting thread for extra strength. The gathering threads form the guidelines for your smocking stitches, so choose a colour that contrasts with your fabric.

Embroidery threads

Any good quality embroidery thread (see page 14) can be used for smocking, as long as its weight is in proportion to that of the fabric. Suitable threads include stranded cotton, coton à broder, perlé cotton and soft cotton, all of which are readily available in a good range of colours. Stranded cotton has a good sheen; coton à broder is a very smooth shiny single-strand cotton, available in a variety of thicknesses; No. 25 is the finest, but you will also find 20, 16 and 12. Perlé cotton is a twisted cotton with a sheen; Nos 3 and 5 are available in skeins and No. 8 (the finest) in balls. Soft cotton is a thick matt embroidery thread.

Danish flower threads are also useful. These are fine dull cotton threads in lovely natural colours. Silk threads may be either stranded or twisted and are available in a range of thicknesses. Linen threads come in a good range of colours – if you can find them. They are twisted, have a sheen, and are very strong. Rayon threads may be either stranded or twisted and are very shiny, catching the light beautifully, but they are rather springy to sew with. Crochet cotton is a rather hard thread, but available in a range of weights.

Knitting yarns in wool, cotton or lurex are all worth trying. For more experimental work, cotton and rayon tapes, ribbons, metallic threads, and space-dyed threads produce very interesting results.

Needles

Crewel needles with a long eye are ideal for smocking. Sizes 7, 8 or 9 are the most useful, but try out different sizes before you start. The needle must be large enough to be threaded easily, without splitting the thread, and it should pass through the fabric easily, without leaving a large hole.

Diamond stitch (see page 64) is a good subject for experiments in random stitching. Stitch the first row at varying levels and with different sizes of zigzag. Form irregular diamonds with the second row, matching the straight stitches at the centre but not mirroring the bottom half of the diamond. Overlay these shapes by making other random diamond stitches, using contrasting textures and colours of thread. Try setting the straight stitches at the top and bottom of the diamonds at an angle, to vary the effect.

Using transfer dots

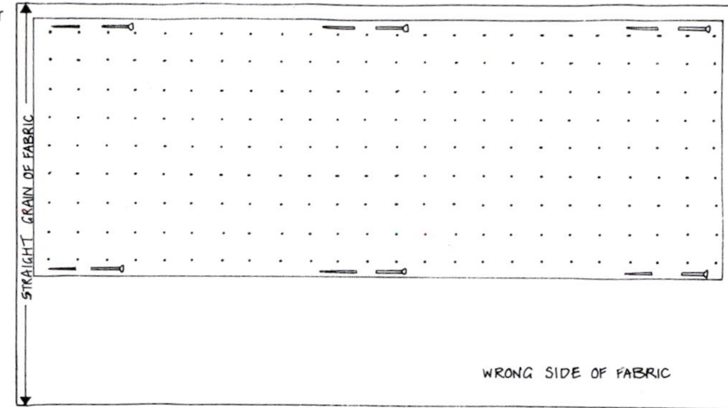

1 **To make sure that your fabric has been cut on the straight grain, pull out a weft thread along the top edge. If there is any distortion, use this line as a guide when cutting away surplus fabric.**

2 **To use transfer dots, first test on a spare piece of fabric, then cut a transfer sheet to the correct size and place it, wax side down, on the wrong side of the fabric. Align it with the straight grain, and allow an extra row of dots at the top and bottom – these will give you greater control when you stitch. Pin the sheet in place; press the iron firmly over it; raise it, then place it on the next section. Do not rub the iron or the dots will be smudged. Lift a corner and check that the dots have transferred before you remove the sheet.**

Preparing the fabric

The folds or pleats on which the smocking stitches are worked are formed by rows of gathering stitches, placed exactly above one another. In the past, this was done by eye, but now there are various methods to help mark the fabric. These mark the picking-up points for the gathering threads and must be placed accurately on the straight grain of the fabric so that the pleats fall straight and parallel.

Care in preparation at this stage is essential and will result in a beautifully gathered piece of fabric. This is part of the charm of smocking, as well as a basis for your stitches. Press the fabric well, so that there are no creases to distort the placing of the dots.

Smocking dot transfers

These are ironed on the fabric and are sold, in a variety of sizes, in sheets about 18cm (7in) deep and 90cm (36in) wide. The size you use depends on the fabric: fine fabrics need shallow folds and therefore closely placed dots; widely placed dots make deeper folds, and allow for the bulk of heavier fabrics. As a general guide, dots 6mm (¼in) apart are ideal for polyester/cotton or lawn. Cut off the manufacturer's name to use for testing on a small piece of your fabric, in order to determine the lowest heat setting at which your iron will transfer the dots clearly. Too hot a setting will make the dots show on the right side, and may distort a man-made fabric. Place the test piece of transfer face down on the wrong side of the fabric and iron firmly. Check also at this stage that the transfer dots will wash out, then mark the main fabric.

Tissue paper

This method is the best for fine, delicate fabrics, through which the transfer dots would be visible, or for patterned materials on which the dots would not show. Mark the dot pattern on tissue paper, using a sheet of transfer dots as a guide. Baste the tissue paper firmly to the wrong side of the fabric, taking care to align the dots with the straight grain. Using the gathering thread, pick up the tissue and fabric together at each dot and gently pull the tissue away when all the gathering is complete.

Water- and air-soluble pens

Semi-transparent materials can be marked with either a water- or air-soluble pen, both of which look like felt tip pens. The dots marked with the water-soluble pen can be sponged away gently with a damp cloth after the gathering has been completed. The dots marked with the air-soluble pen will disappear within 24 hours, so gathering must be completed as soon as possible after marking. This pen is invaluable for marking silk fabrics, which might be stained by water.

Mark the wrong side of the fabric, following the straight grain. Use a ruler or a sheet of smocking dots as a guide. The rows of dots are repeated evenly and are spaced to the required depth. Another method is to baste a sheet of smocking dots to the right side of the fabric; hold it up against a window or over glass with a light underneath, so that the dots show through the fabric, then mark the dots on the wrong side.

A smocking machine is useful for gathering, particularly if you are working in large quantities. The chief disadvantage of smocking machines (apart from the price) is that the depth of gathering is limited by the width of the rollers.

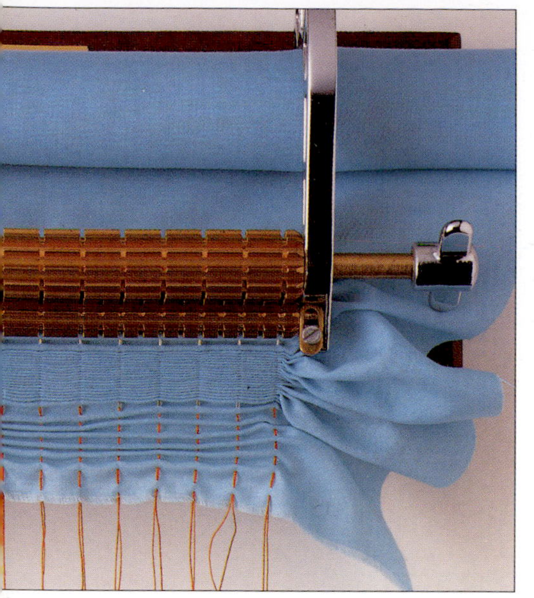

Gathering the fabric

When the dots have been marked, the fabric can then be gathered, either by hand, as shown, or by machine. The latter is available in two widths and has a series of needles that are threaded with cotton and are set between rotating rollers. As the fabric is fed through the machine it is gathered to the required depth.

The machine does, however, have some limitations: only lightweight fabrics can be used, and the pleat depth is set at approximately 6mm (¼in) and cannot be varied. It requires some skill to feed the fabric through the rollers, keeping the grain straight right across the piece of fabric, although this can be helped by rolling the fabric around a thick dowel first. For experimental work, when the position of the straight grain is not so vital, a machine can be used very successfully.

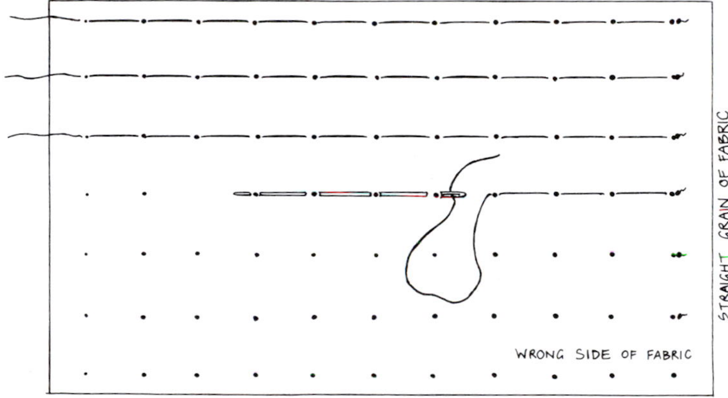

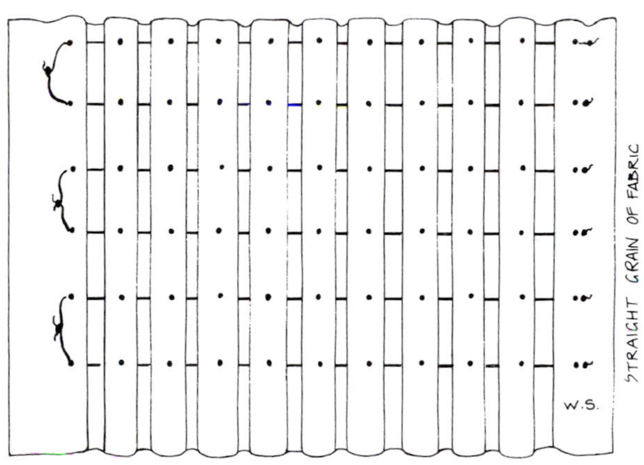

1 **Use a contrasting thread, a little longer than the width of the fabric. Make a firm knot at one end and, working on the wrong side of the fabric, start with a small back stitch at the first dot, to hold the thread securely when you gather. Pick up a small amount of fabric at each dot and work across the row, leaving the thread hanging loose at the end. After a little practice, you can pick up several stitches on the needle before pulling the thread through. Continue across each row in turn.**

2 **When all the rows are complete, hold the thread ends and gently ease the fabric along the threads, forming the folds. Pull the fabric lengthwise every so often, to help to set the pleats. If there is any puckering, pull the fabric lengthwise again and stroke along the pleats with a blunt needle. Wrap pairs of threads around a pin to hold them until you are ready to smock. Then undo the pins, and ease the pleats out to a little less than the required finished length. You should be able to see the gathering threads between the pleats. Knot the threads in pairs.**

Smocking stitches

All smocking patterns are based on the following stitches. Correct tension is essential for a neat finish and the desired amount of elasticity, and practice is the only way to achieve this.

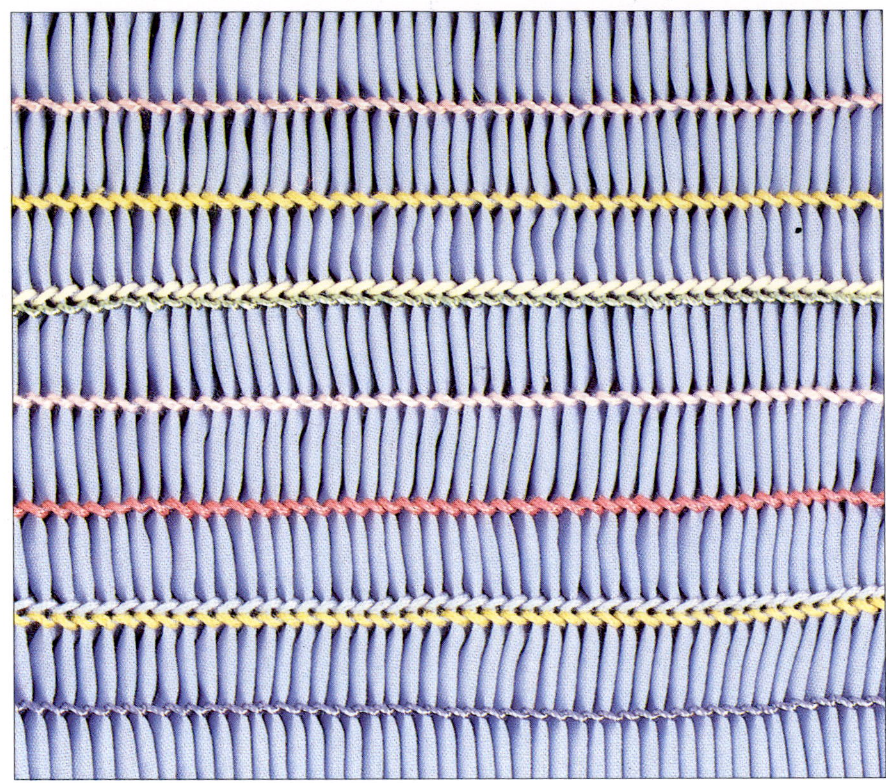

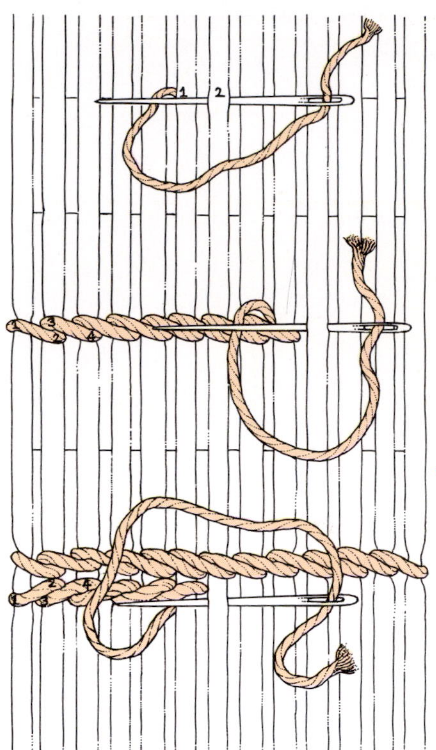

To make a row of outline stitching, take approximately 45cm (18in) of thread and make a knot at one end. Bring the needle up through the left-hand side of the first pleat, level with a row of gathering threads. Keeping the thread below the needle, push the needle into the right-hand side of the next pleat and at right angles to it. Bring it out on the left side, picking up the top third of the pleat. Continue in the same way, picking up each pleat in turn. Keep a straight line, using the gathering thread as a guide. When you reach the end, push the needle down beside the last pleat and fasten off with two or three back stitches on the back of the pleat.

Outline stitch

This is also known as rope stitch and was widely used on the old smocks. It is worked in the same way as stem stitch, in surface embroidery, and is a useful first stitch in a design because it holds the pleats firmly. It forms a continuous rolled line that can be used to outline other stitches.

Other rows can be added to the first, perhaps with the spacing between them varied, to suit the design. When a second row of this stitch is placed just under the first, the thread may be kept above the needle, reversing the stitch to form a wheatear or mock chain stitch.

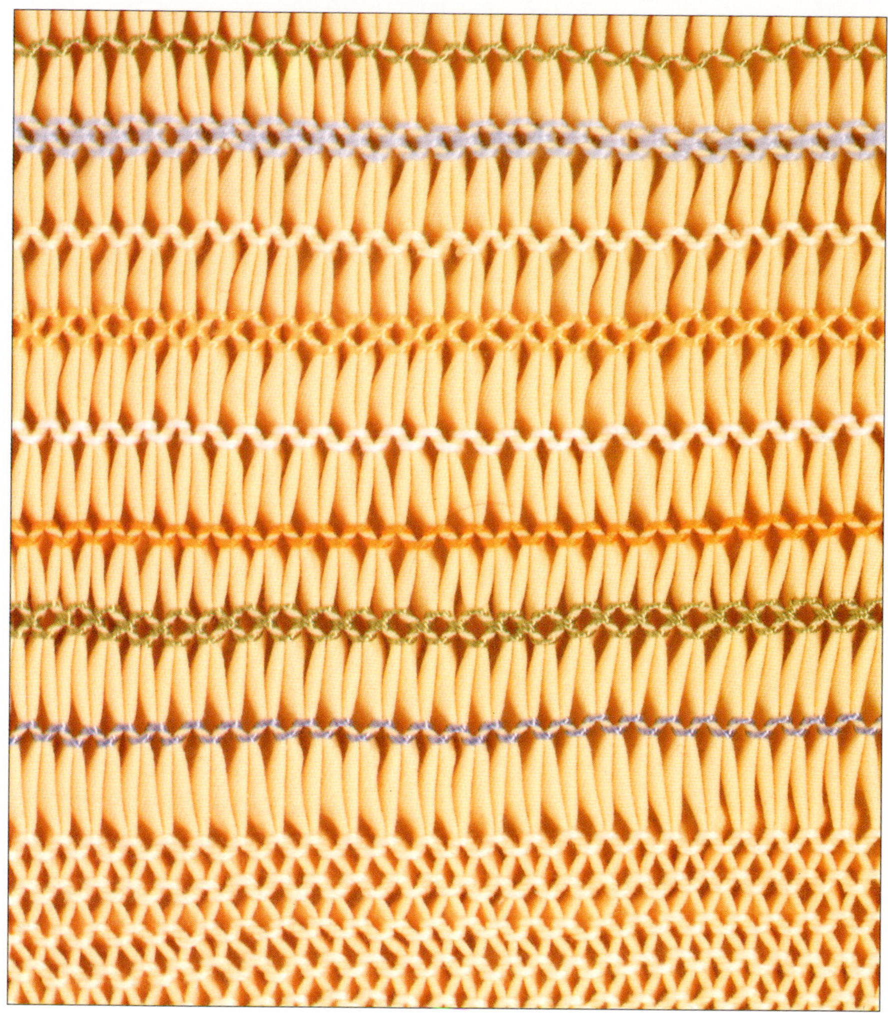

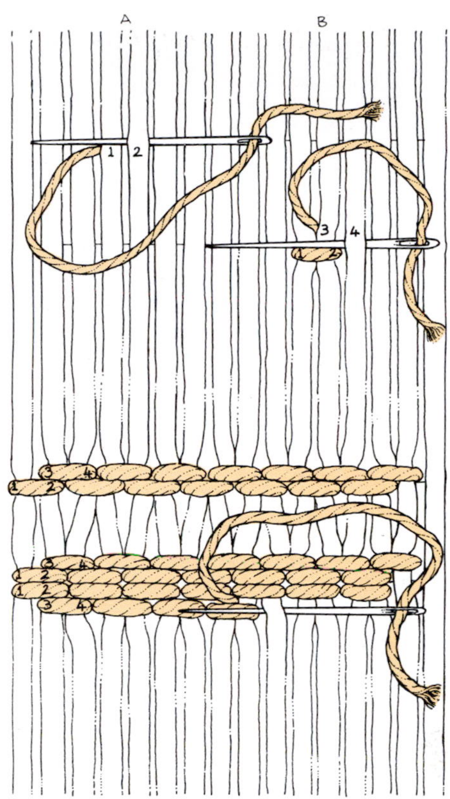

For cable stitch, start off as for outline, taking the first stitch with the thread below the needle (A). Next, place the thread above the needle and take the second stitch (B). Keep your needle at right angles to the pleats, and maintain a straight line across the work, picking up each pleat in turn. The stitches should be rounded and should sit neatly, lying alternately above and below each other. Learn to recognize the shape of the stitch, and you will soon see if you have made a mistake, forgetting to change the position of the thread with each stitch.

Cable stitch

This is worked in the same way as outline stitch, but it appears different because the thread is placed alternately above and below the needle. This is a firm stitch and, like outline stitch, it is a useful way of holding the pleats at the start of a pattern. It can be repeated in spaced rows, and was used in this way on many of the old smocks. It forms an interesting texture, rather like purl knitting.

Double cable

Two rows of cable stitch, worked closely together, make a double cable, looking rather like the links of a chain. The second row is an exact reverse of the first, so if you started the first row with the thread below the needle, start the first stitch of the second row with the thread above the needle. The stitches should lie neatly together, alternately touching and then leaving a space.

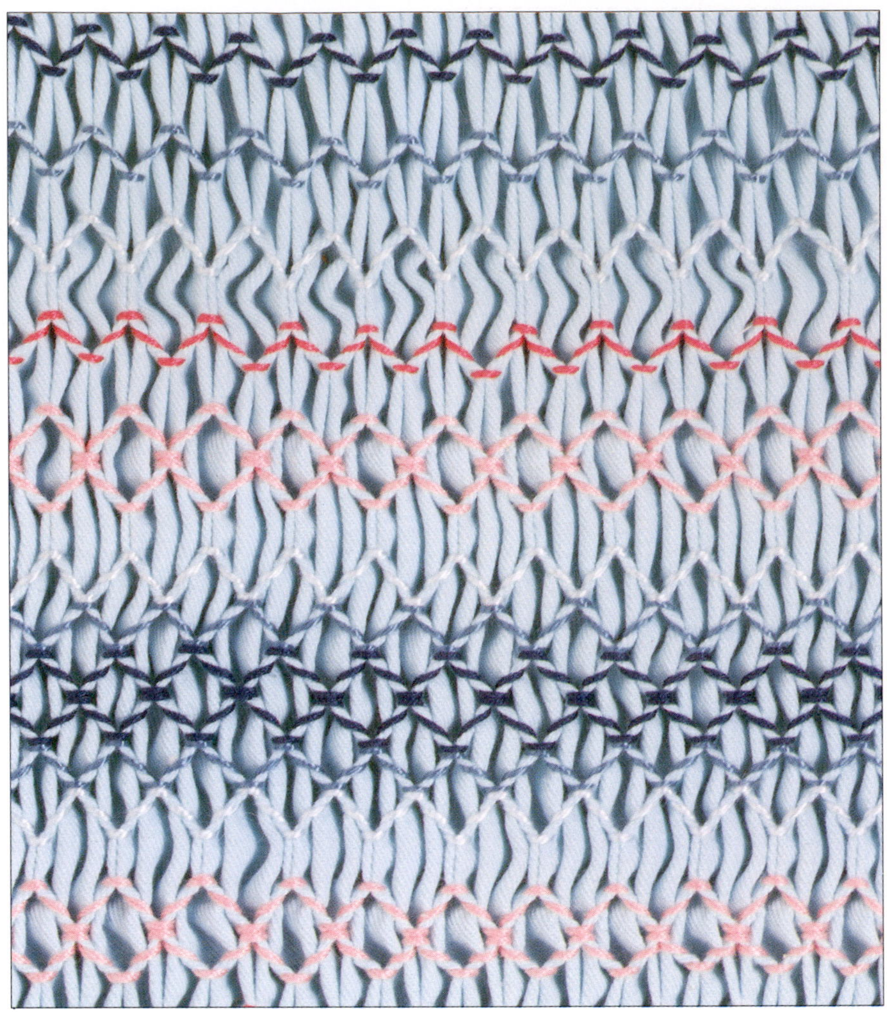

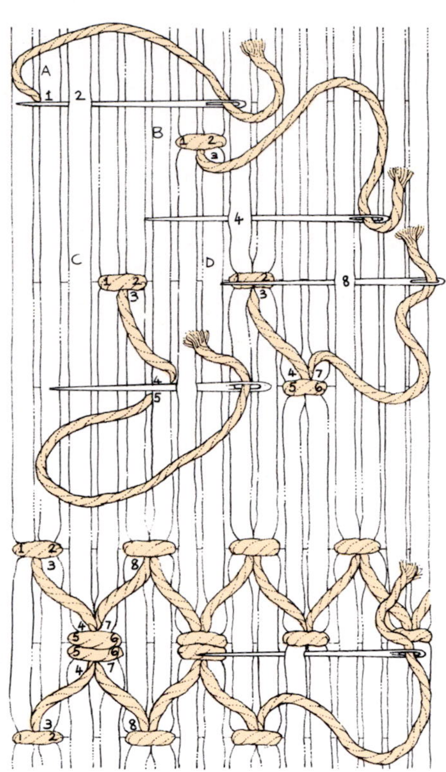

Diamond stitch is worked using two rows of gathering stitches as guidelines. Bring the thread out to the left of the first pleat. Put the needle through the next pleat (A), keeping the needle horizontal, with the thread above it, as for cable stitch. The next stitch is taken on a level with the lower gathering thread: keeping the thread above the needle and the needle horizontal, take a stitch through the next pleat (B). Next, place the thread below the needle and take a stitch into the adjacent pleat, as for cable stitch (C). With the thread still below the needle, take a stitch into the next pleat, level with the top row of gathering threads (D).

Diamond stitch

This is a very versatile stitch, which can be used in blocks, and works well with other stitches. It can also be overlapped, as will be shown later. The instructions describe how to make one half of the stitch, and this can be used on its own, in spaced rows. The diamond is formed by making a second row, reversing the stitch.

This is a quick stitch to work and its wide spacing makes it very elastic. Beware of making the diamond stitches too large, as will be the case if your gathering rows are more than 12mm (½in) apart. If this is so, work the complete diamond between the two rows of gathering threads, bringing the needle down at B to half way between the two rows.

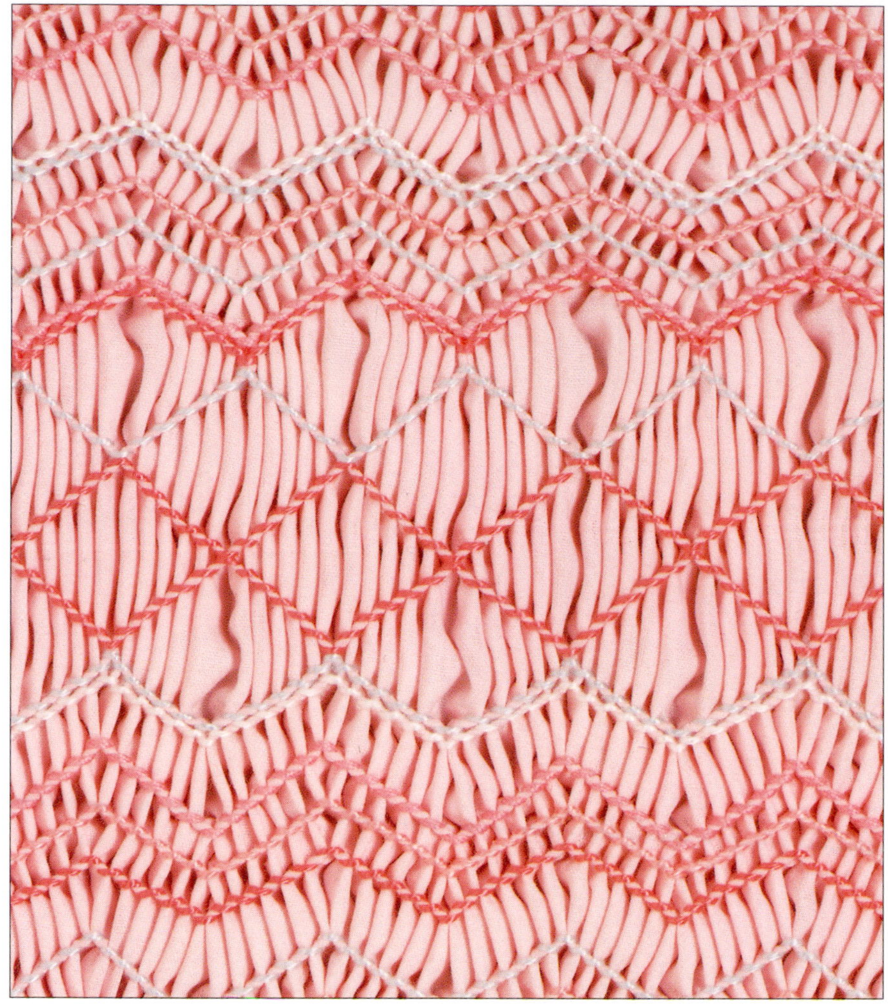

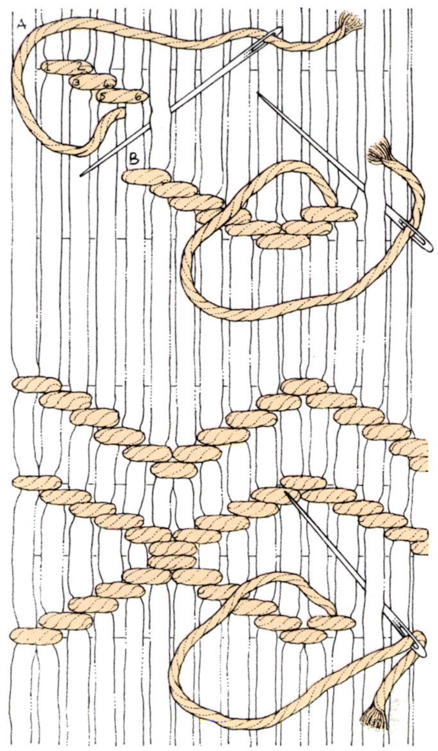

To make wave stitch, start by bringing the needle up on the left-hand side of the first pleat. Keeping the thread up, take a stitch into the next pleat at the same level, but with the needle angled slightly downward. Continue to stitch in this way, making sure that you keep the stitches even, until you reach the lower gathering thread (A). Keeping the thread down, take the next stitch with the needle angled slightly upward. Continue to work up, making the same number of stitches as were made on the way down and keeping them even (B).

Wave and trellis stitch

This is worked diagonally in steps down and up between two rows of gathering threads. To keep the stitches lying straight across the pleats, the needle is angled down when working down and up when working up. As a result, the stitches are stacked step by step. If the needle were to be kept straight when making this stitch, the thread would finish at an angle to the pleats.

The instructions describe how to make one row of wave stitch. The rows can be spaced apart or set close together, which makes a much bolder wave. This can look very attractive if you use a succession of threads in tones of the same colour.

Trellis stitch is formed by reversing the process, creating a row of diamond shapes. These can stand on their own or in combination with wave stitch, and are used effectively in many designs. This is a stitch that takes some practice to perfect, but it is well worth the effort.

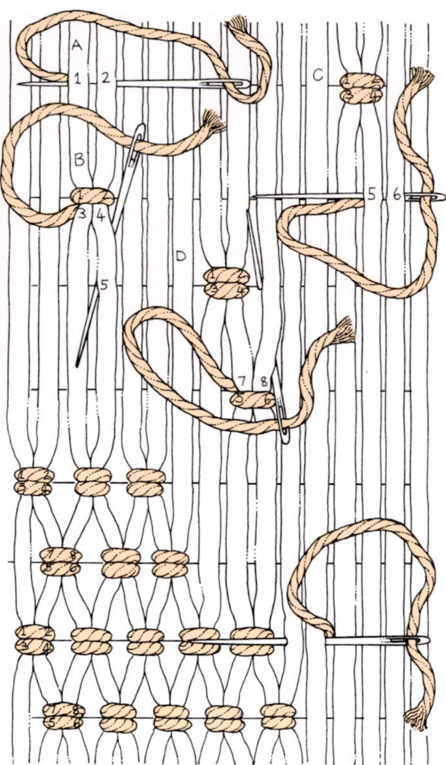

Keep the thread above or below the needle, according to the diagram. Bring the needle out on the left of the first pleat, at right angles to it; stitch into the second pleat and through to the left side of the first, pulling them together (A). Insert the needle into the right side of the second pleat; angle it down under the fabric, bringing it out at the left side of the second pleat, level with the lower gathering row (B). Stitch through the third and second pleats (C). Insert the needle into the right side of the third pleat and angle it up behind the fabric and out on the left side of the third pleat, level with the top gathering row (D).

Honeycomb stitch

As its name implies, this stitch creates a texture that resembles the cells of a bee hive. Because there is very little surface stitchery, honeycomb has a delicate appearance, and it is very elastic. Like diamond stitch, it is worked between two rows of gathering threads or, if the gap between the rows is too large, you can take the stitches to a point halfway between the rows. After you have made the first row, the second and subsequent rows are worked in the same way, building up the characteristic cell structure.

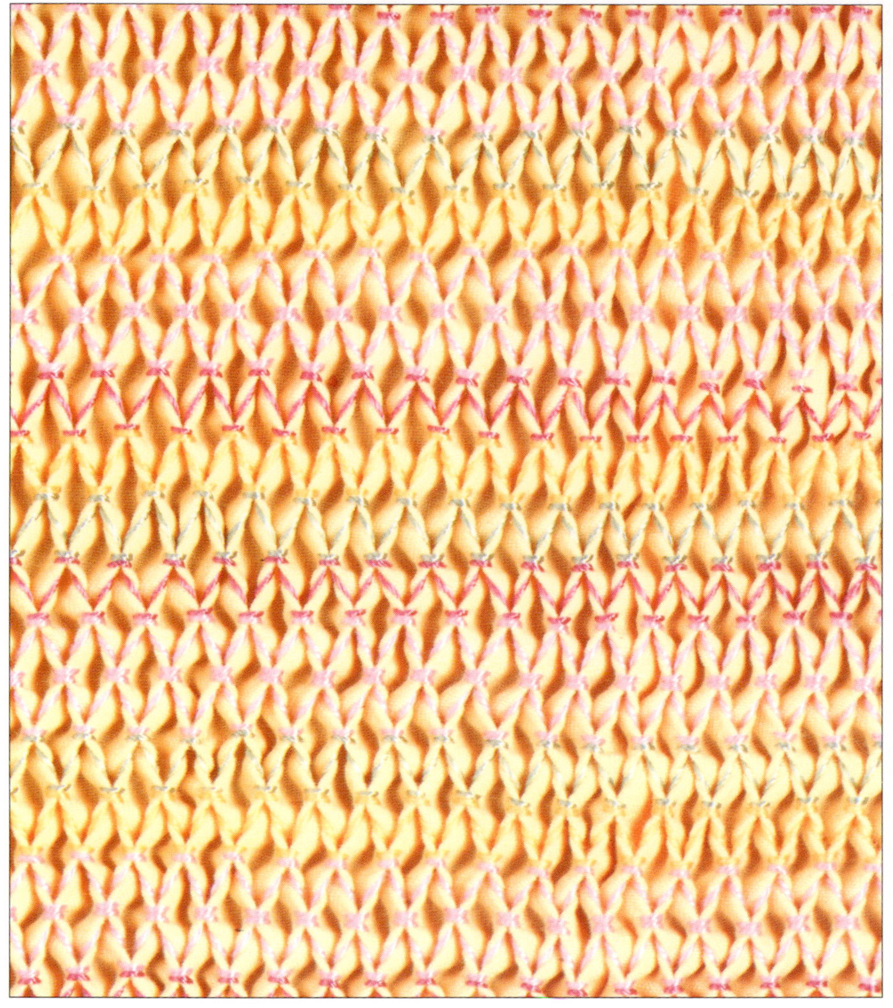

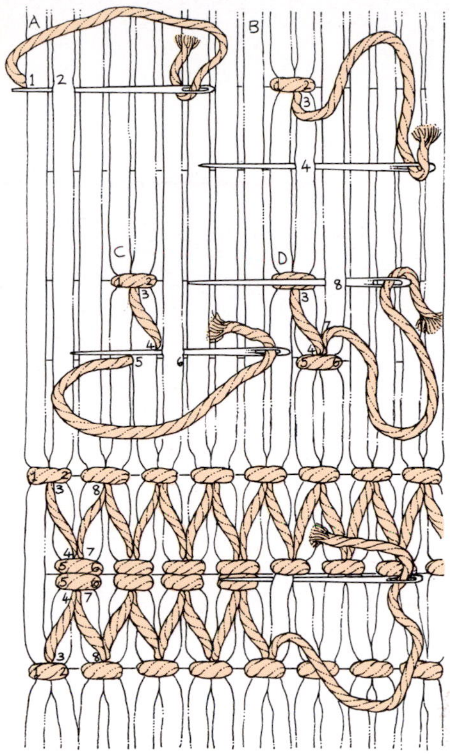

Begin surface honeycomb by bringing the needle out on the left-hand side of the first pleat, in line with the top gathering thread. Keeping the thread above the needle and the needle at right angles to the pleat, pick up a stitch on the second pleat, as for cable stitch (A). Take another stitch on the second pleat, again with the thread above the needle, but this time at the lower level (B). Take a stitch through the third pleat, with the thread below the needle (C). Keeping the thread below the needle, take another stitch through the third pleat, but at the top level of gathering threads (D). Continue across the row.

Surface honeycomb

All the stitchery is on the front of the fabric when you use surface honeycomb: the pleats are stitched across, as with cable stitch, but they are also wrapped with thread, resulting in a highly textured surface. If you follow the first row by stitching the second row in reverse, a wrapped diamond shape will result.

Surface honeycomb is worked in almost the same way as diamond stitch, and consequently the two are sometimes confused. As with diamond stitch and honeycomb, use two rows of gathering threads as guides, or stitch to a point halfway between the rows. The difference between diamond and surface honeycomb is that in the latter case, the stitch is taken over the same pleat, wrapping it with thread.

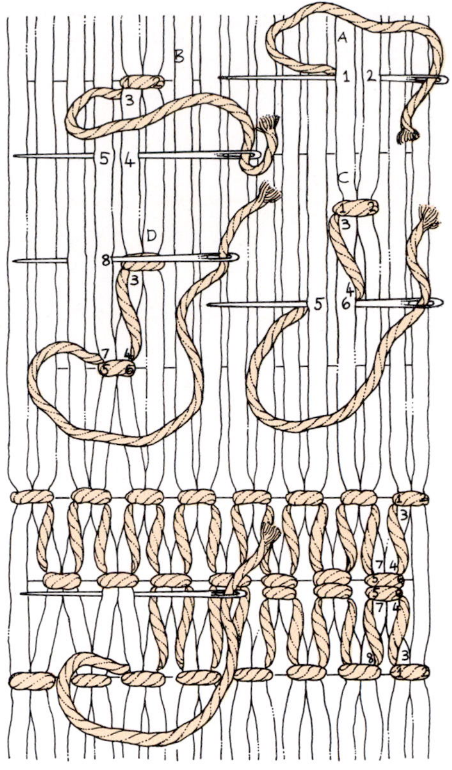

Vandyke stitch

This stitch is worked from right to left. The thread is wrapped around the pleats, as in surface honeycomb, but as it is worked in a different direction the resulting cell shape has a slightly square appearance. Vandyke stitch can be used on its own, in spaced rows, or you can work a second row in reverse, to form a square, wrapped shape.

Keep the thread above or below the needle, according to the diagram. Bring the thread up on the left side of the second pleat from the right end of the work. With the needle horizontal, backstitch through the first and second pleats (A). Drop to the lower gathering row; insert the needle into the right side of the second pleat and through the third, wrapping the second (B). Backstitch through the second and third pleats (C). Wrap the third pleat by inserting the needle into the right side of the third pleat, level with the top gathering row, and through to the fourth pleat. Backstitch these pleats together and continue to the end of the row (D).

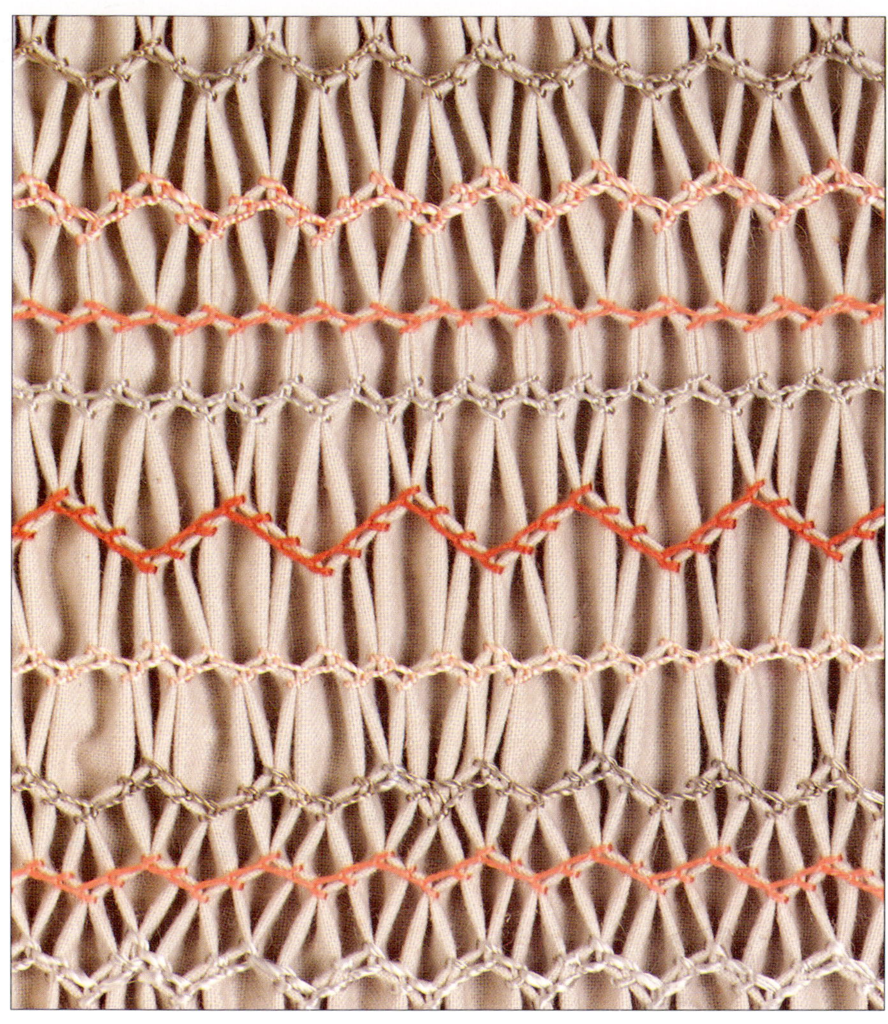

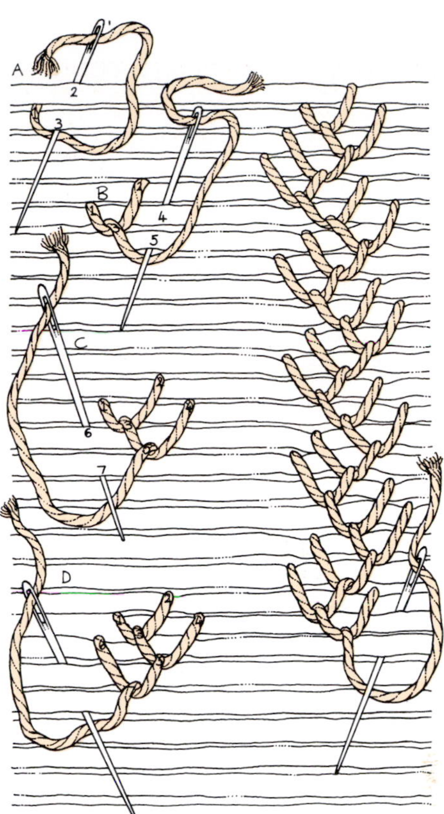

Feather stitch

In pictures of old smocks, you will see this stitch used extensively to form the patterns that decorate the boxes, collars and yokes. It can also be used as a smocking stitch, in which case it is worked in just the same way as on flat fabric.

The stitch is formed with a loop, as with blanket stitch, and it changes direction from side to side, with either one, two or three stitches each way, to create a pretty zigzag line. For a wider zigzag, three stitches each side can be taken, or for a narrower line, just one stitch each side. Try to keep the stitches evenly spaced and the tension constant throughout. This is a light, delicate stitch, contrasting well with the more geometric shapes of the other smocking stitches. In the diagram, the stitch is worked over two pleats at a time, but for a more elastic stitch you can work over one pleat at a time.

Turn the fabric so that the pleats lie horizontally, and stitch towards you. Bring the needle up under the first pleat, then swing the thread down and to the right. Holding the thread with your thumb, take a stitch to the right, through the first and second pleats. Bring the needle out over the thread, forming a loop (A). Take the next stitch in the same way, through the second and third pleats, making a step to the right (B). Now swing the thread down and to the left, and take the next stitch to the left, forming a loop as before (C). Continue, taking two stitches to the left and right in turn, dropping one pleat each time (D).

Finishing and stretching

When you have completed a smocking pattern, place the smocked fabric face down on an ironing board and pin it in position, keeping the pleats straight. Using a steam iron or a dry iron and a damp cloth, steam the smocking to set the pleats and stitches, holding the iron just above the fabric. Never press the smocking, or the pleats will flatten and be distorted. Leave the piece to dry completely; then unpin it, and remove the gathering threads.

If the smocking is to be set into a garment, leave the top gathering thread in place, as this helps to control the pleats while you are making it up. Sometimes the smocking may seem a little too tight to fit into position in a garment, but it can be stretched slightly: remove the gathering threads and pull out the smocking gently and evenly to the required width. Pin the smocked fabric to an ironing board, pulling the pleats straight. Steam the smocking as before and leave it to dry, when it should retain the correct width.

If the tension of the stitches is too tight to allow much movement, you will not be able to stretch the work, even by steaming, without distorting the pleats. For this reason, always make a tension sample before embarking on a large piece of work. A heavy concentration of stitches may also hold the pleats tightly, so try to space the rows of stitches, in order to allow adequate elasticity.

A finished piece of smocking is pinned, right side down, to an ironing board. The steam from the iron, which is held just above the fabric, helps to set the pleats.

Reverse smocking

This technique is used to control the pleats on the wrong side of the fabric in areas where there is no surface smocking. This could be at the centre of a large trellis pattern, where the pleats are not covered by stitching and would stretch out of shape unless held in place at the back. When a space that is wider than usual is required between the rows of a design, the use of reverse smocking is advisable. It can also be used to create a free area on the surface of the pleats where you wish to stitch a motif or to add free surface embroidery. If the pleats are controlled at the back of the fabric in this way, the front becomes rippled and slightly distorted when the gathering threads are removed, producing an interesting texture.

The effect varies from stitch to stitch: look at the back of the stitch samples you have made; stretch them out gently, and see how the pleats become slightly twisted out of line. In this way, you can judge which stitch is the most suitable to use for reverse stitching in order to give you the effect that you want on the front. Cable and outline stitch control the pleats firmly and result in a faint line showing across the surface. More open stitches, such as surface honeycomb and diamond stitch, will give a lighter effect and are more elastic. Honeycomb stitch should not be used for reverse smocking, as the threads that run behind the pleats will be seen on the right side. Whichever stitch is used, only a small amount of fabric should be picked up, or the backs of the stitches may show on the right side.

The body of the fish, formed with surface honeycomb and beading, appears to recede into the background of reverse smocking.

Reverse smocking can be used to distort the fabric into the attractive rippled patterns.

North American smocking

This is really a method of fabric manipulation, and is not elastic like English smocking. The fabric is marked with a grid, and is then pulled into shapes with the stitches. The technique should be worked on a firm fabric that will not flatten or crush, so that the shape of the pattern is maintained.

The lattice pattern creates a woven effect. Regular check fabric, such as gingham, is ideal for this technique, as the squares form the grid pattern and the alternating colours make an interesting pattern. If you are using a plain fabric, mark out the grid on the wrong side with an air- or water-soluble pen, or use a large square dot transfer: the size of the grid will depend on the weight of the fabric. The flower pattern is worked on a grid in a similar way, to create raised shapes like flower heads.

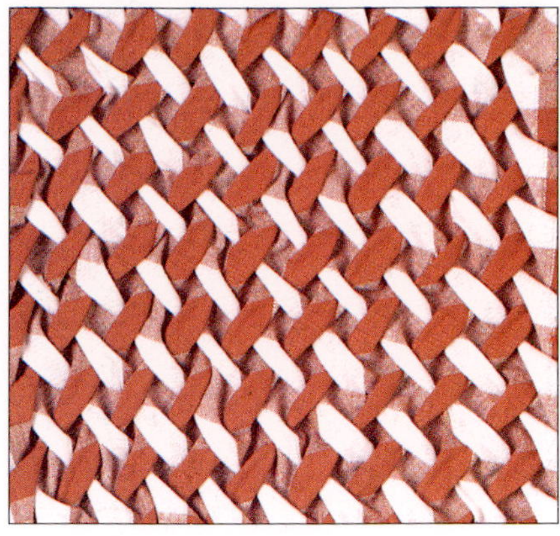

A lattice pattern is here worked on gingham, so that the white and brown squares appear to cross over one another.

Lattice pattern

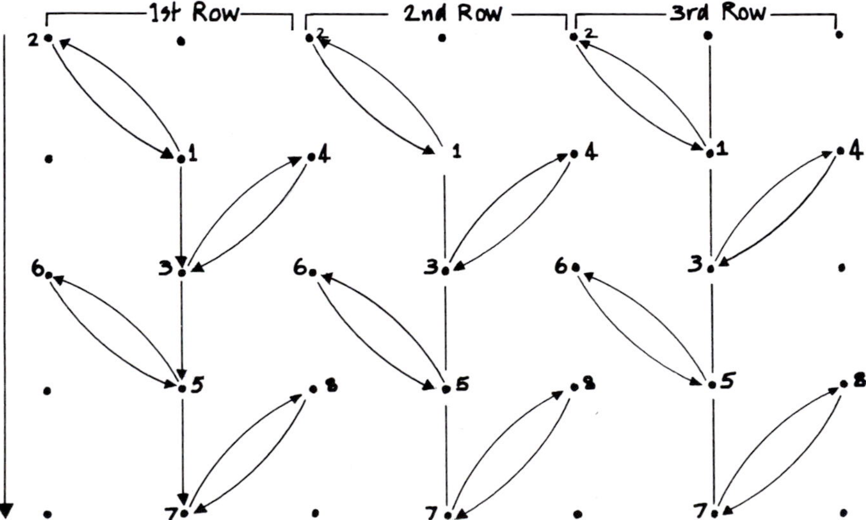

1 **Using strong thread, with a knot at one end, pick up small dot of fabric at dot 1. Pick up dot 2 and pull the fabric down to dot 1, then stitch the two firmly together.**

2 **Take a backstitch at dot 3, keeping the fabric flat between dots 1/2 and 3. Pick up dot 4 and pull the fabric down to meet dot 3. Stitch firmly. Continue down the first row, keeping the fabric flat between the uneven numbers. Work subsequent rows in the same way.**

Flower pattern

For the flower pattern, mark a grid of squares on the right side of the fabric. With strong sewing thread, leave a knot at the back and start at corner 1, box A. Pick up a small piece of fabric at each corner, with small stitches slanting to the centre of the box. Pick up corner 1 again; pull the thread tightly, drawing the corners together, and secure them with a back stitch. Take the thread to the back of the work; bring it out at the corner of box B, and make a back stitch, keeping the fabric flat between A and B. Stitch each box in this and subsequent rows in the same way.

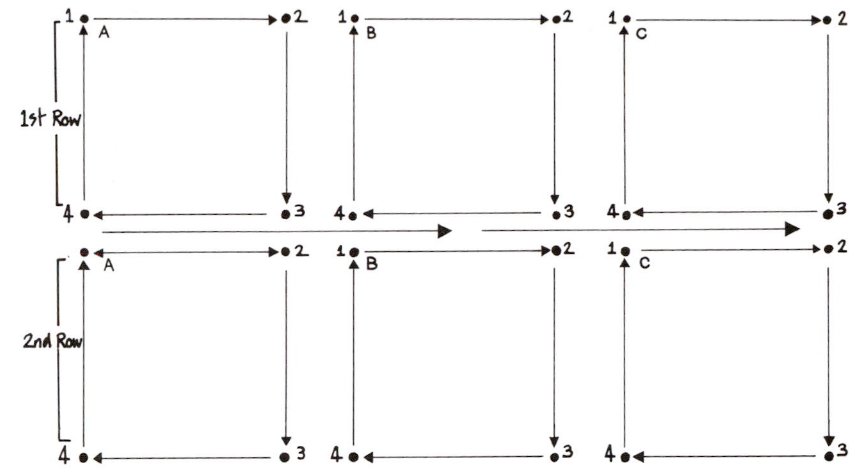

This cushion cover by Jean Hodges is worked in flower pattern, with some of the petals of the flowers pushed back to the wrong side, thus creating a design in which the flowers stand out in contrast against flat areas.

Landscapes and perspective

If you make up some of the samples illustrated here and on the following pages, you will soon discover how fabric manipulation experiments can be a source of inspiration for smocking design. It is not necessary to interpret an idea too literally; the texture of the fabric, the colours and the stitchery should combine to create the image that you wish to convey. Gathering patterns can act as a starting point for innumerable design ideas. In addition to landscapes, for example, random groups of lines can make a stunning surface for the sleeves of an evening jacket.

The linear quality of the pleats can be used to give an impression of perspective. Squeeze the pleats together at one end of a piece of gathered fabric, and spread the other end to make a fan shape. Place the fabric with the wide edge of the fan towards you, and you will see that your eye is drawn along the lines of the pleats towards the narrow end, which could become the horizon of a landscape picture. Dye a piece of fabric to give the impression of a ploughed field, covered with snow, and mark the wrong side in an irregular pattern. Gather the fabric with toning sewing thread and pull up.

Stretch grey background fabric in a frame and place the gathered fabric about two-thirds of the way down. Pull the pleats together at the top and pin them in place. Spread the pleats at the bottom and, when you are satisfied with the position, pin and stitch the whole piece in place.

Use embroidery stitches and knots over and between the pleats in the foreground to convey the feeling of turned earth, stones, roots and plants. Make a line of trees and bushes using hand or free machine embroidery along the top edge of the gathered fabric to indicate the horizon, making sure that the scale is in proportion with the rest of the picture. Remember that at a distance you see only the overall shape.

You might enjoy making another landscape, perhaps a field of poppies or buttercups. Choose a blue or pale grey fabric as a background and, using a sponge, daub the fabric with white and grey to suggest clouds. Gather a green fabric – this might be dyed or machine embroidered – following step 2, page 76. Mount this horizontally on the painted background, with the narrow pleats at the horizon. Indicate the flowers, using embroidery stitches and knots, merging them together in the distance and making them brighter, larger and more distinct towards the foreground. These flowers could be made with applied ruched fabric or ribbon.

1 **Using fabric paints or crayons in several shades of green and brown, paint or draw irregular stripes all over a piece of fabric, merging the colours and stripes into one another.**

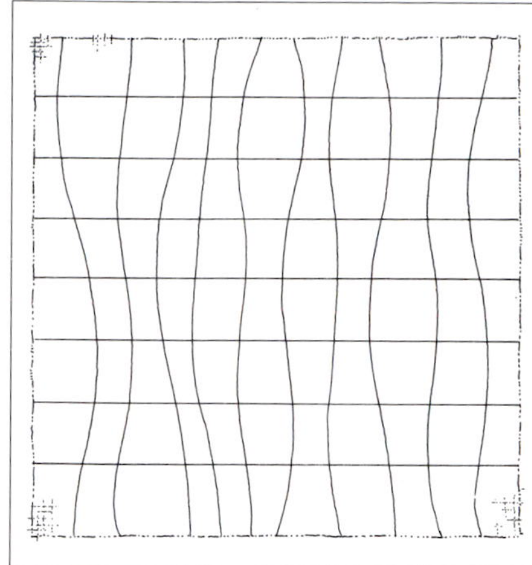

2 **Mark the wrong side of the fabric as shown. Gather with green thread, which will blend into the dyed background, then pull up the gathers. Stretch a piece of firm fabric, such as heavy cotton, on a square frame. Lay the gathered piece on the cotton background and manipulate the pleats, spreading them out or pulling them together until you have a pleasing effect. Hold the pleats in place with pins.**

3 **Stitch the gathered fabric to the background. Use either a matching thread and small stitches, which will not show, or toning threads. These might be of various weights, and you might make long straight stitches at random between the pleats, to indicate more reed stems.**

4 **Choose some shiny threads in a range of blues, whites, greys and silver (space-dyed rayon machine embroidery threads would be ideal for this). Stitch through the pleats at varying depths and spacings across the lower third of the panel, creating an impression of shimmering water.**

This landscape, using pleats to suggest tree trunks, was made with the gathering design shown in step 1, overleaf. The pleated areas were painted a dark colour before pleating.

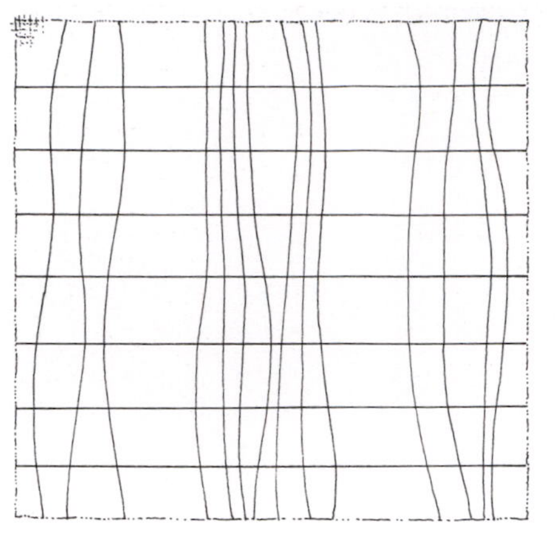

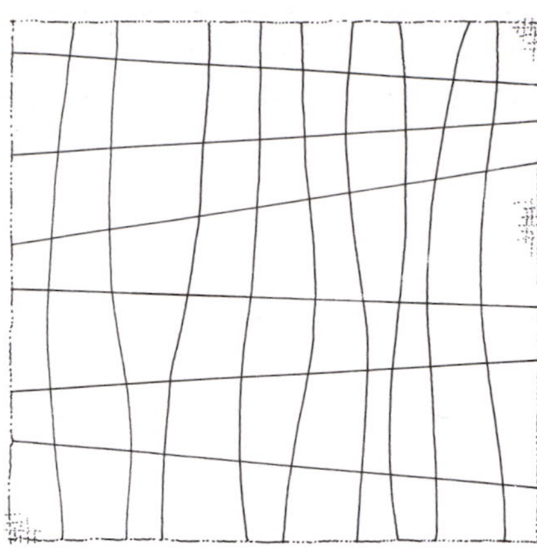

1 **Draw varied groups of lines down the fabric and leave different widths of spacing between the groups. Gather each group separately. This will result in groups of raised pleats on the right side, with flat fabric between. The space between the pleats could be covered with rich slubby threads, couched in position, or you might use it for free machine embroidery, hand stitchery, or beading.**

2 **If you draw lines down the fabric and vary the spacing between them, graduating from a narrow spacing at one side to a wider one at the other, you will end up with graduated pleats, when the fabric has been gathered. Turn the fabric so that the pleats lie horizontally, with the narrow ones at the top, and you will notice a suggestion of perspective, with the pleats appearing smaller in the distance.**

3 **Mark the gathering lines at different angles, varying the spacing between the gathering lines and the (pleat) lines that cross them. This might form the basis for an abstract panel.**

You can create the impression of a snowy ploughed field like this (left) by dyeing the fabric in appropriate colours and gathering it unevenly, to suggest perspective.

Again, the picture on the right uses a gathering variation and a cross-section of embroidery skills. The flowers could be embroidered, or they could be made with either applied ruched fabric or ribbon.

Random and diagonal patterns

When the cell-shaped stitches – honeycomb, vandyke and surface honeycomb – are used in a random way, the cells are pulled and distorted into a wide range of irregular and elongated shapes that are wonderfully interpretative. These shapes between the stitches become as important as the stitches in the design, because the shadows formed by their depth contrast with the play of light on the surface.

You might, for example, elongate diamond stitches, using different sizes of zigzag, ranging threads, and taking extra steps until the whole depth of the gathering has been stitched diagonally. If you repeat rows of diagonal stitching, you will find that the pleats are controlled in the same way as when the stitches are worked straight across the gathering, but the pattern created is quite different. Surface honeycomb and vandyke stitch can also be used diagonally. Contrasting colours will emphasize the diagonal stitchery, drawing the eye down rather than across the smocking.

Double chain stitch, worked over two and three pleats

1 **To make the honeycomb stitch panel, silk fabric was dyed in a random block pattern, using the bright pinks and purples of the flowers, with bands of green running through at intervals, to represent the leaves and stems. Small pieces of fabric, ribbons and textured threads were dyed at the same time.**

2 **The textured threads were laid on the fabric between the blocks of colour and machined in place with zigzag stitch and coloured metallic thread. The whole piece was then gathered into relatively large pleats, in such a way that the textured threads were running along the front edges of the pleats.**

3 **Random honeycomb stitch was used on the pink and purple areas, producing a texture of uneven shapes to indicate the flowers. Each of the green bands of fabric was then regathered separately into much finer pleats, suggesting the stems of the flowers. This process further distorted the fabric, making the flower areas more prominent.**

alternately, makes an elongated chain effect. Honeycomb and surface honeycomb, when stitched over three pleats at a time, make the extra pleat twist and distort slightly as the neighbouring pleats are pulled into place by the stitches, creating an interesting addition to the surface pattern. The same is true of vandyke stitch, which, together with surface honeycomb and honeycomb stitches, can successfully be stitched diagonally over three pleats. In this case different pleats are picked up in successive rows, changing the pattern.

4 **The smocked piece was then mounted on a background fabric and stitched in place. The flowers were accentuated by adding tiny bows of fabric, ribbons and raffia over some of the honeycomb stitches.**

Abstract designs

In all the samples made so far, the gathering threads have been left in place and toning threads have been used so that they do not show. However, they can be made a feature of the design, providing a contrast between the lines of pleats and the lines of thread. You might, for example, make a large-scale abstract panel, based on a random gathering design, and using an exciting colour scheme. Choose decorative threads and pick up more fabric than usual, so that the threads become an important part of the design. Make some more experimental gathering samples of your own, and think how you would use these to decorate clothes as well as for pictures.

Small pieces of fabric, gathered on a smocking machine, are an excellent way of introducing textured areas into an embroidered panel. If the gathering threads are decorative, they can be left in place, so that the piece can easily be manipulated into shape. Depending on the nature of the design, you might choose to stitch the sample securely in place, using free machine embroidery or by hand, or you might attach it with just a few stitches, leaving the fluted edges free to form part of the design.

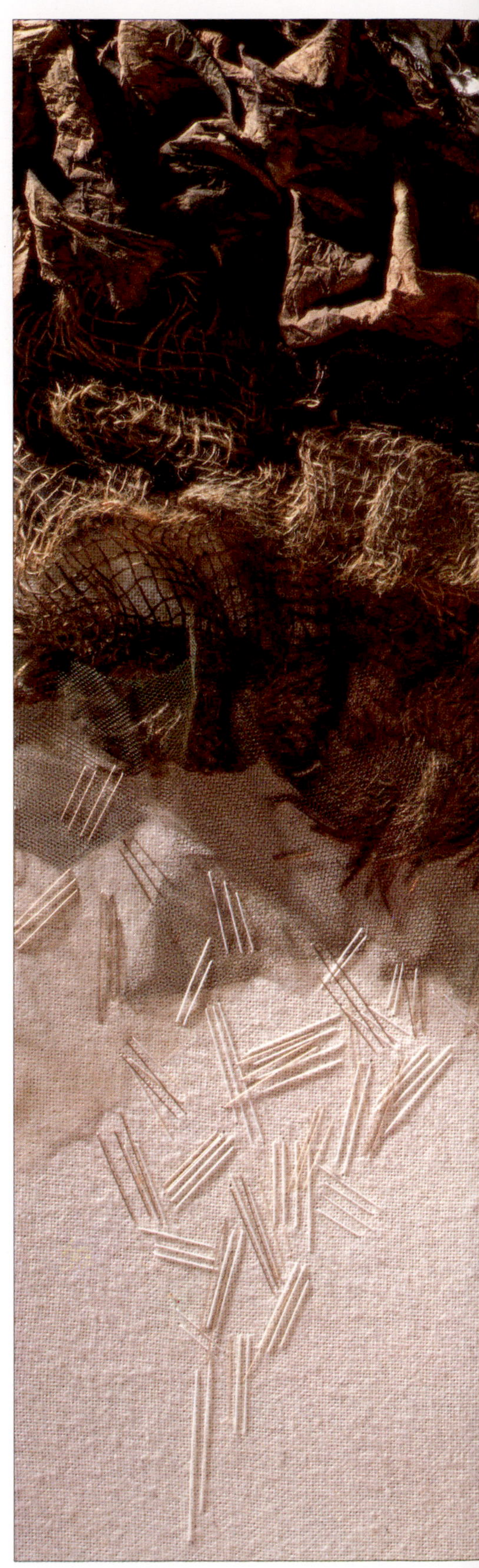

In Abstracted landscape *by Sally MacCabe, textured areas are introduced into the panel by gathering pieces of fabric on a smocking machine, manipulating them into shape, and then stitching them on the background to incorporate them into an abstract landscape. (Photographed by kind permission of Mr and Mrs Jean-Claude Piessel.)*

CANVAS EMBROIDERY

This type of needlework is usually called either canvaswork or needlepoint. Here, it is called canvas embroidery because the traditional styles provide only a starting point.

Materials and equipment

It is preferable to work on a frame (see pages 20–21) to avoid distortion. Use a simple stretcher frame or an adjustable roller frame (slate frame); a ring frame would distort the work.

Canvas

Needlepoint embroidery is carried out on a fairly stiff, open, evenweave fabric, made of cotton or linen and usually white, cream or beige in colour. Its degree of fineness is described by the number of threads or holes to each 2.5cm (1in), and grades range from very fine, with over 30 threads to each 2.5cm (1in), to a large open-mesh rug canvas with 5 or 7 threads. A beginner might choose a single canvas with 12 or 14 threads per 2.5cm (1in). It should preferably be white or cream so that dye may be applied if desired.

About 25 to 30cm (10 to 12in), whatever the width, will be enough for a try-out piece, a sampler of some kind and a small finished piece. Always allow for a good margin of unworked canvas all around your design: 5cm (2in) is the absolute minimum, more is necessary for larger items.

Single canvas Also known as mono canvas, this has single threads interwoven vertically and horizontally. A 12s mono label indicates a fairly coarse canvas – a single weave with 12 threads per 2.5cm (1in). Some canvases have a twisted warp thread, but the count is the same.

Double or Penelope canvas Here, the interwoven threads are grouped in pairs. This canvas is usually described by the number of holes between the double threads, though sometimes the threads are counted as well. A Penelope 16/32 will therefore be a medium double canvas with 32 threads – in pairs – to each 2.5cm (1in), providing 16 holes.

The double threads make it easier to count when cross stitches are being worked, but this canvas is less versatile than single, as you cannot use it for vertical or horizontal stitches. For areas of fine work in a panel – faces, hands, minute details

Sun on Mud Flats, *by Elise Warren, is embroidered in tent stitch. A wide range of unusual threads has been used to convey the effect of brilliant sunlight on darker mud flat areas.*

– the double threads may be prised apart for a fine single mesh.
Rug canvas This is a coarse canvas with 3, 5, or 7 holes to each 2.5cm (1in). It is usually cream in colour and is often marked out in a grid of ten holes, shown by a brown thread.
Plastic canvas A relatively new medium, this has a fairly coarse mesh, which is generally of translucent plastic, though pastel colours are available from specialist suppliers. It is semi-rigid and can be cut to shape easily without fraying. Plastic canvas is usually bought in sheets measuring either 37cm × 27cm (13½in × 10½in) or 45cm × 30cm (17½in × 12in).
Perforated paper Originally used for Victorian card-work, this has 14 holes per 2.5cm (1in). It comes in sheets measuring 31cm × 23cm (12in × 9in) and is quite strong. It may be rolled, in one direction only, without weakening it significantly.
Evenweave fabrics Any kind of evenweave fabric, such as linen, may be used. Such fabrics are more suitable for wearable items because of their flexibility. Other fabrics with a square mesh may be useful for experimental pieces.

Threads

In past times, the criterion for choosing a thread was whether it covered the canvas sufficiently well to produce an even, hard-wearing fabric. This may be what you need, in which case you will require purpose-made threads (see page 14). These are available in a wide range of subtly graded colours, but they are expensive. If you are a beginner, or wish to expand your skills, a more adventurous and economical course is to assemble threads you already have. Anything that will go through the eye of a needle may come in useful. Group them into categories – matt, shiny, fine and thick, and textured and smooth. If you have to go out and buy threads, restrict yourself to shades of one colour, with perhaps one contrast.

Tapestry needles

A tapestry needle has a large eye that can easily be threaded and a blunt point, so that it will not split either the threads of the canvas itself or the embroidery thread, when stitches share the same hole. When threaded, the needle should pass easily through the canvas without pushing the mesh threads out of place. Sizes range from size 13 for very coarse work to 24 or 26 for fine work. A size 18 or 20 is perhaps the best for general purposes; a pack of assorted sizes is also useful.

A tapestry needle is ideal for needlepoint, but if you are tempted to use the sharp pointed version – a chenille needle – turn it around and pass the eye end through the canvas.

Stitches and their uses

This is not a complete stitch dictionary, but a selection of favourite and useful stitches that may be used either formally or experimentally. Needlepoint stitches are not just a way of filling specific areas; they have a beauty of their own when used individually, and once you begin to experiment with them, in the same way that you might experiment with surface stitches, you will discover your own exciting and interesting variations.

Instead of showing the stitches one by one, grouped into categories such as cross stitches or diagonal stitches, we have included possible experiments and variations throughout this section, with the aim of encouraging experimentation with the stitches as you practise them. First, learn and understand the stitch. If possible, try some of the variations illustrated. These may involve an unusual choice of thread, a change of colour within the stitch, a variation of scale, or completing only part of the stitch. Look for variations of your own, and when you have made a stitch, ask yourself: 'What does this stitch look like? What can I use it for?' This is one of the best ways to begin making your own designs.

Many books state that certain stitches are worked from left to right and others from right to left. In some cases, there is a reason: it may be easier to learn a stitch this way; it may be more economical in time and materials, or it may provide a thicker backing for the stitch. In other cases, the direction of stitching may not matter.

Using the diagrams

The needle is not shown in the stitch diagrams, as this may suggest that the stitch is scooped up. Instead, follow the numbers on the diagrams, bringing the needle up through the canvas at 1, down at 2, and so on.

Count the threads of the canvas, not the holes. A 'thread' is one vertical or horizontal canvas thread; an 'intersection' is a crossing of a vertical and a horizontal thread. A square may therefore be described as either 'over four horizontal threads and four verticals' or 'over four intersections' (diagonally).

Starting and finishing

Begin by taking a tapestry needle and threading it with thread that suits the mesh of your canvas, filling the hole without packing it too densely. The thread should not be too long (from index finger to elbow is a good enough guide); long lengths will

Upright Gobelin

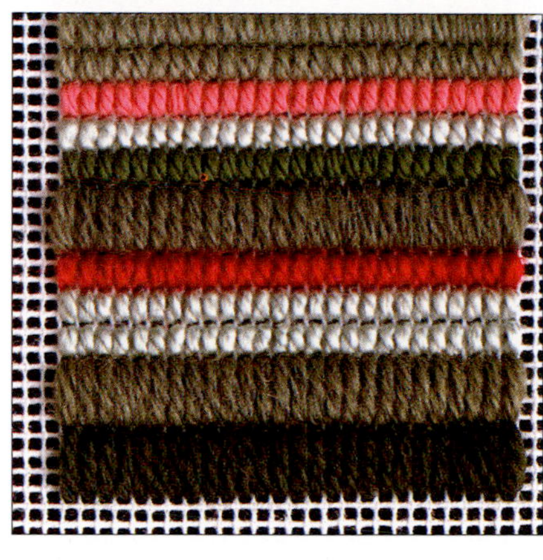

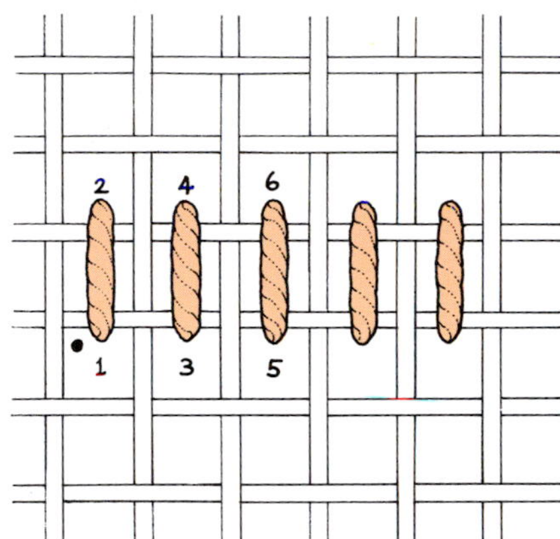

Also known as straight Gobelin, upright Gobelin is a vertical stitch, usually over two threads. It may be worked over a tramming stitch to give a padded effect and to make the finished piece more hard wearing. The threads of the canvas may be seen between the rows.

Encroaching Gobelin

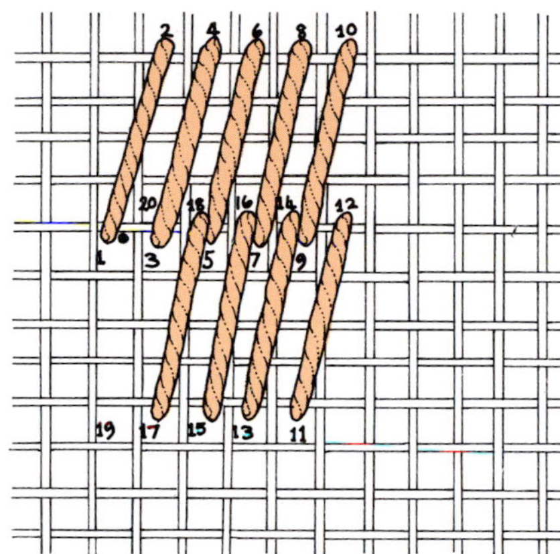

A useful stitch for shading, this has longer stitches than slanting Gobelin. Each stitch runs over five horizontal threads and diagonally over one thread. Each row overlaps the preceding row by one horizontal thread.

Filling Gobelin

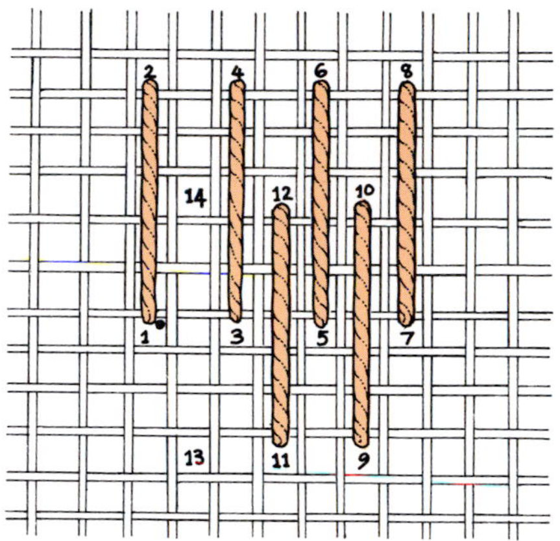

Long upright stitches are worked over six threads, leaving two threads between each stitch. The second row is spaced three threads below the first, the stitches fitting neatly into the empty spaces. Half stitches may be used to straighten the top and bottom rows.

roughen as they pass repeatedly through the canvas. Cut the thread from the skein; if you break it, the wool will stretch and become uneven. If a thicker thread is needed, take two lengths: do not thread the needle with single length and double it back, or the wool fibres will lie in different directions.

Start and finish by running from 3 to 5cm (between 1 and 2in) of thread through the back of existing stitches, or sew the end in as you go. Do not make knots on the back of the work. Keep a piece of canvas as a try-out piece, making it as neat or untidy as you please.

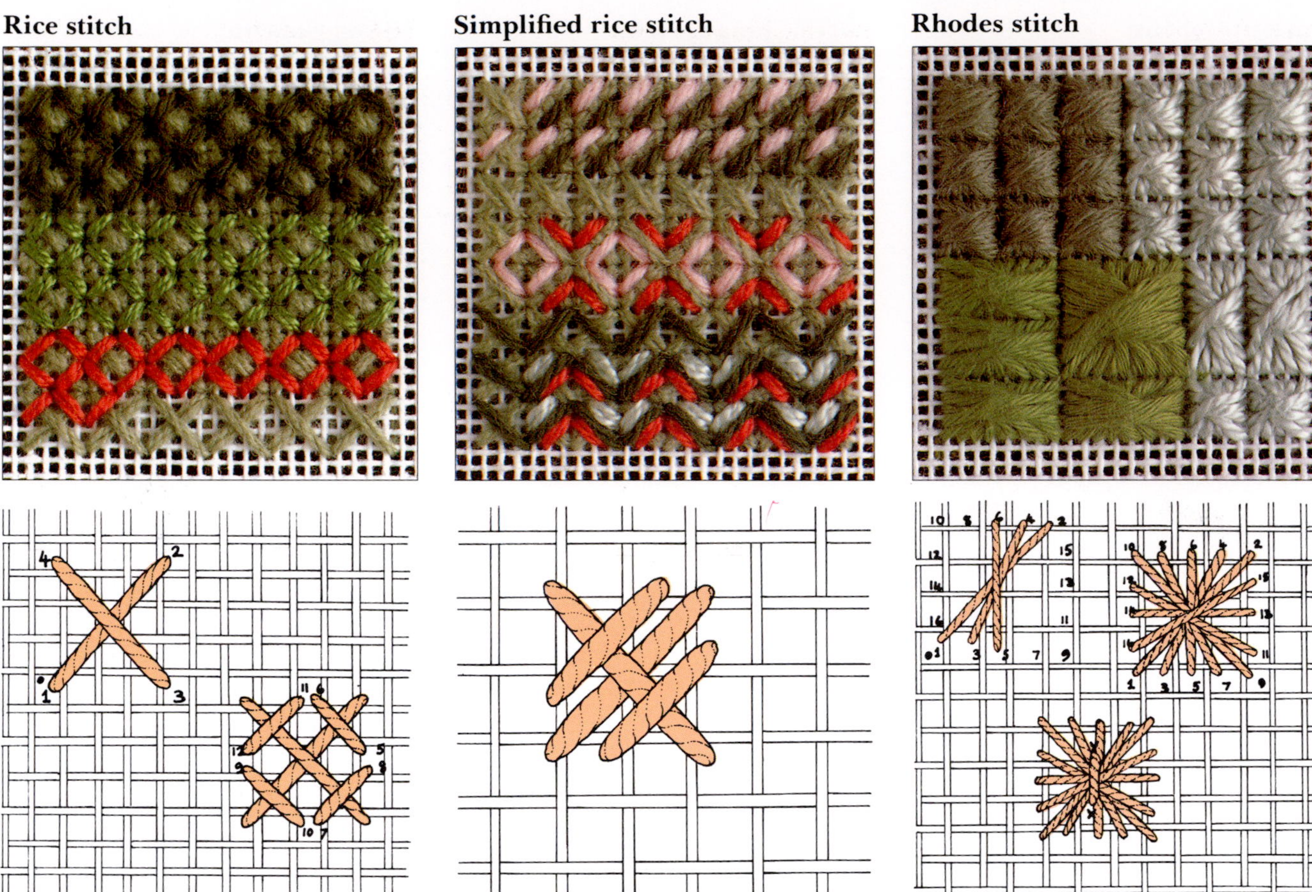

Rice stitch

Also known as crossed corners and as William and Mary stitch, rice stitch is a large cross stitch, worked over a square of two or four threads, with a smaller diagonal back stitch crossing each arm. This is sometimes worked with a finer thread. The small stitches may be worked in any convenient order.

If you are covering a large area, you may stitch all the larger crosses first and then the smaller stitches, making one or more journeys.

Simplified rice stitch

This is worked over three threads, with only two small diagonal stitches across the arms of the cross stitch. Many variations can be achieved with colour changes and mirror images.

Rhodes stitch

This is a raised square stitch, worked over a square of four, six or eight threads. Start with a long diagonal over four (six, eight) intersections of the canvas and work around the square, as shown in the numbered diagram. A small vertical stitch may be added when these eight (12, 16) stitches have been completed: ease the needle through the existing stitches to hold the centre threads at X and Y.

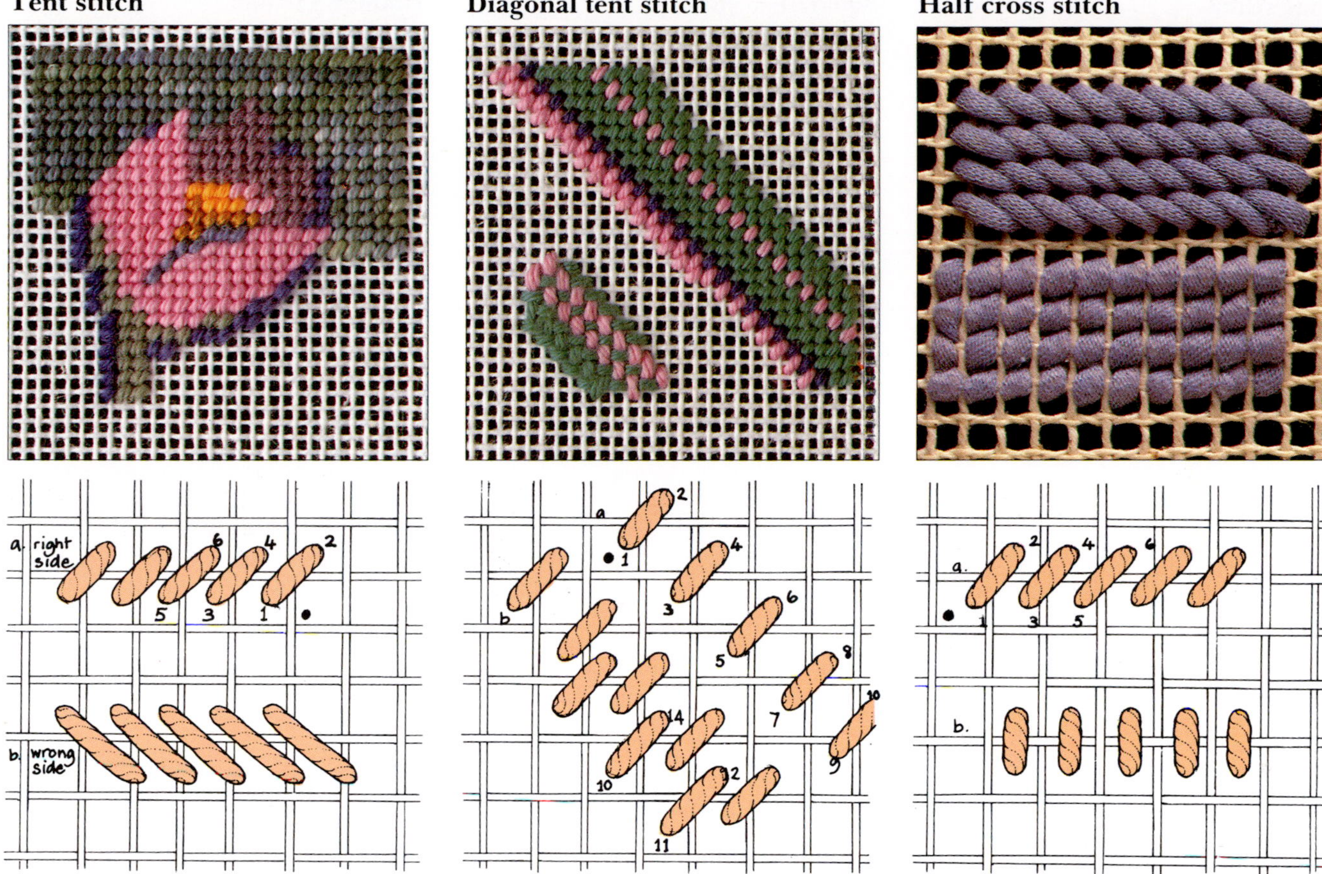

Tent stitch

This looks like half cross, but the wrong side reveals a long slanting stitch. The stitch uses more thread than half cross, but extra padding makes the work more hard wearing.

When you have finished one row, working from right to left, turn the work upside down and work the next row, checking that you are making long slanting stitches on the wrong side, not small verticals. Stitch any motif first, then fill in the background.

Diagonal tent stitch

Also known as basketweave, because of the appearance of the back of the work, this way of working tent stitch causes less distortion of the canvas than the previous version. Begin at the top left of the area to be filled and stitch down to the bottom right. The second row begins at the bottom, to the left of the first row. The small area on the lower left side of the picture shows the reverse of the stitch.

Half cross stitch

A small diagonal stitch, taken over one or two intersections of the canvas, half cross, when made with a thick thread, looks like tent stitch but is not as hard wearing. The difference is only obvious at the back, as shown here. Make sure that all the stitches in each row slant in the same direction.

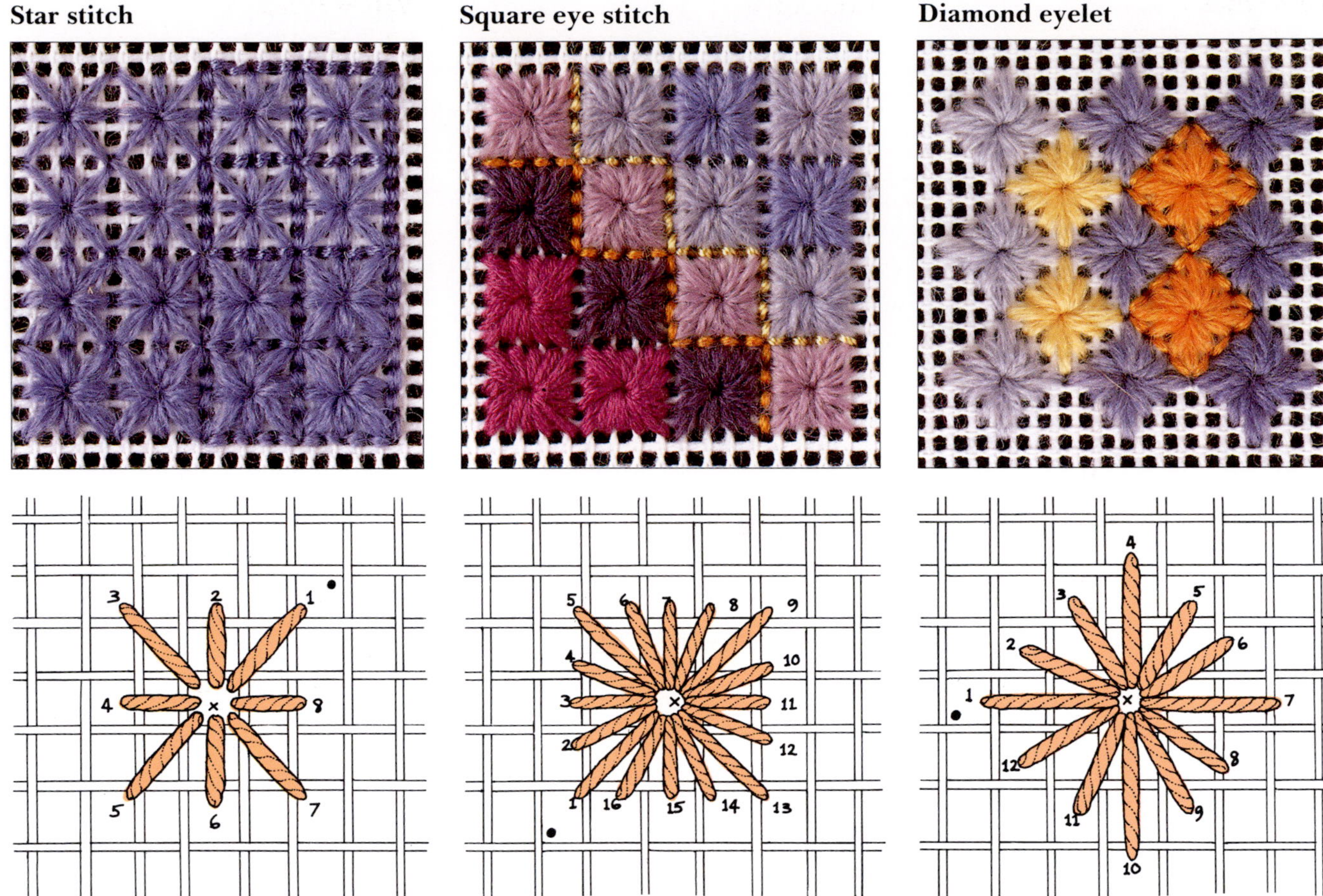

Star stitch

Also known as Algerian stitch, star stitch is a group of eight stitches, all worked into a central hole and arranged to cover a square of four or any even number of threads. The stitches may be pulled slightly to emphasize the central hole. (If each stitch is worked twice into the same hole before passing on to the next, the result is called Algerian eye stitch.) If the canvas is not covered completely, a lacy effect is obtained. Bring the thread up at 1, down at X, up at 2, down at X and so on.

Square eye stitch

Also known as eyelet stitch, this is similar to star stitch, but more densely packed. Based on a square of four threads each way, a stitch is worked into the centre from every hole around the edge of the square – 16 altogether. The stitch may also cover a rectangle, and the central hole may be moved off centre to create an asymmetric effect.

Bring the thread up at 1, down at X, up at 2, down at X, and so on.

Diamond eyelet

Eyelet stitches are here worked in a diamond shape, covering six threads altogether, vertically and horizontally. Follow the diagram, working each stitch into the central hole at X. Count carefully when making diamond eyelet, because some of the stitches must be shorter than others, to create the correct diamond shape. (The stitches on this page are all best worked in soft wool, as many threads must pass through the central hole.)

Fern stitch

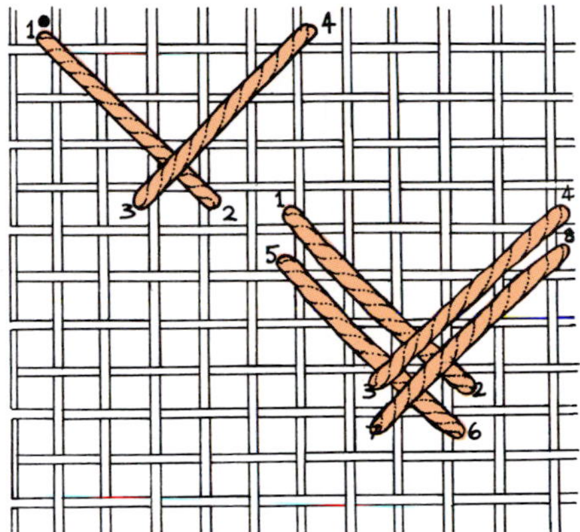

A useful stitch for foliage or for feathers, fern stitch is worked from the top down, over an even number of vertical threads (the width), the central two forming a centre vein or plait. It may be much wider or narrower than the diagram. Bring the needle up at 1, then count four threads down and four across to find 2. Bring the needle up again two threads to the left at 3, and down again at 4, making a large, top-heavy cross stitch. Stitch downward for the required length. The stitch may also run horizontally.

Leaf stitch

Count from the central vein of the leaf. This version is six threads wide (three each way from the centre), so begin at the lower centre and complete the first half of the leaf. The second half mirrors the first, sharing the same holes of the centre vein. If this is used as a filling stitch, the second leaf will begin six threads to the right of the vein of the first. The second row begins six threads below and three threads right of the vein of the first leaf of the first row.

Velvet stitch

This raised pile stitch may be left in loops or clipped to make a thick velvety effect. Make stitch 1–2, the first half of a cross stitch, then make loop 3–4 through the same holes. Complete the cross stitch to hold the loop in place.

When even loops are required, they may be worked over a pencil or strip of card. Begin at the bottom when covering a large area, so that the loops do not get in your way as you stitch. Fill the whole area before clipping any loops.

Cushion

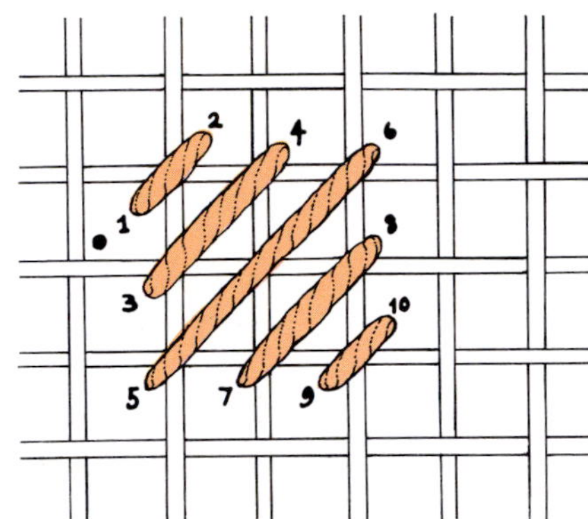

Also known as flat stitch or diagonal satin stitch, this is a group of small diagonal satin stitches, forming a small square over three or four threads. The squares may be repeated exactly or mirror imaged. Interesting effects can be obtained by changing colour halfway through the stitch.

Chequer stitch

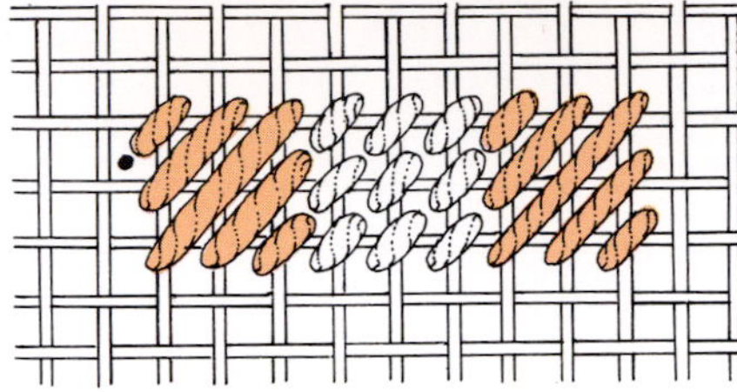

For this pattern/stitch, small cushion stitch squares are alternated with squares of tent stitch.

Scottish stitch

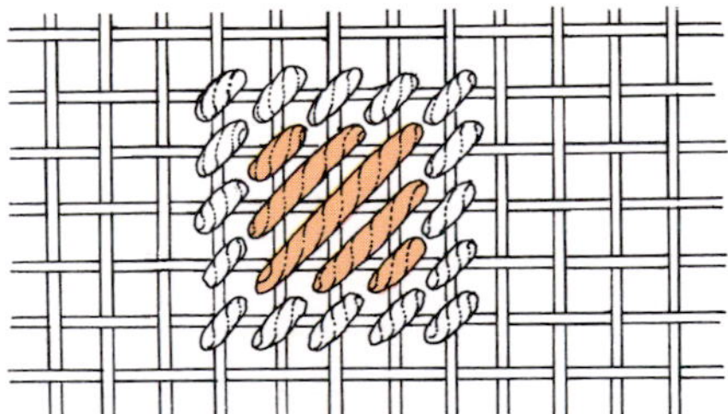

In this variation, each cushion stitch square is surrounded by a line of tent stitches.

Diagonal stitch

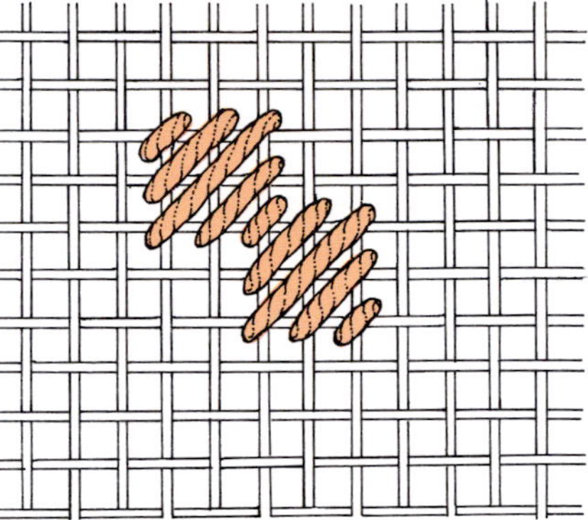

Here, the cushion stitch pattern is extended into long diagonal bands. The small diagonal stitch completing the square is counted as the first stitch of the second square. In the second row, the longest stitch fits into the same hole as the shortest stitch of the previous row.

Jane Trowbridge and Shirley Staniforth were new to needlepoint when they stitched these small garden panels. Groups of flowers are reduced to simple shapes formed with a limited number of needlepoint stitches. Darning and Cretan stitches are used in the background to contrast with the formal stitches.

Long-legged cross stitch

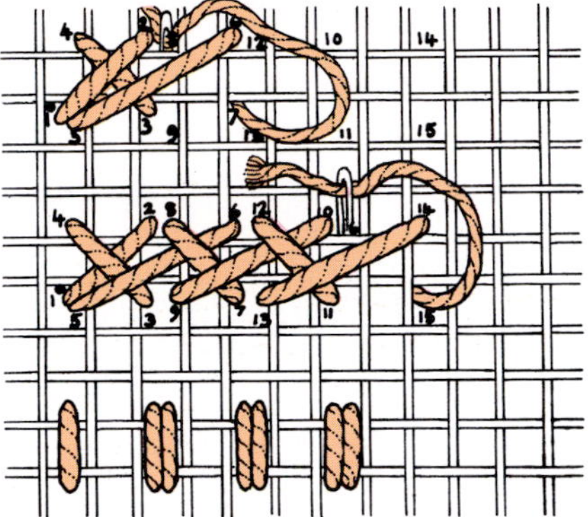

Also known as long-armed cross stitch or plaited Slav stitch, this builds up into a row of lop-sided cross stitches with a plaited effect. Long-legged cross stitch is useful for joining seams, where it gives a braided appearance to the edge, but it requires practice. Start with a small cross stitch over two intersections. This makes a neat beginning, but is not part of the stitch pattern, which moves forward four threads on the first diagonal, and goes back two with the next stitch.

Parisian stitch

This is a useful filling stitch, or grounding, made up of alternate short and long vertical stitches, over two and four threads, worked horizontally.

Hungarian stitch

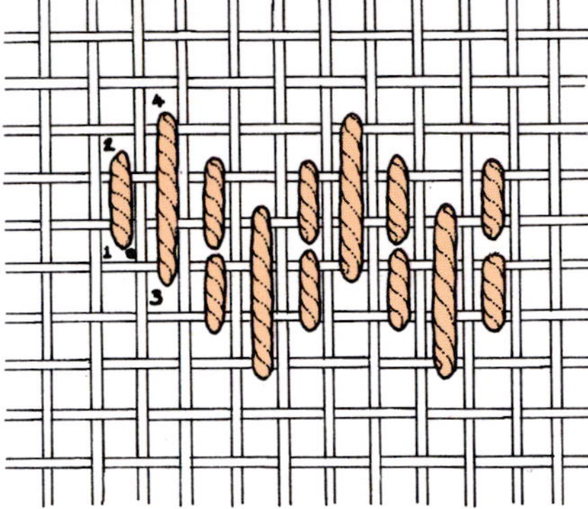

This is worked in a similar way to Parisian stitch, but the stitches are grouped in threes, with a space between each group.

In this first canvas worksheet, Ellen Crawford has experimented with stitches on both a large and a small scale, working on a coloured background with space-dyed threads and fabric strips, as well as with more ordinary materials.

Damp stretching

If your finished work is not quite straight, it may be necessary to block (damp stretch) it before mounting or making up. In any case, damp stretching will improve the general appearance of the embroidery, just as pressing improves dress-making.

The dampness loosens the stiffening element in the canvas, which is stretched, pinned into shape, and allowed to dry naturally. There are several different ways of doing this, but the following works very well. You will need a piece of thick wooden board, larger than the embroidery, and soft enough to take drawing pins or tacks; four or five sheets of newspaper or blotting paper; a top sheet of plain white paper, with the outline of your embroidery drawn out with waterproof marker, and drawing pins (brass, if possible, to avoid rust).

1 **Place layers of paper on a board and wet them thoroughly. On top, lay a sheet of white paper with the outline of your finished piece of embroidery marked on it with a waterproof pen or a pencil. The centre lines should also be drawn on the paper, and centre points marked on each side of the embroidery.**

2 **Lay the embroidery right side up on the paper, matching the centre points. Starting from the top centre and working outwards, insert drawing pins (thumb tacks) outside the embroidered areas at intervals of about 2.5cm (1in), closer if the work is very distorted. Pull the canvas straight, and pin along bottom edge to match drawn shape. Pin the sides in the same way, and then leave the canvas to dry naturally for two to three days. If necessary, repeat the whole process.**

Lacing and mounting

If you are framing a finished embroidery, you will probably need to lace it over hardboard to keep it flat and in shape. If you are using a card window surround or presenting the piece as a greetings card, you may simply staple the embroidery to board or card. The staples will be hidden, though they will eventually rust through.

For lacing, there should be a margin of unworked canvas of at least 5cm (2in), more for larger pieces, to allow for the pull of the lacing, but if you have worked too near the edge you can extend the area with fabric strips: they will not be seen. The hardboard should fit loosely in the frame, allowing for the canvas turnings. Mark the centres of the sides to line up with the centre marks on the canvas.

You will need a piece of hardboard, drawing pins (thumb tacks), a sharp needle and strong thread.

In Sweet Peas, *Peggy Field used two grades of canvas in order to make some of the plants appear to grow behind others. The joins of the overlapped canvas, first secured by herringbone stitch, are hidden partly by the cords stitched on top.*

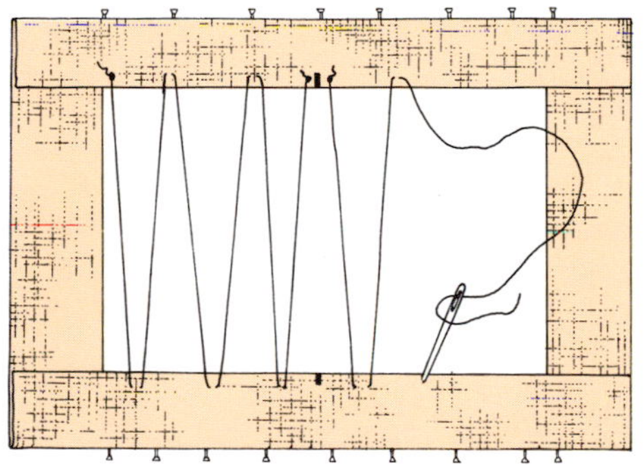

1 Lay the embroidery on top of the board, matching centre points. Fold the top and bottom allowances to the back, securing them temporarily with pins. Fasten a long thread securely at the centre top. Lace from top to bottom, working first to the left. Take up several threads of the canvas with each stitch to prevent them pulling away. Fasten off temporarily, leaving a tail of thread. Return to the centre and with a new piece of thread work out to the right.

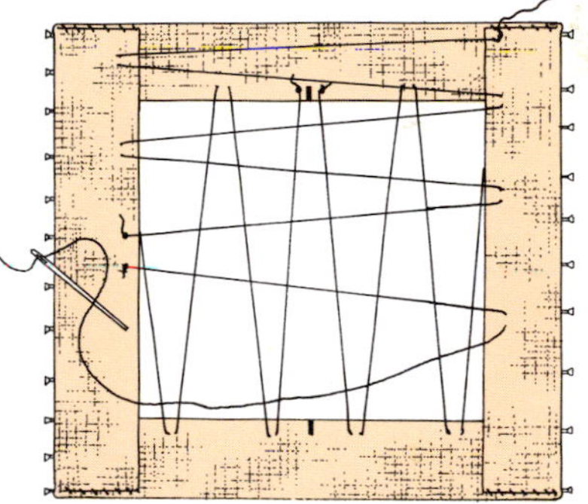

2 When this lacing is complete, remove the pins. Return to the centre and pull each stitch tighter, taking up any slack. At each end, fasten the lacing thread securely. A dab of glue may prevent any slackening. The sides are laced in the same way.

The corners of the canvas may be mitred, but it is sufficient to fold over the edges and secure them with a few stitches. When lacing is complete, a piece of thick paper may be glued in place, to cover the back.

Behold Zion *is a large semi-abstract panel in three sections, by Alison King, evoking the visionary search of the early Mormons for their promised land. The construction of such large panels poses considerable logistical problems for the machine embroiderer, and requires as much manipulation under the arm of the machine as would a full-size quilt. (By kind permission of Jacqueline and Robert Torrance)*

CHAPTER TWO

Machine Embroidery

The development of the computer-age sewing machine and advent of a wide range of new fabrics and threads, together with dyes that can be used at home, have opened up a vast field of experimental possibilities to textile artists. The effects that can be achieved with machine embroidery are often entirely different to those of hand work, and the two can complement each other in a finished embroidery. Used with creativity, even a comparatively basic sewing machine can produce beautiful works of art.

Throughout this section, reference will be made to two terms – automatic machine embroidery and free machine embroidery. In the first case, the feed dogs that feed the fabric under the needle are left up, and functional; in the case of free machining, they are lowered, so that they become inoperative.

The feed dogs can be shifted up or down mechanically on most machines, but if this is not possible on your model, a cover must be placed over the feed dogs so that they do not engage the fabric. Some manufacturers supply these covers, but if they are not available, the same effect may be achieved by covering the feed dogs with a piece of thin cardboard, taped down around the edges, or simply by applying transparent tape over them. (Remember to make a hole for the passage of the needle.)

MACHINE EMBROIDERY BASICS

If you are a beginner, spend some time experimenting until you are fully acquainted with the possibilities of your machine, and the effects of different fabrics and threads. The following section includes a guide to the various types of machine and a buyers' checklist, but a wide range of embroidery techniques can be achieved with even a very simple model.

Automatic machining, using a zigzag sequence, with the presser foot attached.

Know your machine

If you are consistently having problems with your machine, have it serviced. Explain to the service person that you are using the machine for embroidery; describe the types of threads being used and the effects that you are trying to obtain, and make it clear that you will need to adjust top and bobbin tensions. If the machine has any particular limitations, the service person will so advise you. Above all, get to know your machine: no machine will do everything; not even a new one. Your own familiarity with your machine will dictate what is, and what is not, possible.

Free machining is generally covered in manufacturers' manuals under darning. It normally involves only two stitches – running stitch and zigzag – worked with the feed dogs down and the fabric, which is usually held in a frame, moved under the needle by hand. The combination of frame movement and foot pedal pressure allows you to vary the length of stitch and speed of sewing.

Zigzag machines will make both straight and zigzag stitches.

Anyone in the market for a new sewing machine will find that there is a vast number of machines, with manufacturers offering competing claims regarding new capabilities and advances in technology. It would be rather more easy to make a reasoned choice if the terms used by all manufacturers had the same meaning, but unfortunately they do not. What follows is not an exhaustive study of all the machines in the marketplace, but it covers some of the most common terms and capabilities, with the aim of making it a bit easier to understand what is available.

Straight stitch machines

These will only make a straight sewing stitch.

Automatic machining, using the straight stitch sequence, with presser foot attached.

Zigzag machines

Zigzag machines have a needle bar that moves from side to side as you sew, and will do both straight stitch and zigzag.

Semi-automatic machines

These machines will do a basic zigzag stitch, plus other utility stitches. The utility stitches are, generally, accomplished through the use of shaped discs called cams. These may be either built-in or changeable by the user. The shapes on the cam control the side-to-side movement of the needle bar, varying the stitch width and producing patterns.

Fully automatic machines

The fully automatic machines will do straight stitching and zigzag, as well as having the facility to produce a wide variety of decorative stitches.

Electronic machines

The use of the term electronic has developed into an advertising buzz word: it can be used in any number of

Semi-automatic machines will allow stitch width variations while sewing.

Fully automatic machines combine automatic control of the feed dogs for forward and reverse feed of the fabric, with a controlled side-to-side motion of the needle bar. This allows automatic pattern generation. Fully electronic machines will produce all the automatic machine stitches, and they can also vary both stitch width and length while sewing.

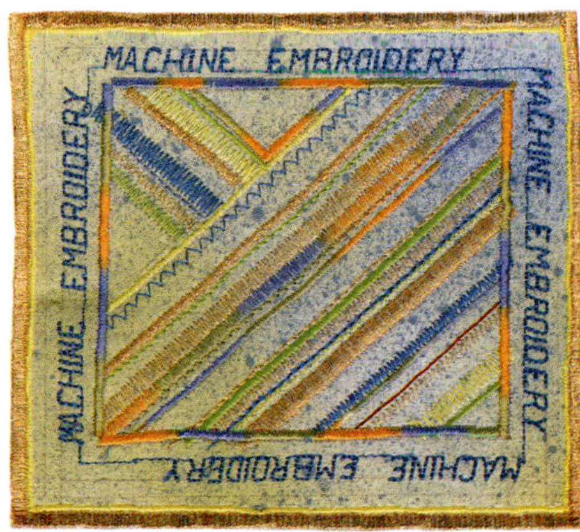

Computerized machines are fully electronic and conform to those capabilities. Some machines allow the user to program individual designs and patterns by creating original instructions to the feed dogs and needle bar.

contexts because it conjures up concepts of technological advancement. Some manufacturers will claim their machine is electronic if any electronic control circuit is used in the machine, but electronic control circuits are used in a number of applications from manufacturer to manufacturer.

In the older electric machines, the sewing speed is controlled by varying the amount of electricity, or power, to the motor. Slow speeds entailed lower power and a loss of needle penetration. Electronic speed control allows full power to the motor, regardless of speed, resulting in full needle penetration power at slower sewing speeds.

Fully electronic machines not only have electronic speed control, but, as far as most manufacturers are concerned, they also have electronic control circuits, operated by push button, for the needle bar and feed dogs. In other words, the sewing speed, the rate at which the fabric feeds through, and the needle bar operation are all electronically coordinated.

Computerized machines

Computerized machines are at the leading edge of sewing machine technology and are the most expensive models available. A wide variety of patterns are pre-programmed into micro-chip control circuits which, for the most part, replace the cams used in automatic machines, controlling feed, needle swing and speed. Some machines have a memory that stores and recalls stitches and patterns, so they can be programmed to create individual patterns and store them in the memory for later use. Some machines will have replaceable, plug-in, pattern modules, available as an option at extra cost.

Buyer's checklist

Free machine embroidery may be done on almost any sewing machine, but the following are points to consider before you buy a new machine.

- Check whether the feed dogs can be lowered into the needle plate or not.
- If the feed dogs cannot be lowered, ensure that there is a cover plate that can be used to cover the feed dogs. Check for protrusions that might catch or snag the embroidery frame.
- For machine embroidery, a flat bed is preferred. If the bed is sloping, ensure that the embroidery frame can be held tightly to the bed of the machine, with no gaps.
- Ensure that the bobbin tension can be varied. Some bobbin cases may be removed from the machine and adjusted by

Cover plate/darning plate: different names may be given to this plate, which is normally supplied as an accessory with the machine. The plate is used to cover the feed dogs when darning or – in the case of models that do not allow the feed dogs to be lowered – during free machining. The plate may be attached by clips or a screw.

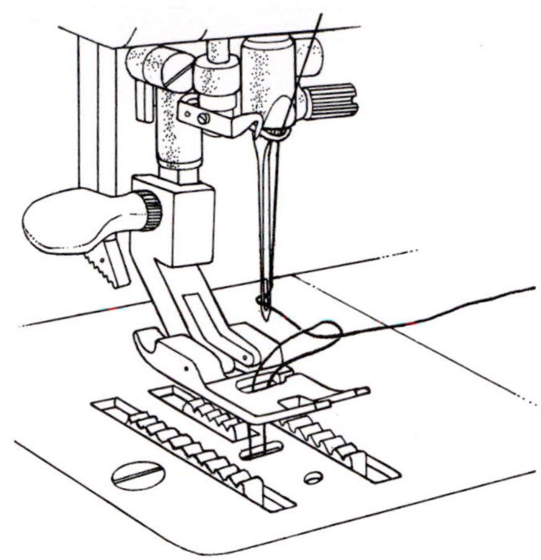

The presser foot applies pressure to the fabric so that the feed dogs engage the fabric, feeding it at the correct rate as the machine makes automatic stitches. (Some machines have a pressure control, to vary the pressure applied to the presser foot.) The presser foot should be raised for threading the top of the machine. When free machining with the presser foot removed, the presser bar *must* be in the lowered, or down, position.

The feed dogs move back and forth in a cylindrical, up and down motion, feeding the fabric under the needle during conventional or automatic stitching. They are lowered or covered for free machining.

Needle plate/throat plate: different manufacturers have their own names for this plate, which has slots through which the feed dogs and needle operate.

turning the set screw on the side of the bobbin case. Other cases are fixed in the machine where the bobbin is fitted. Some of these are adjusted with a set screw with a graduated tension scale, while other machines have a tension screw but no numerical scale. Since bobbins are changed and tension varied with great regularity, it also pays to make sure that the bobbin is easily accessible.

Perfect straight stitch

Before beginning to embroider, always set your machine up for a test, adjusting it to produce *perfect straight stitch*. Experienced machine embroiderers have all learned the importance of stitching small trial pieces as a check on machine operations and techniques.

Threading With the presser bar up, to open the top tension discs, thread the top thread (needle thread) through the guides, according to the manual for your machine. Load the bobbin with thread, of the same size and of a contrasting colour to the top thread, and put it in the machine. Ensure that the needle is straight and sharp. Bring the top and bobbin threads to the sewing surface and place the fabric under the needle.

Machine controls Lower the presser bar; check that the feed dogs are up; set the tension to normal (between 3 and 5), and set the stitch control for straight stitch.

Machining Sew a line of straight stitch. If the top thread shows through the bottom of the fabric, gradually increase the top tension and sew another row of stitching until no top thread is visible on the bottom. If the bobbin thread appears on the top of the fabric, gradually increase bobbin tension until the bobbin thread is no longer visible on the top.

Top and bottom tension for normal sewing

It is essential to be able to adjust tensions on your machine, although some manuals may advise against this. Some machines have what is termed universal tension, and in theory such machines do not require adjustment, but in practice it is vital to be able to adjust tensions for specific techniques.

Top (upper) tension

Top tension may be adjusted through the use of a numbered dial or knob. The scale usually ranges from 0 to 10: 0 represents no top tension; 3 to 5 normal tension, and 6 to 10

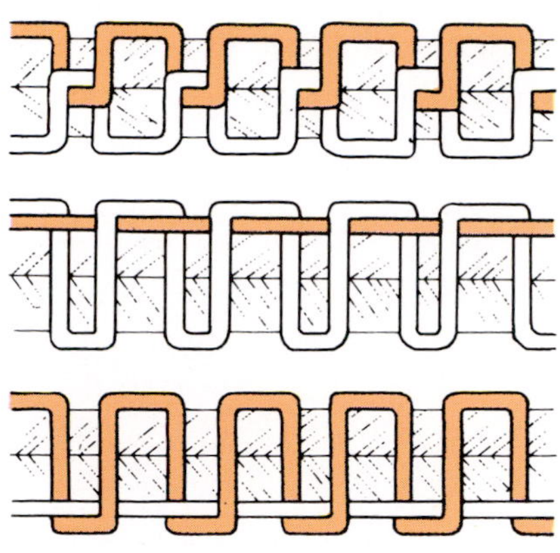

When no contrasting thread appears on the top or bottom of the fabric, the perfect straight stitch has been accomplished. Some machines may not make a perfect straight stitch.

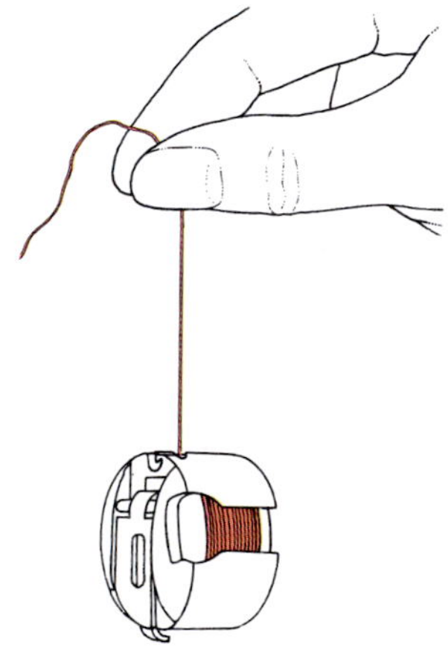

The bobbin thread should not spool out through the weight of the bobbin case alone. If the thread spools rapidly, the bobbin tension is too loose. If the thread does not spool out, the tension is too tight.

very tight or high tension. Some machines have no numerical scale at all, having instead a simple '+' or '−' indication on either side of a central or normal setting.

Bobbin tension for removable bobbin cases

Wind the bobbin with the required thread and insert it into the bobbin case.

Most bobbin cases have a set screw and a tension screw. The set screw holds the tension band in place. The tension screw is the one that may need adjustment. When adjusting the tension screw, only turn the screw a half turn for each adjustment. Holding the bobbin case with the open side (the side where the bobbin is inserted) facing your body, turn the tension screw – clockwise to increase tension or anti-clockwise to reduce tension. Take care: this tiny screw has a tendency to pop out and is easily lost.

Some machines have a built-in, non-removable bobbin case, which lies flat in the machine, under the needle plate. There will generally be a tension screw alongside a numbered scale. To adjust the tension, use the machine screwdriver: '0' indicates little or no tension and higher numbers indicate increasing tensions (other machines use a '+' or '−' system).

Fabrics for machine embroidery

A medium- to heavy-weight cotton fabric is ideal for first attempts at machine embroidery. Polycotton is not generally recommended for machine embroidery, due to its lightness and tendency to pucker.

After your first efforts, once you are beginning to feel at ease with the technique, it is useful to experiment with as many types of fabric as possible. This will encourage creative ideas about the applications of various fabrics. Try cottons of all weights, silks, satins, acetate, linen, net, 100 per cent nylon, curtaining, rayon, plastic sheeting, paper, net bags from the grocer, scrims of all weights, butter and cheese muslin, leather, vinyl, lace, ribbons, velvets and interfacing. In other words, anything through which the needle will pass is suitable for machine embroidery.

Embroidery materials may include silk, silk cotton, mercerized cotton, cotton muslin, cotton organdie, nylon organza, pelmet vilene, acetate satin, light-weight wool, cotton velvet, silk taffeta, leather, nylon net, felt, heavy-weight cotton, ribbons and machine embroidery threads.

You will find that every fabric has its own particular properties, and slight machine adjustments may be required for each of them.

Some fabrics will require backing in order to provide the stiffness necessary to support satin stitch or heavy automatic embroidery. For this purpose, iron-on or paper interfacing may be used.

Where very stretchy fabric is used, it may be advisable to baste it to a firm, medium-weight, cotton backing, before framing and stitching. Fabrics with a lot of stretch will be very difficult to frame evenly, and when the fabric is removed from the frame and the tension is released, the stitching may disappear into the fabric. You will find that some fabrics are too thin to be used on their own for machine embroidery. In these cases, the fabric may be doubled to provide support for the embroidery. If the thread shows a tendency to drag through a particular fabric or paper, it may help if you change to a needle of a larger size.

Take note of the effect of using heavy threads on light fabrics: very fine fabric, unless mounted on a backing, will pucker if a very heavy thread is used to cover the whole piece. If the weight of the thread is matched to that of the fabric, a more even and consistent stitch will be produced. It is useful, at this stage in the development of your machine embroidery repertoire, to begin a reference book. Use a loose-leaf binder for samples of fabrics, threads, techniques, tensions and settings.

Interfacings

It happens so often: someone watches a sewing machine demonstration; sees wonderful stitches being created; purchases the machine and takes it home, only to find that the stitch patterns are not quite up to the quality of the demonstration. What that person has probably failed to observe is that the stitch demonstration was worked on very stiff fabric or on several layers of fabric.

Often, automatic decorative stitching will be very heavy and can pucker the fabric upon which it is produced. One must therefore ensure that sufficient stiffening or backing is present to offset this tendency. Fortunately, there are products that can assist machine embroiderers with these problems. A number of manufacturers produce paper interfacings variously known as Stitch-and-Tear or by other trade names.

Satin stitch and many of the intricate computerized patterns

1 **To use paper interfacing, or simple typing paper, to strengthen the fabric during stitching, place an appropriately-sized piece of interfacing under the fabric to be embroidered, between the fabric and the needle plate. Stitch the pattern or design on the fabric.**

2 **Turn the fabric to the reverse side and carefully tear away the interfacing. The product will neatly separate from the work, leaving a consistent pattern without puckers.**

available on a wide range of machines require backing of this type. If these products are not readily available, ordinary paper may be used, but it will not tear away so neatly.

Other products that may be used are the iron-on, or fused, interlinings. These, however, will alter the feel and pliability of the fabric to which they are applied.

Experiment with all the options. Fusible interfacings are available in light, medium and heavy weights: your local fabric shop should be able to offer you a good selection.

Pelmet interfacing is a very thick, stiff product, intended to give pelmets more rigidity. Because of this stiffness, it can be used without a frame for both automatic and free embroidery techniques. Creative stitching can be done on this fabric.

Double-sided fusible interfacing is ideal for bonding appliqué shapes to a background fabric. This obviates the need to baste appliqué pieces to the background.

If you choose, you can use an interfacing as the background fabric on which to embroider. Most interfacings are very receptive to dyes. In this panel by June Lovesy, interfacing has been dyed, torn into strips, and reassembled as a background fabric. The top lace panel is worked on hot-water-soluble fabric.

Vanishing muslin

This is a stiffened, chemically treated material that disappears when it is heated with an iron. Because of this property, stitches may be applied to the material which, when ironed, will leave behind only the stitches that have been applied. As an aid in designing, patterns may be drawn on the fabric. This material may be used to stiffen or support other fabric while doing machine embroidery. Instead of using a hot iron, you can dissolve the muslin by placing it in an oven heated to 150°C (300°F). When the muslin turns brown, it may be gently brushed away with a soft toothbrush.

Threads for machine embroidery

Machine embroidery threads are quite different from ordinary sewing threads. Threads manufactured exclusively for machine embroidery do not normally have the high twist required of ordinary threads. Because they do not have this high twist, they lack tensile strength amd are thus unsuitable for dressmaking; they are softer, and have a tendency to spread and cover areas with fewer passes of the needle.

The numbering system used for machine embroidery threads is the same as that used for dressmakers' threads, being based on weight, but because of the looser twist, the end result is very different. A No. 40 dressmakers' thread, for instance, is much too heavy for machine embroidery and would tangle and clog hopelessly as stitches piled up. A No. 40 machine embroidery thread, by comparison, would pass through the machine with ease and would cause no problems. A No. 50 dressmakers' thread could be used for machine embroidery as this is a medium-weight thread, finer than No. 40 dressmakers' thread, and would pass through the machine. A No. 50 machine embroidery thread would, however, appear much finer than the No. 50 dressmakers', and is in fact the finest grade that is readily available. When machine embroidery threads are not readily available, it is possible to use dressmakers' threads.

The properties of the two types of threads have been developed for their very specific purposes. Machine embroidery threads – except for the heavier weights – lack strength, so it would not be advisable to use them for ordinary sewing. On the other hand, the soft, pliable nature of those very threads provides a nice, even, lustrous coverage when used in embroidery.

Special machine embroidery threads may be used on the top of the machine (above), but other threads may also be used for special effects. This includes heavier threads, such as tatting, perlé or crochet cotton (right).

Machine embroidery threads are produced in a wide variety of fibres. These range from 100 per cent cotton, viscose rayon with a high tensile strength, nylon, polyamide and silk, to wool and wool-and-acrylic mixes, as well as metallic threads. This allows the present-day machine embroiderer to select a thread with a matt, sheen or metallic finish – whichever is preferable.

When it is desirable to use heavier threads, they should be wound onto the bobbin. Six-stranded hand-embroidery cottons, floss or silk may be used in this way, as may perlé threads (all weights), and some knitting and crochet yarns, as well as heavier metal threads, provided that the latter are not so wiry that they will not feed properly.

Some heavier threads, such as tatting cotton, buttonhole twist and heavier machine embroidery threads, may be used on the top of the machine, providing a larger-sized needle or a needle with an enlarged eye (a topstitching needle) is used.

Bobbin thread

Regardless of the type of thread used on the top, and unless special effects are required, use machine embroidery cotton Nos 30 or 50 in the bobbin. Since this thread is not seen, it does not matter what colour is used. If the back of the work is to be seen, use the same thread in the bobbin as on the top. Any type of machine embroidery is finer and easier to work with machine embroidery cotton in the bobbin.

Hints on thread usage

Top thread breakage This usually occurs because machines are set up for general sewing with high-strength sewing threads and the top tension is too high/tight for machine embroidery.

Try reducing top tension by degrees. You might start at tension 3, but it could be necessary to reduce to 1. Each machine is different, but remember that adjusting the tensions does not harm the machine.

Needles Some of the specialized threads will require the use of larger needles, but for normal embroidery try a size 90 (14 US/ Eng.). It is good practice to change needles often when using metallic threads. Ensure that needles are not bent nor 'burred', in other words with nicks or sharp edges. You can find these by running a finger down the needle. Be sure, when inserting needles, that they are seated as high in the needle slot as they will go and orientated in the proper direction.

Uncontrolled thread spool-off Some of the metallic and rayon threads have a tendency to spool off the reel in an uncontrolled fashion. Some machine manufacturers have dealt with this problem by adding an extra thread guide. This is often designed to clip on the reel holder. If this is not available, the problem may be solved by taping a tapestry needle alongside the reel, or behind it and set slightly higher than the reel. Alternatively, a piece of felt, cut to fit under the reel, will sometimes help the problem. Some of the newer machines have horizontally mounted reel holders. These can often solve spool-off problems and are helpful to machine embroiderers.

Threads shred on the last guide If this is a problem, do not use this guide, which leads to the needle, if at all possible.

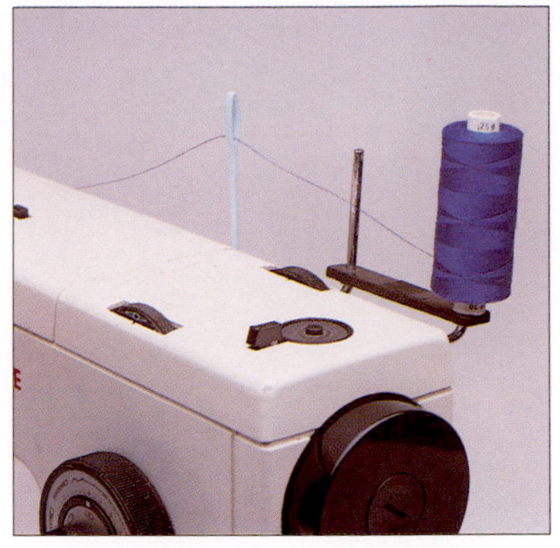

The addition of an extra thread guide is a useful aid if threads have a tendency to unreel in an uncontrollable fashion.

Machine embroidery needles

It is important to the machine embroiderer to have a good understanding of the full range of sewing machine needles, which includes several designed for special applications.

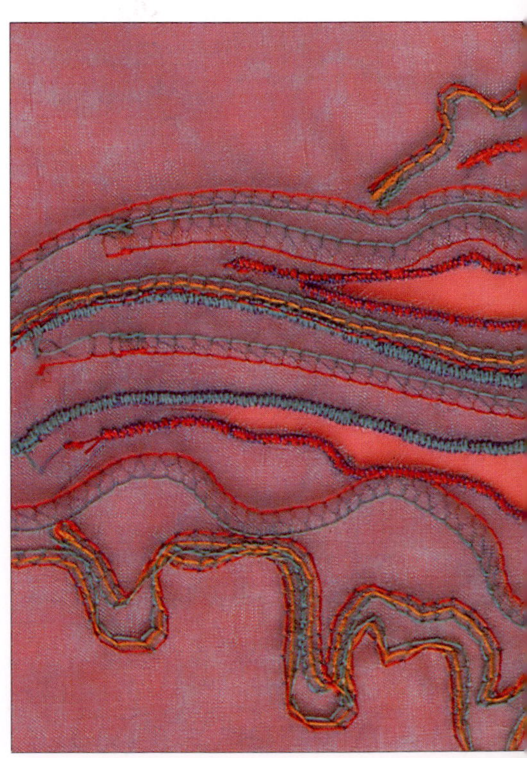

Continental and US/English needle sizes

Continental	60	65	70	75	80	90	100	110	120
US/English	8	9	10	11	12	14	16	18	20
	Very Fine				Medium				Very Heavy

The needle size is normally selected according to the weight and type of fabric being used. Size 90 (14) is the middle of the range and is used for sewing fabrics of medium weight. A medium size is a good choice for machine embroidery beginners, because it is more resistant to flexing and bending during free machine embroidery than a finer needle. Fine needles have a tendency to bend, break, miss stitches and shred machine embroidery threads. One of the most common causes of skipped stitches is that the needle has been inserted backwards or not high enough, so take care to insert needles correctly. It is important to change needles frequently when sewing on synthetic fabrics.

While the general charts matching needle sizes to fabrics are useful for dressmakers, they do not normally apply to machine embroidery. The machine embroiderer must select a needle that will allow the use of modern machine embroidery threads. These may incorporate fibre blends and twisted metallic threads and, as a result, a heavier needle may be required to accommodate them. Even though you may use a 90 (14) needle initially, it may be advisable to increase the size or use a topstitch needle if you encounter problems with threads.

In addition to US/English and Continental sizes, needle selection is further confused through the use of different sewing systems. Thankfully, only one system is used on most modern zigzag machines. This is designated on needle packaging as 130/705H. Caution must be exercised, however: check your own machine manual for the correct needle system identification. The following lists a selection of special needles, with some of their embroidery applications.

Twin needles These are produced in various sizes and with the needles spaced varying distances apart. In addition to the system number, the spacing and needle size will be noted on the packaging. For example, the notation 1.6/80 indicates size 80 needles, spaced 1.6mm apart. To thread twin needles, two threads are routed through the top of the machine in the same way as for single needle sewing. The two threads are then threaded through separate sides of the tension discs and each is taken through one needle. The bobbin contains one thread.

Twin needles may be used to produce unusual and creative machine embroidery effects. The distance between the shafts varies, as does the size of the needles. Triple needles may not be usable on all machines, so check your manual. Many fine effects are possible with these special needles.

The effect of the twin needle is to create two parallel rows of stitches, and it may be used to create some decorative and zigzag stitches.

Take care to check, manually, that the needle will pass through the needle plate, before making automatic zigzag stitches. Some machines may have special threading instructions for twin needle operations, so read your manual.

Triple needles Not all sewing machines will accommodate triple needles, so be sure to refer to your own sewing machine manual. The effect of the triple needle is to create three parallel lines of stitches, with three threads through the top of the machine. These needles may be used for decorative and zigzag stitches.

Ballpoint Synthetic fabrics and knits can resist 'sharp' needle penetration and cause skipped stitches. Ballpoint needles were developed to overcome this problem: the ballpoint pushes the fibres aside rather than piercing and splitting them. Always be sure to buy the correct type for your machine.

Jeans needle This needle, with its sharp and tapered point, was designed to pierce dense fabrics, such as denim. It is a very useful needle for embroidery on heavy fabrics.

Leather needle The leather needle has a wedge-shaped cutting edge which helps it to pierce tough materials like leather, oil cloth, vinyl and other plastic materials.

Topstitch needle This is a special design with a larger eye than a needle of its size would normally have. The needle is used for automatic and free machining and is ideal for accommodating heavier threads.

Single wing The 'wing' refers to a flattening and widening of the needle shaft, which enables this needle to make an enlarged entry hole and decoratively perforate the fabric as it sews fine fabrics, such as lawn and organdie. This is a very good needle for free machining.

Double wing The double wing needle is similar to a twin needle, except that one of the needles is shaped like a single wing needle.

Double wing needles (above) are normally used in hemstitching, but, again, the experimenting machine embroiderer will be able to produce exciting patterns.

Single wing needles (above) perforate fabrics such as lawn, organdie and muslin, creating interesting decorative effects.

Some of the more useful feet and attachments used for machine embroidery, clockwise from the top left: darning foot, eyelet plate, tailor tacking foot, regular sewing foot, pin tuck foot, open appliqué foot, teflon foot.

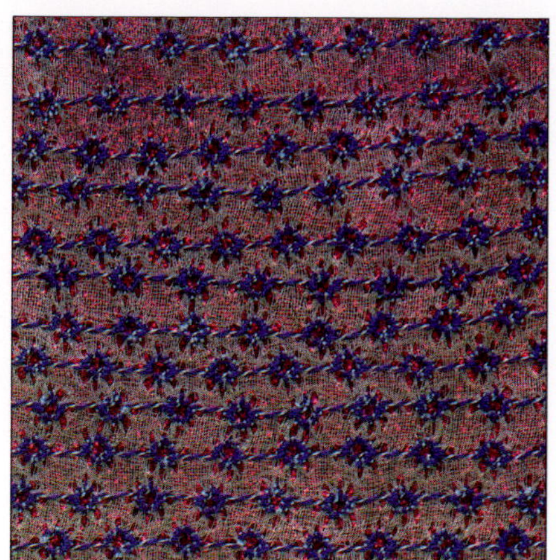

Feet and attachments

The feet and attachments named here are particularly applicable to automatic, decorative and free machine embroidery.

Satin stitch foot The satin stitch presser foot is designed with a shallow groove on the underside of the foot to allow clearance of the high pile created by the stitches. This allows the fabric to feed through evenly.

Darning foot Although most machines will allow free machining without the use of a foot, the idiosyncrasies of individual machines may demand the use of the darning foot for free machining. The darning foot assists in stabilizing fabric and also acts as a safety guard to keep fingers from passing under the needle.

Tailor tacking foot This foot is also used for making fringes in the automatic stitching mode. It has a high ridge in the centre,

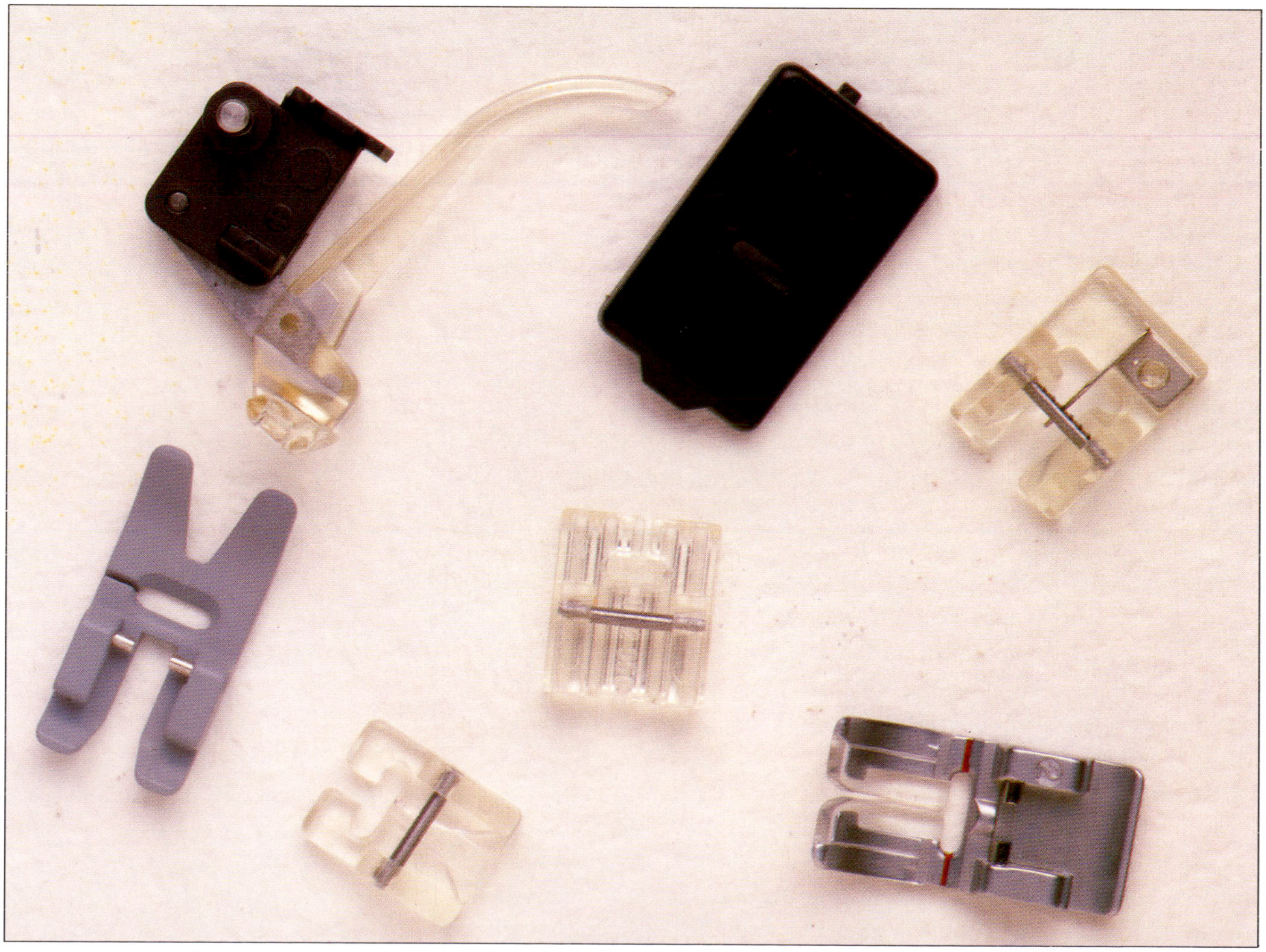

which creates a high looped fringe when satin stitch is applied.
Teflon foot/roller foot Either of these may be used for automatic stitching on such fabrics as vinyl, plastic or leather.
Open toe foot This foot is sometimes called an embroidery foot or appliqué foot. The toe of the foot is shorter than other feet to allow the embroiderer to see the production of the stitch.
Pin tuck foot Used in automatic stitching, this has from one to seven grooves on the underside to facilitate sewing raised seams with a twin needle. The grooves engage previously sewn line(s), while the needles sew further, parallel lines.
Eyelet plate Usually attached to the sewing plate, this has a small cylindrical protrusion that is placed through a small hole pierced through the fabric. Zigzag stitch is sewn around the edges until an even satin stitch is achieved. This plate is used only on swing needle machines.
Fringe and rug making fork The fork is used to produce a fringe in the automatic stitching mode. This fringe may be left as it is or clipped to produce an unlooped fringe.
Circular sewing attachment In the automatic stitching mode, this attachment is used to produce precise circular patterns. Fabric used with this attachment must be placed in an embroidery frame. A pin is inserted through the fabric to a locating hole some distance from the needle. Any automatic stitch may then be sewn, while the work rotates about the pin, creating a circular pattern.
Walking foot Sometimes called an even feed attachment, this feeds layers of bulky or slippery fabric through evenly.

Machine embroidery frames

Unless the fabric is very stiff, it is essential to use a frame to secure it for free machining. A frame will hold fabric tightly to control the material any time the feed dogs are lowered or disengaged and the presser foot is removed. Frames are also an aid in manipulating fabric during free machine embroidery.

As a general rule, the smaller the frame, the more tightly the fabric may be mounted, but whatever the size of the frame, you must allow an adequate overlap around the sides.

Round frames

Round embroidery frames or hoops come in a variety of sizes and materials. They may be made of wood, plastic or metal. Wood and metal frames generally have a knurled screw on the outer ring to adjust the frame for varying fabric thickness and

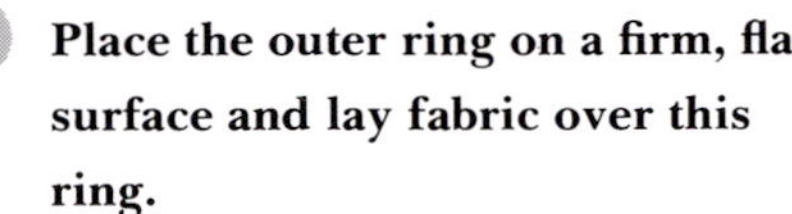

1 Place the outer ring on a firm, flat surface and lay fabric over this ring.

2 **Press the inner ring into the outer ring. Ensure that the fabric is stretched taut by gently pulling and stretching it around the ring. It may be necessary to tighten the tension screw on the frame. Press the inner ring slightly below the outer ring so that the fabric makes close contact with the needle plate.**

tightness. Some wooden types are too deep to pass under the needle with ease. If this is the case, cut a notch in the edge to allow the needle to pass into the centre of the frame.

It is advisable to bind around the inner ring of wood frames with narrow bias tape, stitched at the end to secure it. The tape binding helps to reduce slippage of the framed fabric, a problem which can frequently occur, especially with synthetic fabrics.

Plastic frames are made with a groove on the inner face of the ring, which receives a metal, sprung, inner ring. These frames are recommended for finer fabrics, such as fine cotton and silks. However, the largest size that will adequately secure the fabric for free machining is about 12cm (5in). Ensure that the frame allows the fabric to lie directly on the needle plate, with no gaps.

Free machining without a frame

Very stiff fabrics may sometimes be free machined without a frame. Fabrics generally suitable for stitching without frames include canvas, pelmet interfacing, buckram or lighter fabric that has been stiffened with roller blind spray. For safety's sake, it may be advisable to use the darning foot to protect your fingers.

Other equipment

Scissors Use dressmakers' for fabric cutting and small sharp scissors for appliqué and other intricate cutting requirements.
Tweezers Useful for removing threads that may be wound around the bobbin case or jammed in the feed dogs.
Lint brush These are usually supplied with the machine to remove the lint that builds up around the bobbin case and feed dogs.
Sewing machine oil Some newer machines are self-lubricating. Others require oil. Use oil sparingly and use only sewing machine oil.
Bobbin case It is very convenient to have an extra bobbin case. Retain one case at normal tension, the other at much looser tension for special effects.
Bobbins It is very convenient to have several bobbins wound with thread for rapid exchange.
Spray glue Very light applications of spray glue are useful to hold fabrics together for stitching and help to hold appliqué shapes in place as you sew.

AUTOMATIC STITCHING

The numerous automatic stitches, both utility and decorative, that have been available on sewing machines for many years, can be used for creative machine embroidery. It is possible, however, to vary the application of these automatic stitches to create some very individual pieces of work. Automatic patterns may be shortened or lengthened, made wider or more narrow, depending upon the creative imagination of the embroiderer. In the case of computerized machines that allow individual pattern programming, it is possible to program unique stitches or stitch sequences.

In this photograph, taken to show the effects of loose bobbin tension, silver thread has been used and the bobbin tension has been loosened. The top – blue and pink thread – brings up the silver thread to produce a variegated effect. The top tension can also be tightened to produce the same effect.

Satin stitch

One of the most frequently ignored stitches on the machine seems to be the satin stitch. Satin stitch may be used for decorative purposes, edgings, appliqué or quilting. The following are some ideas for working with satin stitch.

Satin stitch is a variation of the zigzag stitch. The width of the stitch is set on the stitch width control, but the stitch length control must be set for closely spaced stitches, to achieve full coverage without spaces between stitches. Some machines allow width and length variations while sewing. This facility permits a varying width of the satin stitch line. The sheen of the closely spaced threads creates a lustrous effect.

Fabrics Any fabric may be used for satin stitch, but unless it is a heavy fabric, such as heavy cotton or denim, it will pucker under the stresses of stitching. Steps must therefore be taken to reduce those stresses on lighter fabrics: depending upon the weight of the fabric, either place under it one or two layers of paper interfacing, of the type that can easily be torn away, then remove it after stitching; or stiffen the fabric with iron-on interfacing. The latter will, however, alter the feel of the fabric.

Threads Fine, soft embroidery threads, both on the top of the machine and in the bobbin, make the nicest satin stitches. Heavy threads can look clumsy and will have a tendency to clog the machine through stitch build-up.

Needle The needle size is dependent on the weight of fabric and the thread being used. Begin with a size 80(12) needle and experiment; the thread should not shred and the fabric should not cause the needle to flex back and forth. If these problems

Satin stitch can be worked over typing or tracing paper or paper interfacing. The paper is torn away from either side of the very close satin stitch. If your satin stitch is not sufficiently close, go over the lines a second time.

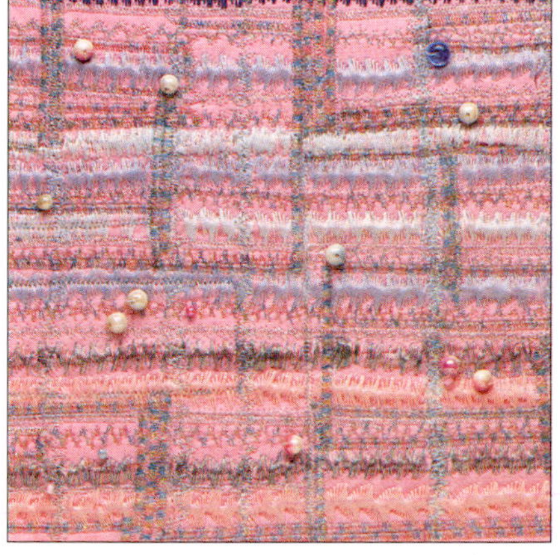

Rows of satin stitch have here been worked by pivoting the fabric rapidly from side to side in an arc while the machine is operating, in this way distorting the stitch.

occur, change to a larger size of needle. A topstitching needle, with its elongated eye, can be used to combat thread shredding.

Foot Use the zigzag (satin stitch) presser foot.

Tensions Decrease the top tension so that only the top thread shows on the fabric.

Stitch width What you wish.

Stitch length This should be close enough for the stitches to lie side by side without gaps. If stitches pile up on each other and the fabric does not feed properly, extend the stitch length slightly.

Satin stitch variations

The satin stitch instructions just given are for traditional applications, but if you experiment with top and bobbin tensions, with different weights of threads and fabrics, and with stitch widths and lengths, you will discover your own original satin stitch variations. Even though the machine produces a straight line of satin stitch, the fabric does not have to follow that straight line, as you can manipulate it while the satin stitch is being formed.

Satin stitch edging for shapes

Satin stitch may be used to finish edges of fabric, either to prevent fraying or to provide a decorative edge. The machine is set up as for satin stitch, with certain exceptions, given below.

Fabric Almost any fabric may be used, though it is best to use a reasonably firm fabric for practising if you are a beginner. If the fabric is very light in weight, it may be advisable to double it and use featherweight non-woven interfacing or vanishing muslin.

Needle Start with the smallest needle that will allow the thread to pass without shredding: try 65(9) or 70(10) to start with. Large needles have a tendency to perforate and weaken the fabric along the stitching line.

Tensions It is desirable for the stitches to lock along one side of the row on the underside. To achieve this, the tensions must be adjusted so that the top thread is pulled to the underside and therefore covers both sides of the fabric. Gradually reduce the top tension until it is possible to see the locked stitch on the underside of the fabric along one edge of the stitching. If this

Satin stitch edging

1 **Using a pencil, transfer your pattern outline to the fabric. Attach two layers of paper interfacing to the back of your fabric. These may be either lightly sprayed with glue or hand basted. Sew a straight stitch, with a stitch length of approximately 1.5mm ($^1/_{16}$in), along the pattern line marked on the fabric.**

2 **If it is desirable to be able to bend the shape into a particular form, a wire may be laid inside the line of straight stitch. Make a narrow zigzag stitch over the wire, then cut away the excess fabric from the shape, closely following the line of stitching. Do not cut away the paper interfacing.**

3 **Sew a close satin stitch along the inside edge of the shape. Ensure that the satin stitch covers the straight and zigzag stitches. If your machine will not produce a close satin stitch, increase the stitch length slightly and sew around the shape a second time.**

4 **Gently tear the interfacing from the back of your shape. This will leave the three-dimensional shape. The success of this technique lies in the closeness of the satin stitch, which conceals the fibres of the interfacing.**

effect cannot be achieved through reduction of the top tension alone, the bobbin tension may need to be increased. Some machines may lock the satin stitch down the centre of the stitching at the back, rather than along one edge. If your machine falls into this category, use threads of the same colour on the top and in the bobbin.

Raised satin stitch – loops and fringe

This technique employs the tailor tacking foot, sometimes called a fringe foot. This foot was originally designed to enable dressmakers to make basting stitches. Embroiderers can use this foot in a much more creative way by sewing a satin stitch over it to produce loops and fringing. Experiments with tensions and threads will create some very individual effects and textures, and these can be combined with other techniques. Start by setting your machine up as for satin stitch.
Fabric Use a heavy-weight fabric or add a backing.
Threads Any type of machine embroidery thread may be used. Stiff or metallic threads will produce a loop or fringe that stands erect. Machine embroidery cotton is recommended for the bobbin.
Foot Use a tailor tacking foot.
Stitch width Narrow satin stitch will produce a full fringe or loop; a wide satin stitch will produce a more widely-spaced fringe or loop: experiment with stitch widths for different effects.
Stitch length The stitch length should, generally, be closely spaced. If stitches begin to pile up and the fabric becomes difficult to manipulate, try lengthening the stitch.
Preparation Framing is optional, but if the fabric is framed it will be easier to manipulate the work as you sew, producing curves and patterns. Framing is not necessary if you are stitching fairly straight lines.
Machining Sew satin stitch over the tacking foot in any desired pattern. Since these stitches will easily pull out of the fabric, it is necessary to secure them. To achieve this, push the finished loops to one side and sew a very narrow satin stitch over the line where the stitches enter the fabric. Alternatively, place a piece of iron-on interfacing at the back to secure the stitches. To produce a fringe, carefully clip the loops that are formed, or leave the loops as they are for a softer textural effect.

Satin stitch has been worked here with a tailor tacking foot, and the fabric was moved from side to side under the needle to produce flowing curves.

Satin stitch cords

Cords are produced by sewing satin stitch over a cord or string, so the machine is set up for satin stitch. No fabric is placed under the cord while the satin stitch is being sewn.

Cord Use any heavy string, drapery cord, heavy wool, thread, crochet cotton or wire.

Threads Machine embroidery threads are used, with the same thread in the bottom as on the top of the machine. Some shiny threads, such as rayon threads, will resist this technique and are thus unsuitable.

Foot Either a general sewing or a zigzag foot may be used. A walking foot is an aid in feeding the cord, but it is not essential.

Tension Set the top tension looser than normal; the bobbin tension should be slightly increased. Threads should lock on the bottom of the cord, allowing the top thread to wrap completely around the cord. Adjust the tension so that the threads are tightly wrapped around the cord.

Stitch length If the stitch length is too closely spaced, stitches may pile up on the cord. If this happens, lengthen the stitch setting. Try to keep stitches as close together as possible without piling up.

Stitch width The stitch must be wider than the diameter of the cord, covering it without sewing into it.

1 **Place the string or cord under the presser foot. Leave a long tail on the cord so that one hand can grip the cord to apply a gentle pulling pressure, assisting the feed dogs along the sewing line. More than one pass through the machine will be necessary to achieve full coverage of the cord.**

2 **Interesting effects may be produced by stitching over soft embroidery threads or wool. Almost any decorative utility stitch can be used to apply interesting patterns, and threads can be bunched to create heavily textured cords.**

Cable stitch

Cable stitch is actually a heavy thread couched to a fabric by an ordinary sewing thread. The stitch is made with the underside of the fabric upwards, and the right side of the fabric facing the feed dogs. It is often difficult, on heavy or thick fabric, to create a good outline, as many stitches simply disappear into the fabric: cable stitch not only solves this problem, but does so easily, while using ordinary straight stitch. This stitch is normally used as an outline stitch on velvet, wool, cotton, upholstery or other heavy fabrics. Cable stitch may resemble simple hand couching, and can also be used as a quilting stitch. Since the stitch is worked upside down, the design may be drawn directly on the reverse side of the background fabric.

Fabric Try using heavy-weight cotton, wool, silk, velvet or, perhaps, upholstery fabrics.

Thread For the bobbin thread, use a perlé thread, 6-stranded embroidery thread, or fine knitting or crochet wools. Thread the top of the machine with dressmakers' No. 50. If it is desirable for the couching thread to be unseen, use invisible (nylon) thread.

Needle Begin with a size 90(14) and change if necessary.

Stitch Use straight stitch.

Foot Use the general sewing presser foot.

Tensions The top tension may require no adjustment to form a neat, tight, couching stitch. For most heavy threads, the bobbin tension will normally have to be loosened so that the thicker thread will spool off the bobbin with about the same tension as normal sewing thread.

Stitch length Normal stitch length is generally satisfactory, but experiment for different effects.

Machining Before beginning this stitch, bring the bobbin thread up through the fabric. As machining is begun, check tension to ensure that a proper stitch is being made. The bobbin thread should lie neatly secured to the fabric with a tight couching stitch.

Inspired by the reflection of light on snow, this cotton velvet fabric was first airbrushed with fabric dye, and then quilted, using cable stitch.

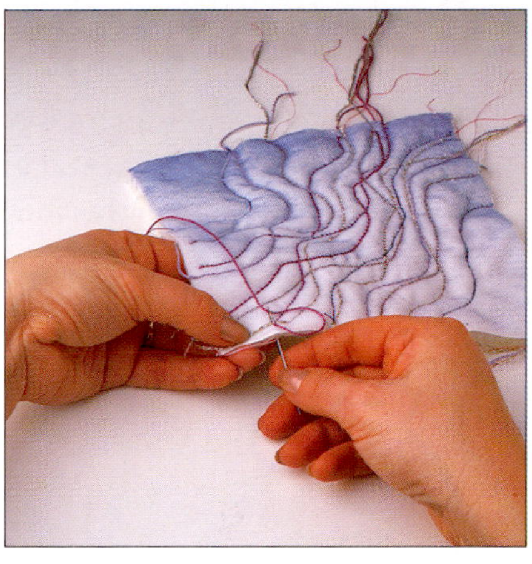

1. Hand baste the three layers – top fabric, batting and muslin backing – securely together. Transfer the design to the back of the fabric.

2. Place the right side of the fabric face down over the feed dogs. Bring the bobbin thread to the surface and begin stitching with straight stitch.

3. Do not backstitch at the beginning of this technique; leave the long tails of the bobbin thread hanging loose; then, using a needle, bring the tails to the wrong side of the fabric and tie them off to finish the piece.

Exploring decorative stitches

Most machine embroiderers tend to dismiss the fixed or programmed decorative stitches as being too traditional for use in creative machine embroidery. But although the stitch may be programmed, the manner in which it is used can express creativity. Programmed stitches, when used with unusual combinations of threads and fabrics, can be the basis of interesting work, especially as many machines allow up to 10 stitch lengths and around 20 stitch widths. These elements allow ample scope for experimentation and individual creativity.

To use decorative stitches free style, frame the fabric and, using the general sewing presser foot, move the frame from side to side. Since the feed dogs are up, it is inadvisable to move the frame backward and forward during sewing. Pivoting the fabric about the needle, without pushing or pulling as in free machining, experiment with a broad selection of stitches in varying widths and lengths. Automatic decorative stitches may be used or satin stitch, as in the sample.

Couched fabric strips

A new fabric may be created by couching torn or cut fabric strips. The technique may be used to embellish clothing or it can be incorporated in a design for a panel or quilt. This is an excellent opportunity to use up scraps or odd pieces of fabric, which can be re-dyed or bleached to change colour and character.

Fabric The background fabric should be of medium or heavy weight, or have a backing attached so that the fabric is stiff enough to support the applied strips and the heavy machine embroidery. The applied fabrics may be of any type and should be torn or cut into strips from 3 to 6mm (⅛ to ¼in) wide. In some places, the background fabric will be seen, perhaps through semi-transparent fabrics, so the colour of the strips should relate to the colour scheme of the background.

Thread Again, coordinate colours with the overall scheme. Variegated threads can create very interesting effects.

Needle Choose a needle to suit the size of thread and type of fabric.

Stitch Select an automatic decorative stitch, such as zigzag or one of the more complex options.

Foot Use either the general sewing presser foot, the satin stitch foot or the open toe foot.

Stitch width Vary the stitch width on successive strips.

Stitch length Some machines allow the stitch pattern to be lengthened. If yours has this capacity, vary the stitch length of the decorative pattern on successive strips.

Mirror image Some machines will allow the decorative stitch to be produced in mirror image format. If so, apply this technique as well.

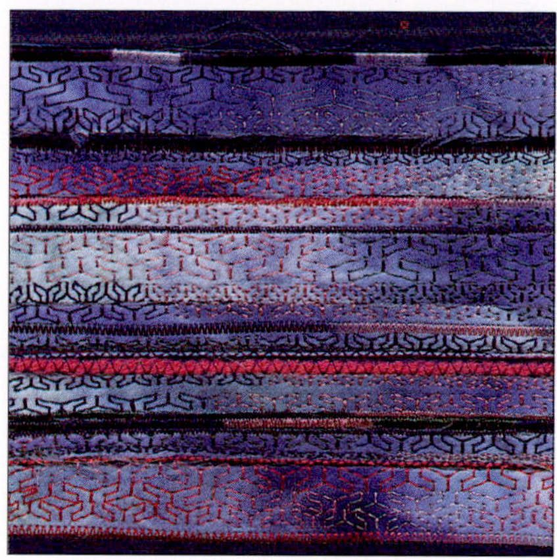

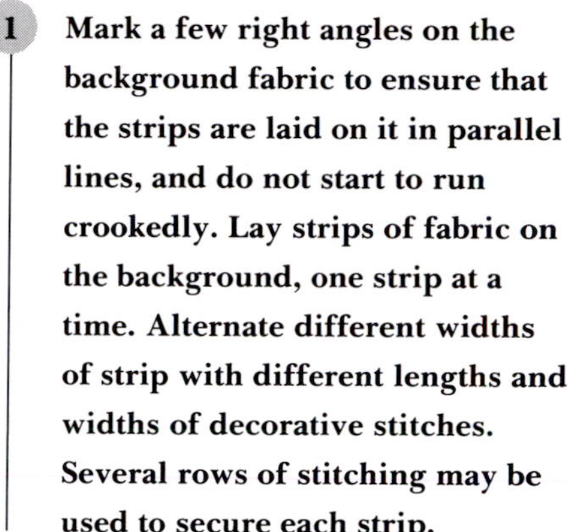

1 Mark a few right angles on the background fabric to ensure that the strips are laid on it in parallel lines, and do not start to run crookedly. Lay strips of fabric on the background, one strip at a time. Alternate different widths of strip with different lengths and widths of decorative stitches. Several rows of stitching may be used to secure each strip.

2 Stitch in parallel rows and occasionally couch a thread or two, blending these in with the general colour scheme. Sew a few rows of satin stitch at random, regardless of any other stitch applied. Let some of the background fabric peek through the fabric strips and stitching.

Fabric strips have here been couched to a background with many variations of stitch pattern. (Embroidery by Gail Harker; cushion made by Chris Bentley)

FREE MACHINE EMBROIDERY

Free machine embroidery opens the door to a whole new world of artistic expression. Try to visualize the needle as a pencil or a paint brush: moving your framed piece of fabric under the needle is like drawing on a sheet of paper or painting on a canvas. Free running stitch, zigzag and some of the automatic stitches will produce lines of wide, narrow or variable width, and textures from an enormous palette of coloured threads. The movement of the framed fabric is within the full control of the artist.

Ensure that the machine is sewing properly – in other words that stitches are forming correctly and are not being skipped – and that tensions are set for general sewing. If not, adjust your machine for the perfect straight stitch. It is usually easier for the inexperienced to begin with a machine adjusted in the automatic mode. However, as one gains experience and acquires a feel for the adjustments, simply set your machine up for free running stitch (see below) immediately, without this preliminary stage.

As you become more experienced you will be able to stop using the embroidery frame. Try stiffening your fabric by using a roller blind stiffener. This can be bought as a spray or a liquid, which needs to be diluted with water. Alternatively, layer a few pieces of fabric and baste them together. Place your hands on either side of the needle to support the fabric; you can then move the fabric in any direction.

It is important to start by adjusting your machine for automatic stitching. After this, the transition to free machine embroidery will require only minor adjustments. In both modes of operation, the presser bar must be lowered while sewing. Always return the tensions to the normal settings after using either mode.

Gail Harker layered fabrics and then decorated them with a wide range of threads to create the wintery feel of Ice Angels.

Persian Pot of Flowers, *by Margaret Townley, represents an attempt to create an embroidery with a rich, mysterious, oriental atmosphere and an icon-like quality.*

Setting-up for free running stitch

Free running stitch (also called straight stitch) is the basis for most free machine embroidery. The most effective method is to maintain a fairly high machine running speed. Too low a running speed can result in needle breakage, drag on the fabric, skipped stitches, or stitches too closely spaced.

It is better to move the frame at a rate that does not allow too much thread to build up on the fabric. Practise lines, circles or curves. Move the frame rhythmically, avoiding jerks and rapid movements.

Fabrics Use medium- to heavy-weight cotton. Lighter fabrics should be backed with a layer of fabric or interfacing.

Threads Any machine embroidery thread may be used on the top of the machine. Use machine embroidery cotton thread or dressmakers' No. 50 in the bobbin. Do not use No. 40 dressmakers' cotton for free machine embroidery.

Needle Use a size 90(14) needle – this breaks less readily and is good for practice.

Foot Start by experimenting without a foot, lowering the presser bar and removing the foot altogether. If you find it difficult to sew without a foot, attach the darning foot.

Stitch length Set the stitch length to '0', to stop the feed dogs moving. The stitch length setting controls the back-and-forth movement of the feed dogs. Although the feed dogs are lowered, any movement may still snag the threads or fabric. If you cannot set your machine at '0', select the lowest number.

Stitch width Set the stitch width to '0'.

Tensions Adjust tensions as for the perfect stitch. If the perfect stitch cannot be achieved on your machine, it is better to have a bit of the top thread showing on the bottom of the fabric, than for the bobbin thread to show through on the front.

Preparation Lower or cover the feed dogs. Ensure that the material is tightly framed in an embroidery frame.

1 **Lower the presser bar, as if lowering the foot. Bring both threads to the surface of the machine.**

Textured stitches based on free running stitch

Many patterns can be developed from free running stitch, and these can be further developed in many different ways – to fill in a design, to secure collages of fabric and thread, for appliqué and quilting – the design possibilities are endless. After you have experimented with some of the stitch patterns shown here, it might be fun to sketch out some ideas of your own, using pencil and paper.

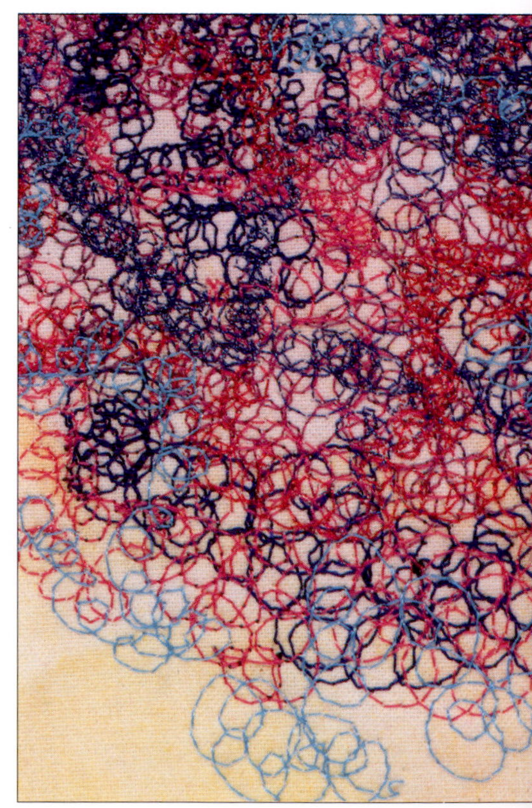

2 **Begin to stitch, moving the frame in any direction. By coordinating the movement of the frame and speed of sewing with the foot pedal, you will be able to control the size, length and direction of stitch.**

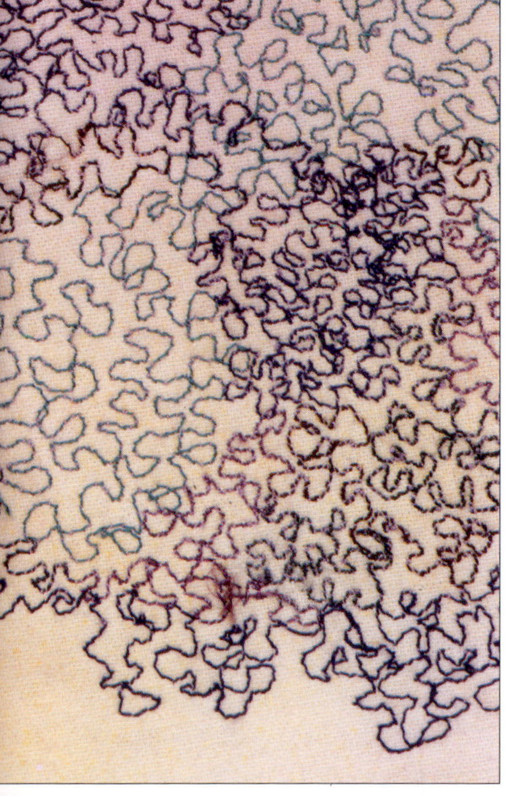

Early machine embroiderers used granite, or seed, stitch (left-hand side of the picture), in which circles overlap.

Vermicelli, or crazy, stitch (right-hand side) is another of the popular patterns used to cover large areas of fabric. The pattern is worked in a series of half circles.

This masterly pillow, drawn and painted by hand, is part of the counterpane and pillow set Creation, *commissioned from Paddy Killer for the crafts house in the Gateshead Garden Festival. Made in silk, cotton, velvet and hand-printed cotton, the embroidery includes machine quilting with cotton and rayon thread and the background stitch is vermicelli. (Photograph courtesy of the Tyne and Wear Museum Service)*

Drawing with the needle

Drawing with the needle is similar to putting pencil to paper or brush to canvas. Once you have acquired confidence, you can mix stitches and techniques, allowing your creative instincts to decide the direction that your work should take. You might, for example, try making your own background fabric, or you could dye or quilt the background, and for the embroidery itself you might choose to combine machine work with hand stitches.

It is advisable to use a firm, heavy cotton or upholstery fabric, which will be easy to stitch. If your chosen fabric is relatively light-weight, it may be necessary to stiffen the fabric by backing it with additional fabric, interfacing, or heavy fusible interlining. Ensure that you leave a sufficient border of unworked fabric around the design to allow for framing.

Prepare your machine in the same way as for free running stitch. Use the smallest frame that is practical and the smallest needle that will accommodate the thread and fabric.

1 **Cut the embroidery fabric and a piece of light-weight fusible interlining to the design size plus a margin. Using a light box or window, trace the design onto the interlining.**

2 **Fuse the interlining with the design traced on it to the right side of the fabric, following the manufacturer's instructions. Cut a second piece of interlining, the same size as the first, and apply it to the back of the fabric.**

3 **Frame the fabric tightly and set your machine for free running stitch. Begin sewing and move the frame to create the desired effect. Work some straight lines, so that they overlap, meet each other and so on. Work small sections at a time, filling in background areas to suit the design.**

4 **The fabric will become very heavy with thread. If difficulty in sewing with the foot off is ever a problem with your machine, it will probably be encountered with this technique. If so, try using the darning foot. A clear plastic darning foot is particularly helpful, enabling you to see the stitching as it is applied to the design.**

In Winter Flowers, *by Gail Harker, free zigzag stitch was worked from side to side on canvas. The petals were cut away and free running stitch was worked across the open areas. No frame was used for this work.*

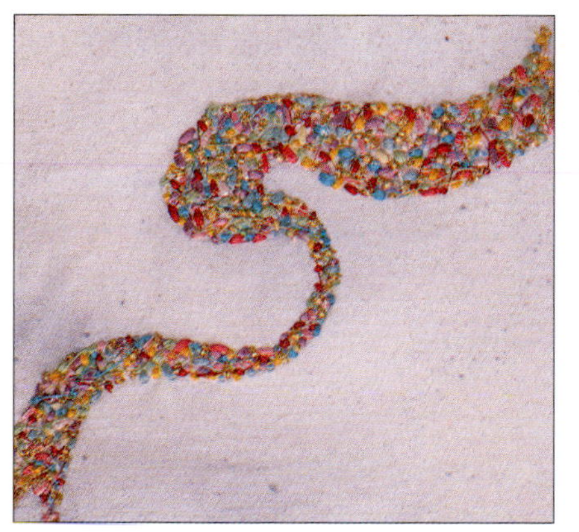

Satin stitch beads are made by working satin stitches closely together.

Free zigzag stitch

Frame the fabric and set your machine up as for free running stitch; the only exception will be the stitch width, which can be set at whatever suits your purpose. To accomplish complete coverage of the fabric by the top thread, you may require a slight reduction in top tension. It is advisable to use a heavy fabric or one that has been backed with an interfacing. The frame can be moved in any direction as you work. If you move the frame slowly, while applying full power to the foot pedal, a satin stitch will be produced. If the frame is moved more quickly and less power is applied through the foot pedal, an open zigzag can be produced.

Satin stitch beads

Satin stitch beads can be densely packed together or spaced further apart. A thread, which may be left as it is or clipped, will run between each bead. Place the framed fabric under the needle; then lower the presser bar and select the preferred stitch width. Begin stitching, but hold the frame in place. A bead of built-up satin stitch will begin to form. When the bead reaches the desired size, raise the pressure bar; move to the next position, and continue the process. Do not allow the build-up to clog the machine.

If it is desirable to clip the connecting threads, a few stitches, made with the width setting set at '0', will secure the thread at the beginning and end of each bead.

Couched threads with loops

Free machining techniques can easily be used for couching threads. These may be arranged in loops or other designs and may be of any length. Almost any type of thread can be used, as can cord, ribbon, fabric strips, string or knitting wool. The (top) sewing thread is not intended to be seen and should therefore be the same colour as the couched thread. The bobbin thread may be any thread of your choice.

Stitches Free running stitch or free zigzag.

Foot Use the darning foot, or sew without a foot.

Preparation The background fabric should be framed for this technique. Paper or other interfacing may be used to provide additional stiffness if required.

An example of couched cords applied at random and embellished with satin stitch beads.

1. **Draw with a pencil or transfer a design to the top fabric. Form a loop of the thread that is to be couched. With the left index finger, hold the loop on the top fabric and stitch over the protruding ends to the right of the finger. Continue this process, forming loops as required.**

2. **Continue to add loops until the desired amount of build-up is accomplished. This is not continuous stitching, but a start-stop process as each loop is formed and attached. Make small stitches over the edges of the couched thread. It is important to ensure that the loops are close together in order to get even coverage.**

Eyelets

Eyelets are traditionally the basis of broderie anglaise, but with free machining you can expand upon this conventional use, creating wonderful clusters of textured motifs, perhaps with eyelets of different sizes combined on one fabric.

Eyelets may be used in many creative ways: they may be overlapped and varied in size or shape, or small roundels may be cut from fabric and glued or basted to the background fabric in random patterns. You can punch holes through both fabrics to create raised eyelets, though if the roundels are cut from very thick fabric, the eyelet stud may not engage the fabric.

When the satin stitch is applied to the roundels, it creates the eyelet as well as attaching the roundel, which may protrude beyond the satin stitch. You can create interesting textures and patterns with roundels and it is well worth experimenting with different fabrics.

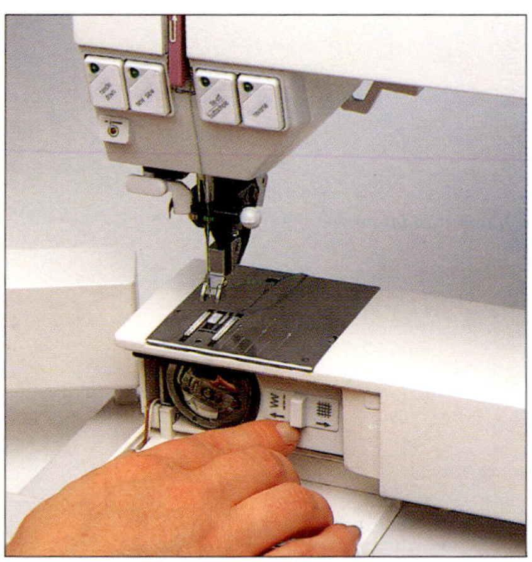

1 **Remove the presser foot and lower the feed dogs. Secure the eyelet plate over the feed dogs. Frame the fabric tightly with a small frame, about 8 to 9cm (3¼ to 3¾in) in diameter, unless heavy fabric such as pelmet Vilene or belting is being used.**

2 **Punch a small hole in the fabric with a pointed instrument, and position the hole over the eyelet stud. Lower the presser bar and adjust the stitch width. Begin stitching, while pivoting the fabric about the eyelet stud. Check your machine manual for any special instructions for your machine.**

Eyelets with a plate

There are several variations on this technique, but it is best to start with the comparatively conventional method outlined here. Prepare for machining by fitting in the eyelet plate and – unless the fabric is very stiff – by setting the work in a frame.

Threads Use any machine embroidery thread.

Stitch Use satin stitch throughout.

Foot Remove the foot.

Tension You may find that it is necessary to adjust the bobbin tension in order to ensure that no bobbin thread is visible on the right side.

Eyelets without a plate

Do not throw up your hands in despair if you do not have an eyelet plate; this attachment will, in any case, produce only one size of eyelet. The following instructions will enable you to make eyelets of any size.

Start by preparing your machine as already described, but do not use the eyelet plate. Use a firm fabric, held in a small frame, and draw on the fabric an eyelet of the required size and shape. Using free running stitch, stitch two or three times around the border of the shape to strengthen the edge. Remove the fabric from the frame. With small, sharp scissors, carefully cut a hole inside the stitched area and re-frame the fabric. Set the stitch width at the desired setting and carefully stitch round the hole, pivoting about the centre of the hole as sewing progresses. Finish stitching on the outer edge of the eyelet; take the top thread to the back, and tie it off.

You may find it easier to stitch if you place a piece of paper interfacing under the eyelet, tearing it away when you have finished.

This sample shows large eyelets, made without the use of an eyelet plate.

Whip stitch

Whip stitch is a raised stitch that intentionally shows only the bobbin thread on the surface of the fabric. The top of the machine is threaded with a heavy thread and the top tension is increased; as a result, the bobbin thread is pulled up through the fabric and whips around the top thread, creating a beautiful 'looped' effect. Whip stitch requires very slow movement of the frame.

Fabric Use a firm fabric, tightly framed in a small embroidery frame.

Threads For the top thread, use ordinary dressmakers' cotton thread No. 40 or No. 50. Alternatively, two threads can be used simultaneously, though if you opt for this you may find that you need to fit a special topstitching needle to prevent the threads from shredding.

For the bobbin thread, finest machining embroidery thread is ideal, but some machines will accommodate metallic threads, rayons and mixtures.

Needles Use a size 90(14) or choose a needle to suit the thread and fabric.

Foot The foot is normally removed for whip stitch, but you

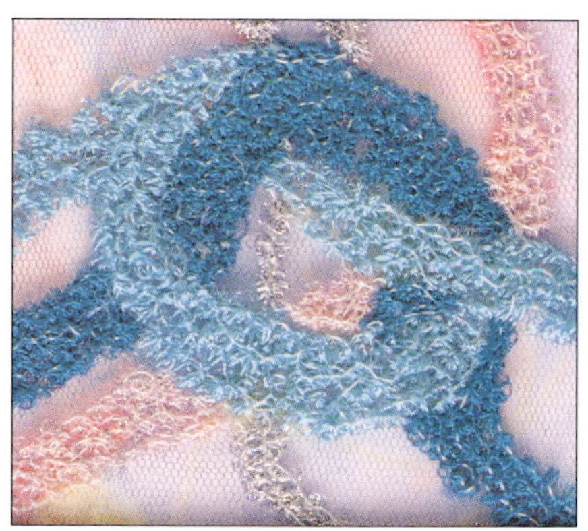

The three samples seen here show feather stitch, a variation on whip stitch (see page 135). In the first, feather stitch has been worked on net, using a loose bobbin tension so that the bobbin thread shows on the surface of the net.

Feather stitch has been worked on cotton muslin – a circular movement creates lace holes.

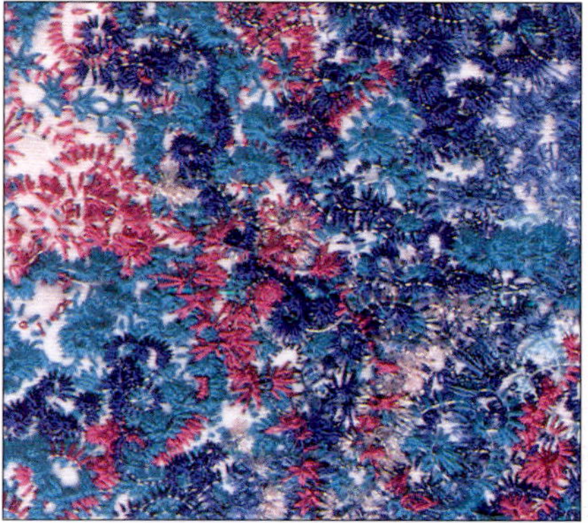

For basic feather stitch, the frame is moved in a circular motion, more quickly than for whip stitch. A tight top tension and loose bobbin tension draw the bobbin thread to the surface.

may use a darning foot if it proves difficult to stitch without a foot.

Tensions Increase the top tension in small steps until the bobbin thread is visible on the surface of the fabric. This will be tighter than for 'normal' sewing. Normal sewing tension will, usually, be indicated by a number on the dial between '3' and '5', or by a coloured line. Tension adjustment could go as high as '9'. If the top thread breaks, reduce tension. Decrease the bobbin tension so that it is slightly less than for 'normal' sewing. Some machines allow bobbin tension to be bypassed – read your manual.

Tension adjustment for this technique is all important. On some machines, high top tension will result in continual breakage of the top thread. If this occurs, reduce the bobbin tension slightly. If the finished stitch is irregular or lumpy, either the top tension is not set tightly enough or the bobbin tension is too tight, so readjust tensions.

Some machines with drop-in bobbins do not permit the

1 ***Lightning Strikes Twice*** **was selected as the design theme for this piece. To translate the feeling of lightning and dark skies, small shapes were torn, cut, and glued to a sheet of paper, and this arrangement of shapes and colours became the design for the finished embroidery.**

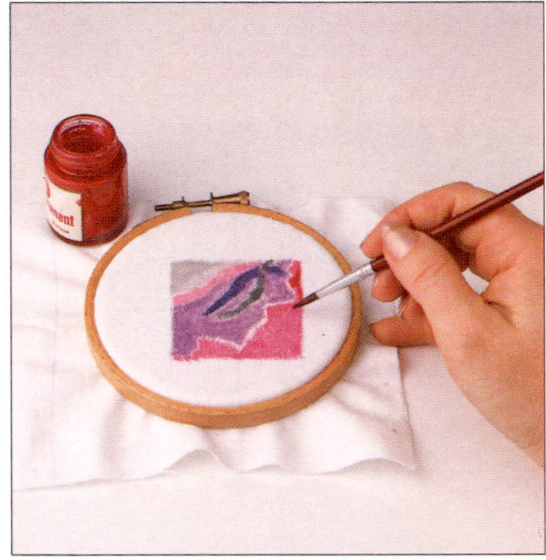

2 **Using cotton fabric dye, following the manufacturer's instructions, the design was painted on the background fabric. The dye transferred the design to the background fabric and provides the background colour where the fabric peeks through the stitches.**

3 **The machine was prepared for whip stitch and the tightly-framed fabric was positioned under the needle. The frame was moved very slowly, with the foot pedal depressed so that the machine ran very fast. Rows of bobbin thread, forming in loops, appeared on the surface.**

required degree of low tension. This condition may be compensated by the use of a heavier thread on the top or by wrapping the top thread, once or twice, around a second spool pin on the top of the machine.

Preparation Prepare your machine as for free machine embroidery, by lowering or covering the feed dogs and removing the foot altogether or fitting the darning foot.

Variations on whip stitch

Whip stitch is one of the few stitches that places great strain on the top tension. Each machine reacts a little differently to the next, and only by experimenting will you discover the possibilities of the stitch on your machine.

Feather stitch, which is demonstrated on the preceding page, is a variation of whip stitch: follow directions for whip stitch, but increase the top tension to the maximum, reduce the bobbin tension to the minimum and move the frame more quickly in a circular fashion.

Gail Harker's finished piece, Lightning Strikes Twice, *is composed of nine patches, each approximately 4.5cm (1¾in) square. The background fabric is dyed cotton twill.*

Free cable stitch

Free cable stitch is used to create a high, three-dimensional, textured build-up of heavy threads on fabric. This is accomplished through the use of hand-embroidery threads, wound on the bobbin and applied with the fabric right side down. The obvious difficulty is that you cannot see the progressive build-up of threads. It is therefore necessary to draw the design on the reverse side of the fabric so that you can follow the design lines during sewing. It is advisable to try an experimental piece to ensure that tensions are properly adjusted to achieve the desired result. This experimental piece can also be used to try out different threads.

Fabrics Experiment with a variety of fabrics, including cotton, velvet, organdie, organza, and other unusual types. Ensure that the fabric is tightly framed.

Threads The top thread may be dressmakers' thread, size 50, or machine embroidery thread.

For the bobbin, use hand embroidery threads, perlé, six-stranded threads, fine knitting and crochet yarns. Try some of the new and exciting combinations of metallic and twisted threads. To wind the bobbin, unroll a length of thread from the ball or skein, but do not cut it until the bobbin is full. Use the bobbin winding mechanism on the machine, but use your fingers as an extra thread guide to ensure that the thread winds on the bobbin evenly. This will prevent sewing problems later. Do not overfill the bobbin.

Needle Choose a needle to suit the thread and fabric.

Stitch Use free running stitch, working in any direction. For a heavy build-up of texture, overlap the stitches.

Tension Adjust tensions as for couched threads. Most heavy threads will require a decrease in bobbin tension, which should be adjusted so that the heavy thread spools off at about the same rate as normal sewing thread. For a loose, looping stitch, the bobbin tension can be set very low. Some machines will have a tension bypass for very loopy cable stitch.

The top tension may require some adjustment to ensure a neat, tight couching stitch. This adjustment of top tension secures the bobbin thread to the fabric. Start at normal tension, and increase as required.

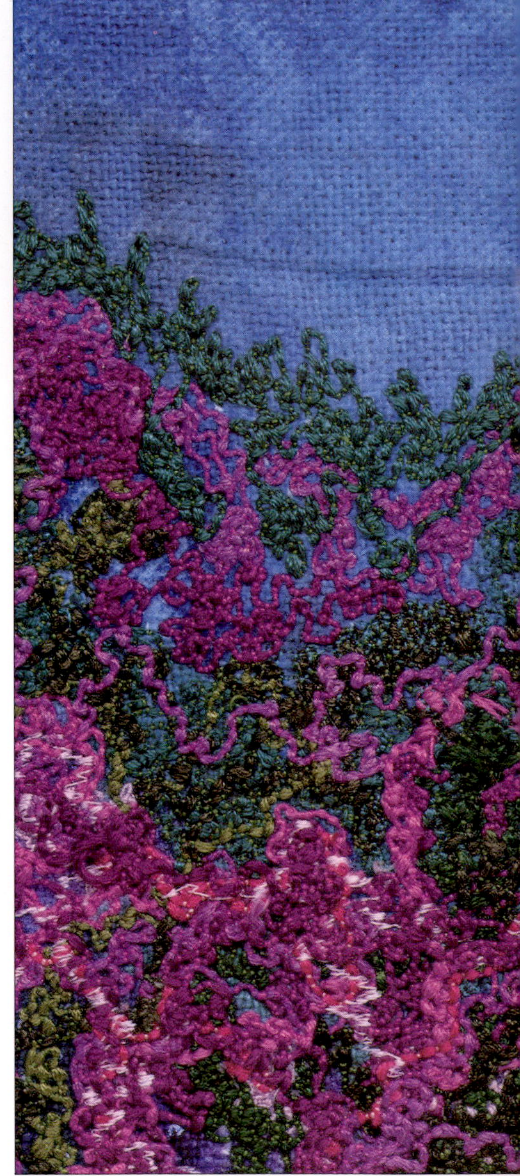

For Lilac Time, *Gail Harker used six-stranded cotton in the bobbin. Approximately six shades of purple and green were used to give a depth of colour. Heavy stitching was worked in the foreground until a dense build-up of colour and texture was achieved.*

Variations with cable stitch

Try increasing the top tension until a suitable amount of bobbin thread is visible on the surface of the fabric. In this variation, the finished side of the fabric may be up.

Alternatively, decrease the top tension below normal, until the top thread is visible on the wrong side of the work.

This technique can also be used to create richly textured lace effects, when worked on vanishing muslin, as demonstrated on pages 142–3. In this case, the reverse side of the vanishing muslin will be the finished side of the work. Use a machine embroidery thread on the top, and experiment with a wide range of hand embroidery threads and knitting yarns in the bobbin.

Free cutwork with lace filling

Cutwork is a traditional hand embroidery technique, in which parts of the background fabric are cut away and filled with lace, with satin stitch worked around the edges of the cut. Generally, closely-woven fabrics, such as cotton, linen or organdie, were used. The most imitative technique is done in the automatic mode, using satin stitch. The technique described here uses free running stitch and lace insertion.

Fabric It is best to use a closely woven fabric that does not fray easily. Try organdie, nylon organza or cotton, and frame the work tightly in a small frame of 12 to 14cm (5 to 6in) in diameter.

Threads Use machine embroidery threads for both the top and

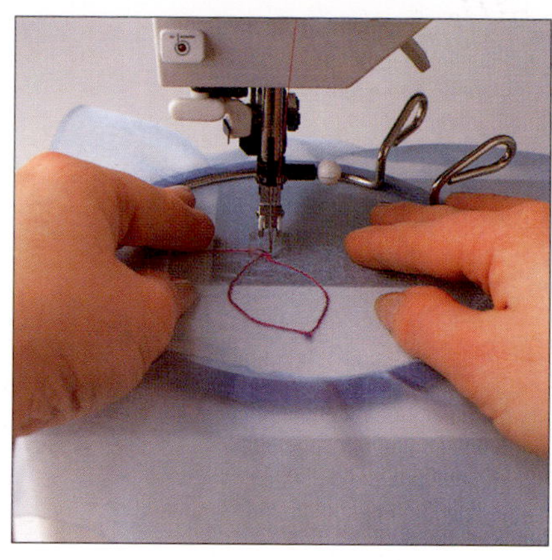

1 Plan a design with a series of shapes to be cut. If you keep the shapes small, the fabric is less likely to be distorted by the embroidery; something worth bearing in mind, especially if a number of cut-outs are to be made. Frame the fabric. Using free running stitch, stitch around the outline of each shape.

2 Remove the fabric from the frame. With very sharp scissors, carefully cut away the inside area of the shape, cutting close to the stitching. Reframe the fabric and sew a decorative stitch around the edge of the cut-out: seed stitch has been used in this example.

Feathers were trapped between two layers of nylon organza to make Gail Harker's Snow Queen Cape. *Free cutwork with lace filling was used, in addition to free running stitch. Twenty shades of machine embroidery thread were used.*

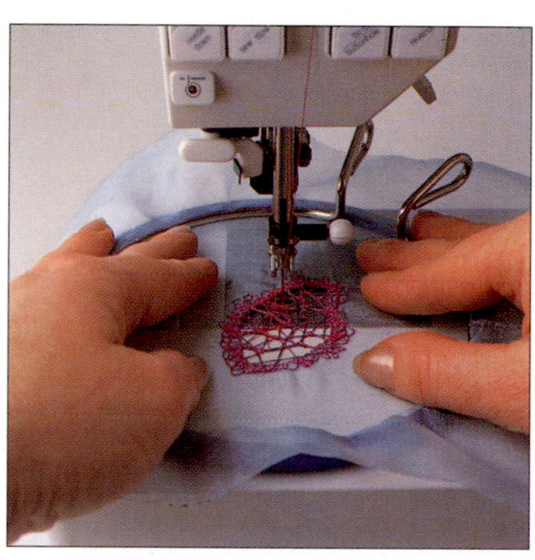

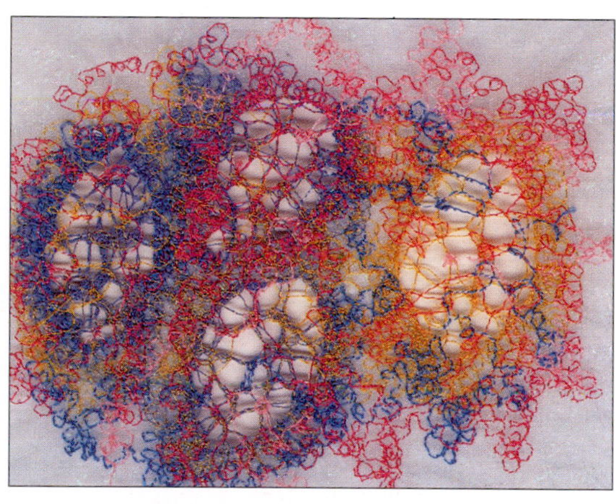

3 Depress the foot pedal for a very fast sewing speed and move the frame from side to side across the open shape. The fast sewing speed will ensure that both the top and bobbin threads twist evenly together as stitches cross the open area. Continue until the desired density is achieved.

4 After the open area has been covered with stitches to the desired density, try stitching swirls or other patterns on the framework of threads. Continue stitching until the desired effect is achieved, and then move on to the next shape, repeating the process.

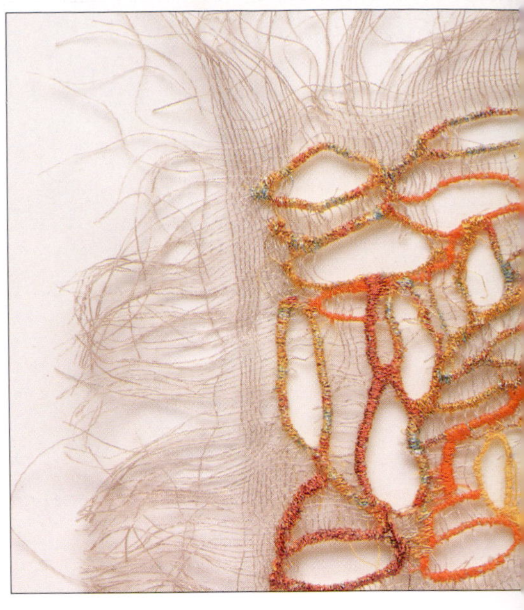

This sample shows open work on linen scrim. The first slit was cut in the fabric and filled with zigzag stitch, after which another slit was cut, and so on.

the bobbin. Some shiny threads may resist crossing open spaces. If the threads are not of the same size, it may be necessary to adjust the top and/or bobbin tensions. Adjust the tensions until the top thread does not show on the bottom of the fabric and the bobbin thread does not show on the top.

Needle Use any needle that will penetrate the fabric without snagging.

Stitch Use free running stitch.

Tension Unless you are using two different weights of thread (see above), the bobbin tension should be normal and the top tension should be decreased slightly.

You will also require a very sharp pair of embroidery scissors.

Variations on free cutwork with lace filling

Try a wide variety of cut-out shapes. After outlining a shape with stitching, any number of patterns may be used to cross the empty areas. When the shape is filled, satin stitch may be applied to the outline, using either free or automatic satin stitch (automatic stitching is usually easier for the beginner).

The lace cutwork filling may be accomplished without a frame if a stiff fabric like pelmet Vilene or canvas is used.

Open work

Open work lends itself to some very creative machine-embroidery designs. The technique is used with fabrics, from very coarse to fine, that have a very open weave; typical fabrics would be gauze, cheesecloth, scrim, linen and hessian. The loose weave of these kinds of fabric allows the needle to alternately catch one thread (weft or warp), skip to another, and draw them together, creating an open space resembling a buttonhole or eyelet.

The technique may be used where a slashed opening in the fabric is made. The slashed area is then stitched around the edges, drawing two or three threads together to create large open areas in the design.

Threads Use machine embroidery threads for both the top and

Open work on very fine cotton muslin has been worked with a free running stitch. T-shapes were cut in the fabric, and the spaces were filled.

bobbin. If viscose or metallic threads are used on the top, use cotton, machine embroidery thread in the bobbin.

Tension Decrease the top tension slightly. Try normal tension for the bobbin, but you may need to increase the tension slightly.

Machining

For fabrics like hessian or burlap, free zigzag or satin stitch may be used. Set the stitch sufficiently wide to catch two or three threads on each stitch – as the stitching proceeds, the fabric threads will draw tightly together.

On finer, more closely-woven fabrics, such as cheesecloth or gauze, much finer designs are possible: circular shapes are easier to accommodate; the fabric may be slashed in any direction, and free running stitch is easier to work on close weaves. Do not slash more than one or two areas before stitching.

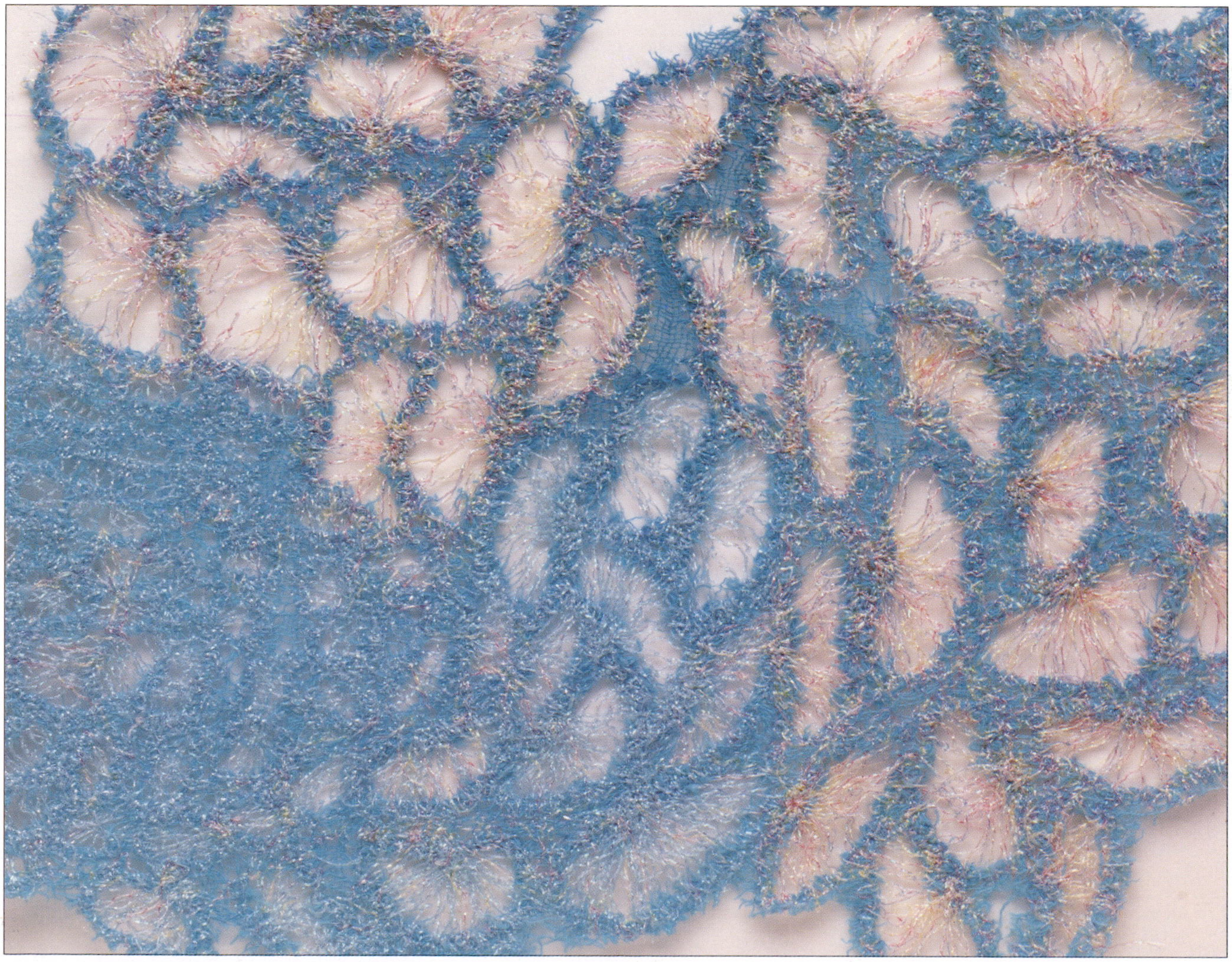

Lace on vanishing muslin

Beautiful lace effects may be created through the use of a special material called vanishing muslin. Vanishing muslin is a stiffened material that disappears when it is heated with an iron. Either straight or circular stitching patterns may be used. Because zigzag stitches are much looser than straight stitches, it is best to select a very narrow stitch width setting and to intersect the lines of stitching frequently if you are using zigzag.

Frame An embroidery frame is recommended.

Threads You can use any natural-fibre thread, such as cotton, cotton perlé, silk or wool. For heavy lace, use crochet cotton or perlé cotton in the bobbin. Synthetic threads are sometimes sensitive to a hot iron, but some may be used in the oven-heat method (see below), and some metallic and shiny threads may be suitable; experiment when in doubt.

Needle Use any needle that is large enough to carry the thread without shredding it.

Colours Try threads in many shades of a few coordinated colours.

Tensions Adjust tensions to form as perfect a free running stitch as possible.

Machining Stitch over a wide area, building up a supporting network over the pattern; then go back over the network to fill

Very small pieces of lace were laid on vanishing muslin and secured with spray glue. Free running stitch was then used to make patterns.

1 **Place vanishing muslin in an embroidery frame. Be gentle – the muslin is quite fragile and will not withstand tight stretching in the frame, nor will it be able to take heavy stitchery until an overall network of supporting threads has been worked.**

2 **Begin sewing with a free stitch that can be intertwined to create a lacy effect. After stitching is completed, trim the excess vanishing muslin close to the embroidery.**

3 **Place a thin pressing cloth over the stitching and press with a hot, dry iron until the muslin turns a grey brown. The vanishing muslin rapidly deteriorates with the heat. Gently remove the ash using a soft toothbrush to clear away stubborn pieces.**

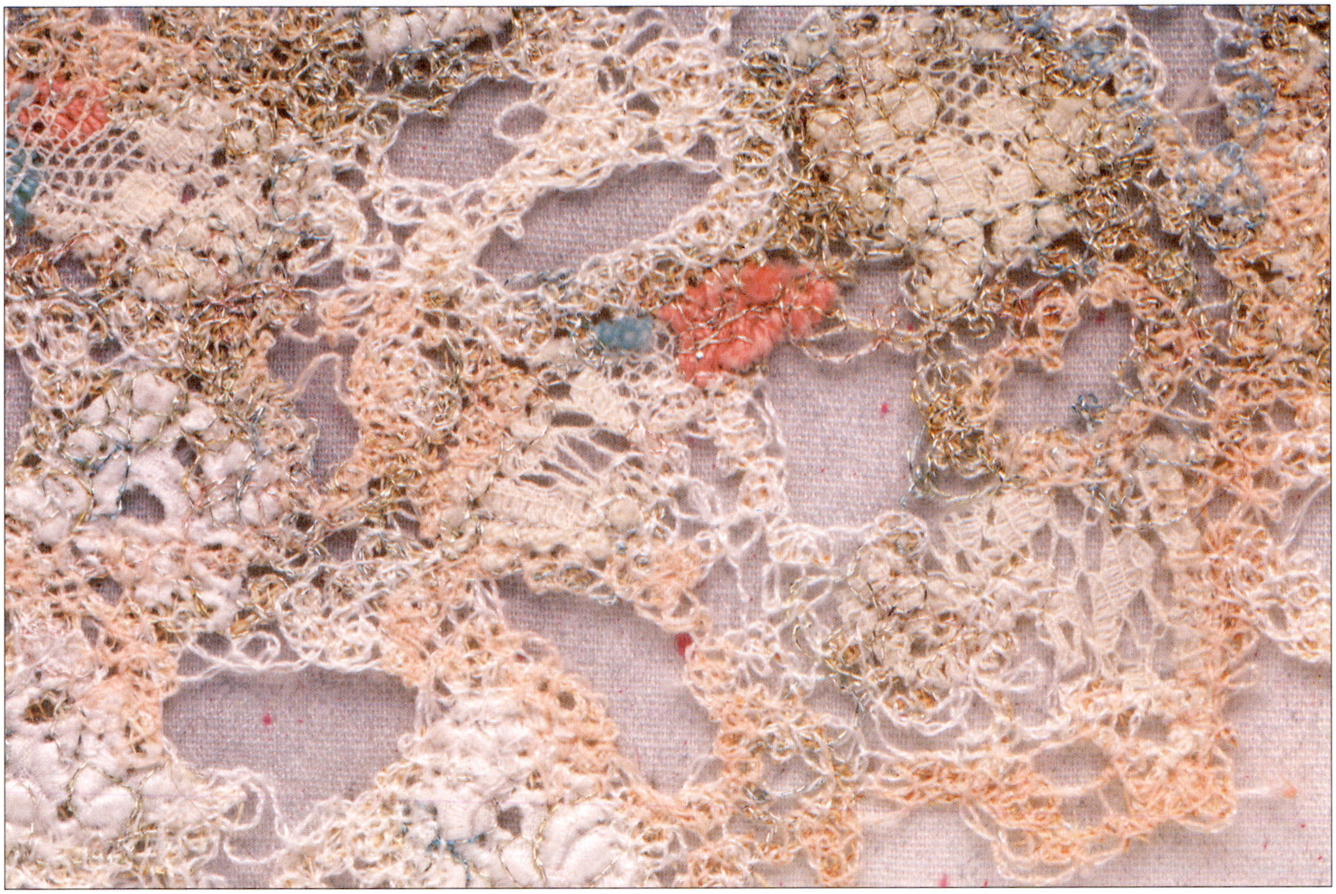

4 **The finished lace may be used as it is, appliquéd, or starched and formed into three-dimensional shapes.**

in spaces. Do not work stitches too densely in one area until the network is laid down or you may tear the muslin. Move the frame evenly and rhythmically while applying stitches. After all the stitching is applied, cut away the excess muslin, trimming close to the pattern.

Burning away muslin Place a thin pressing cloth over the work. Press with a dry, hot iron until the muslin turns a brown colour. Brush away the dissolved muslin gently, using a soft tooth brush or nail brush to work the remaining pieces of muslin out of the stitching.

Alternative The vanishing muslin may also be removed by heating it in an oven. Pre-heat the oven to 150°C/300°F. Wrap the work in a sheet of foil and place it in the oven for five to six minutes. The muslin will turn a brown colour and gentle rubbing will cause it to disintegrate. As with the ironing method, stubborn pieces can be removed with a brush. Do not be tempted to leave the embroidery in the oven for a longer period of time.

The technique can be used with free cable stitch, as described on page 137, though care must be taken to ensure that lines interconnect.

Free machine lace on cold-water-soluble fabric

Cold-water-soluble fabric is a spun alginate, woven into sheets that have the look and feel of thin plastic sheeting. This fabric can be embroidered in the same way as vanishing muslin. However, only machine embroidery threads are recommended for this technique, because larger, thicker threads have a tendency to split the fabric. The fabric can be used to produce very fine, delicate lace.

While the manufacturers recommend dissolving the fabric in cold water, experience indicates that warm, soapy water, followed by a cold rinse, is an effective way of removing the soluble fabric. After removing the soluble fabric, lay the piece of lace on a towel to dry, blocking if necessary. Starch may be applied to the piece if it is to form a three-dimensional shape.

Needle To suit the thread; if problems are encountered, try a ballpoint needle.

Stitch Use free running stitch only; zigzag stitches will tear the fabric.

Stitch length Ensure that the stitch length is set at '0'; even though the feed dogs are down, they will move and may come into contact with the fabric, tearing holes, unless you take this precaution.

Variations on cold-water-soluble fabric

Lay a single layer of soluble fabric on a work surface. On the fabric, lay small pieces of lace, net, transparent fabrics, bundles of thread and so on: a trace of spray glue applied to each piece will help to secure them temporarily. Place a top layer of soluble fabric over the pieces to create a 'sandwich' of materials. Frame the sandwich and, treating it as one piece of fabric, machine free running stitch over it, being careful to intertwine the stitches to create a supporting network. The soluble fabric is very fragile and is easily split, so it is important to avoid dense stitches and stitching in one spot. Be sure to hold the fabric close to the flat bed of the machine while stitching, keeping the foot pedal depressed.

For these samples, various pieces of fabric, lace, ribbon and net were laid on a background of cold-water-soluble fabric. Another layer of cold-water-soluble fabric was placed on top. The layers were then placed in a frame and free running stitch was used to stitch them together.

Lace and other textured fabrics on hot-water-soluble fabric

Hot-water-soluble fabric is much sturdier than cold-water-soluble fabric, and can take much more dense stitching and added layers of other fabrics. The fabric may be worked both framed and without a frame, and cable stitch may be applied. If you work without a frame you will need to set your machine for automatic stitching with the sewing foot on. Zigzag stitches may be applied, but as with the lace techniques already described you must be sure to stitch over the zigzag with two or three lines of straight running stitch or the zigzag will unravel when the fabric is dissolved.

After the stitches have been applied, place the work in a pan of gently boiling (simmering) water for about five minutes or until the fabric is dissolved. The work will appear to be shrivelled up, but do not despair. Rinse under warm flowing water. After rinsing, lay the work on a dry towel and gently stretch and shape the piece, leaving it to dry naturally.

Automatic stitches were used to make lace on hot-water-soluble fabric: net was laid over the fabric and was decorated with straight and zigzag stitches. A frame was not used. The technique can result in a slight shrinkage of threads, which can be very attractive.

Letter to Milano, *by German quilt artist Dorle Stern-Straeter, is cleverly constructed from crazy patchwork triangles to simulate an envelope. Using a variety of fabrics for the pieced design, she has hand-quilted the piece in a pattern of irregular wavy lines which are sometimes referred to as 'wrinkle' quilting. Size: 148cm × 106cm (57in × 42in). (Photography by Patrica Partl)*

CHAPTER THREE

Patchwork, Appliqué and Quilting

The techniques covered in this section are usually associated with quiltmaking, either for practical purposes or for use as large-scale wall-hangings, and you will find here all the information that is required to make your own patchwork or appliqué quilt. The same skills, however, are frequently incorporated into their work by contemporary embroiderers, while today's quiltmakers, though they may draw heavily on past traditions, use patchwork, appliqué and quilting, either on their own or in combination, for large-scale exercises in colour, shape and texture.

Patchwork provides a wonderful vehicle for dazzling geometric exercises, while appliqué techniques have a versatility which covers the entire range from raised embroidery miniatures to large-scale quilts. The subtle lines of hand-stitched quilting produce an entirely different effect from clear-cut machine stitching, and both have their own validity. The fabric dyes now available for use at home add further possibilities, while appliqué, in particular, can make full use of the wonderful new fabrics that have been developed over the last few decades.

Freed from conventional restraints of utility or room decoration, quiltmakers have evolved a form of artistic expression that has its exponents in every part of the world. Freedom, too, from the symmetrical constraints of traditional quilts has allowed quilt-makers to develop a variety of forms in which to express both their individuality and the stylistic fashions of the times. Traditional quilts remain a source of fascination and inspiration, but this has been expanded to embrace a whole new field of creative ideas.

MATERIALS AND EQUIPMENT

For patchwork, the best choice of fabric is good quality, dressweight, pure cotton. Easy to handle, cotton fabrics also wear well and are readily available in a variety of colours and patterns. For appliqué, the choice is broad though fabrics which fray easily can be difficult to work. For quilting, choose closely-woven fabrics to prevent the filling (batting) working through; for handquilting, they should also be sufficiently pliable to stitch through with ease.

The colour and character your fabrics will bring to your work is crucial to the design, so be aware of this when making your choice. Fabrics should also be colourfast and it may be necessary to test for this. For patchwork and appliqué, pre-shrink fabrics by washing.

Where batting is required for quilting or padded appliqué, there is a variety of choice both in fibre and weight. Polyester battings are inexpensive, easy-care and widely available but battings made from natural fibres (cotton, wool and silk) are softer and more fluid. Thicker battings give more 'loft' but are harder to stitch through.

Equipment

Needles For hand sewing patchwork and appliqué, sharps 8 or 9 needles are best; for hand quilting, choose between needles size 8 or finer. For machine stitching, use size 90(14) for most dressweight fabrics but the finer size 80(12) for fine cottons and silk. Long milliners' needles are useful for basting.

Sewing machine A good quality, well maintained sewing machine is an important tool. Though not essential, swing needle and embroidery stitches add to the decorative potential of your work.

Threads Although dressmaking threads can be used for hand sewing, it is preferable to use pure cotton quilting thread for its strength. For machining, a No. 40 cotton or cotton/polyester thread can be used. Use silk threads for silk fabric when either hand or machine sewing. Always choose a designated quilting thread for hand or machine quilting unless using decorative threads. When hand sewing, run your thread through a beeswax block to help to strengthen it and ease it through fabric layers.

Pins You will need fine dressmakers' pins or fine brass lace pins. Long glass-headed pins are useful for thick or layered

Fabric choice is vital to the success of your work so choose quality fabrics. A wide variety of patterned fabrics and 'solids' (self-coloured fabrics) is available from specialist shops.

Although many tools and gadgets can be bought for patchwork, quilting and appliqué, basic sewing equipment is modest and inexpensive.

fabrics; safety pins (size 2) can be used to pin-baste fabrics for machine quilting.

Thimbles A wide variety is available where protection is needed for hand quilting.

Frames A suitable device for holding the work is necessary for quilting and for appliqué (see page 19–21). Full-size quilting frames hold the whole work in place whilst quilting progresses; hoops and frames hold only part of the work but have the advantage of being small and portable.

Scissors Good quality dressmakers' scissors are essential; smaller embroidery snips are useful for cutting away thread ends and intricate appliqué work.

Rotary cutter Now the universal tool for multiple cutting of patchwork pieces, it must be used with a suitable cutting mat and the blade guard replaced when the cutter is not in use.

Rulers A quilters' ruler, a large, wide plastic ruler marked with angles and a grid, is essential for speedcutting of patchwork pieces. It is also invaluable in marking out any large-scale design. A tape-measure is another convenience; a flexible rule is useful for curved shapes and patterns. Rolling rulers and long-rule compasses are useful for pattern marking.

Pencils A variety of lead, coloured and chalk pencils are used for marking but the precise choice will vary with colour and fabric type. Always keep pencils well sharpened or use mechanical pencils. Powdered chalk markers, available in different colours, are also popular.

PATCHWORK

Now that the wonderful design possibilities of exploring shape and colour are recognized, patchwork has shed its utilitarian, scrap craft image. With a variety of well-chosen fabrics, knowledge of patchwork techniques – and a little imagination – exciting and innovative work can result.

Patchwork templates

Templates are used to mark the outlines of geometric shapes on fabric before cutting; they can be bought, but making them from card or transparent plastic gives more flexibility in design, and is cheaper.

For hand piecing using the running stitch method, templates are made to the *exact* size of the geometric shape, with seam allowances added when cutting out. The line drawn around the templates represents the *stitching* line. When machine piecing or piecing over papers, the template has a 6mm (1/4in) seam allowance added and the line drawn around

1 **With a fine, hard pencil and ruler, draw shapes on squared or isometric graph paper.**

2 **Leaving at least 1cm (1/3in) around the marked line, cut out each template shape required. Spray glue the back of the paper shape and stick to card or template plastic.**

3 **Carefully cut the shapes along the marked line. For window templates, cut along both inner and outer lines. For curved templates, cut matching notches along curved seam edges. If required, glue fine sandpaper to the reverse of the template to give adhesion on fabric.**

the template represents the *cutting* line. *Be sure to make the appropriate template for your chosen method of sewing.* Window templates are templates with an open centre (the finished patch area) which allow you to draw the sewing *and* cutting line at the same time and enable you to select particular areas of patterned fabric for each shape.

Cutting out

Before cutting patchwork shapes out of fabric, it is essential that all fabrics should be washed and pressed flat. Use a steam iron on cotton fabrics or press while damp.

Patchwork shapes are cut and marked individually for hand piecing by the running stitch method, but can be cut in multiples (batch cut) for machine piecing, or piecing over papers. Consider carefully the pattern and grain of your fabric when positioning templates; in general, keep bias seams to a minimum. You may need to reverse assymetric templates for mirror-image shapes.

Cutting single shapes

On a flat, hard surface, lay the template on the wrong side of the fabric and draw around with a sharp pencil (never use an ink pen). If hand piecing with a running stitch, cut around the drawn line leaving a 6mm (¼in) seam allowance; otherwise, cut exactly on the drawn line.

Multiple scissor cutting

Layer up to four even-sized fabric pieces, wrong side up, matching the fabric grain and orientation. Using templates, mark shapes on the top layer, then pin layers together through the centre of each shape. Cut along the marked lines with sharp scissors. For mirror image shapes, alternately layer right and wrong sides.

Multiple rotary cutting

With six to eight fabric layers, follow instructions for multiple scissor cutting but do not pin. On a cutting mat and holding ruler and cutter firmly, cut along the marked lines. Simple shapes (squares, rectangles, triangles, and strips) can be cut without templates, using the grid and angles on a quilters' ruler.

Piecing by hand and machine

Patchwork can be sewn by hand or machine. Machine stitching is quicker and stronger, but hand stitching is more relaxing and portable. Both have their champions but both are equally valid techniques.

There are two basic techniques for hand piecing. The running stitch method is appropriate for large shapes and for piecing blocks. Piecing over papers is a very accurate technique used for intricate mosaic designs; popular in nineteenth-century Britain for hexagon and other mosaic patchwork, it is often called 'English paper patchwork'.

For most machine piecing, a straight line stitch is all that is required, so the most basic sewing machine will suffice. It does help to have a backstitch facility to finish seams. For machine stitching crazy patchwork, a swing needle is required.

Piecing over papers

1 **Two master templates are required – one without seam allowances, for papers, and one with, for fabrics. Alternatively, use a window template. Using appropriate templates, cut a paper and fabric patch for each shape in the design.**

2 **Centre the paper shape on the wrong side of the fabric shape and pin. Fold over the seam allowance and baste in place; with small shapes baste only through the seam allowance, not through the paper. Leave long ends to the basting thread for easy removal. Remove the pin and press.**

3 **Place adjacent patches right sides together, matching the edges carefully. Using a knotted, matching or neutral coloured thread, sew the edges together with tiny overcast stitches, taking care not to catch the papers. Finish with a few reverse stitches. When all the shapes have been sewn together, remove basting threads and papers, and press.**

Machine piecing

1 Pin adjacent shapes together, carefully matching the raw edges, with pins at right angles to the seam. If sets of shapes are pinned ready, they can be sewn at the same time.

2 You will need a line guide to the right of your machine needle equivalent to the seam allowance (6mm or ¼in). If your machine has no scale on the needle plate, use tape. With matching or neutral coloured thread, set the machine to sew about five straight stitches per centimetre (10–12 per inch) and check the tension.

3 Set the raw edges of the pinned shapes against the line guide and sew a straight line seam, removing the pins as you sew. Begin and end each seam with a few back stitches, but batch sew sets of shapes without cutting the threads. Once sewn, the shapes can be separated and pressed.

Running stitch method

1 Place two adjacent patches right sides together and matching the sewing lines. First pin at the corners, then at intervals along the edge. All pins should be at right angles to the seam.

2 Using a sharps needle and knotted, matching or neutral coloured thread, sew a line of small, even running stitches along the marked lines. Finish with a double backstitch. Press the seam to one side.

Piecing and pressing

Piecing sequence

Before sewing any patchwork shapes together, it is necessary to consider the piecing sequence. This is especially important when piecing a quilt top; it is better to break the design up into manageable units or blocks, so that only in the finishing stage will you need to deal with a large and perhaps heavy area of fabric. Colours and the balance of light and dark shades may change across a quilt top, but most designs can be broken down into repeated units, joined in either straight or diagonal rows.

It is also better to sew patchwork shapes together with straight-line seams wherever possible, rather than trying to set shapes into an angle, especially with machine piecing.

The piecing sequence for every design will be a little different but, in general, the following rules apply:

- join the smallest shapes first
- join shapes together into rows (horizontal, vertical or diagonal)
- join rows together to assemble each block or unit
- once units are assembled, join these into rows then join rows together, add borders and finish.

The example (opposite) shows the piecing sequence for the traditional American *Anvil* block.

1 **Lay the fabric shapes out in the finished block or unit pattern.**

2 **Pin and stitch the small triangle shapes together then press seams to one side. These are now squares.**

3 **Pin and stitch rows of squares together. Press seams to one side, making sure that seams on adjacent rows are pressed in the opposite direction.**

Pressing

Pressing between each stage of piecing is an important part of the patchwork sewing sequence. It is essential to press each seam *after* it has been sewn and *before* the shapes are joined to other shapes. Normally, seams are pressed to one side to minimize pressure on the stitching, but there are exceptions. If a quilting design is planned which involves stitching across the seams or if quilting 'in-the-ditch', it helps to press them open.

Like piecing, some general rules apply to pressing:

- with light and dark fabrics, press to the darker side wherever possible to avoid seam allowances showing through
- when joining rows of shapes, or rows of blocks, press seam allowances on adjacent rows in opposite directions to minimize bulk
- when pressing fabrics with a pile or nap, place something soft, such as a soft towel, underneath to absorb pressure
- when pressing on the right side of fabrics, use a pressing cloth to avoid glazing
- set the temperature of your iron according to the fabrics used.

4 **Stitch rows together, carefully matching the seams of adjacent rows and pinning the seam allowance in position. Press seams to one side then press the finished block on the right side with a pressing cloth.**

Block patchwork

Block patchwork patterns are grid patterns where the patches are usually, though not invariably, grouped into grids of even-sized squares. Many hundreds of block patterns exist, categorized according to the basic grid on which they are based. For example, nine-patch blocks consist of nine equal squares but each square can be further subdivided.

The huge variety of patterns, and varied methods of setting blocks together, developed in 19th-century North America, where making patchwork quilts developed into a true folk art. There, dynamic quilters learned that the visual impact of block patterns could be dramatically changed within a design according to the colours and light tones used, and the method of 'setting' blocks together. They developed representational and curved seam blocks as well as the simpler four-patch and nine-patch grids, and gave them all names – sometimes practical, but often romantic or biblical.

Always plan your block design on graph paper before stitching. This allows you not only to experiment with colour and block orientation, but also to plan how to set the blocks together and to consider the borders, which are often crucial elements in the overall design. Block patterns can be pieced by hand or machine. If sewing by hand, either method is suitable, but the running stitch method is the quickest and most widely used.

1 **Draw and colour your chosen design of blocks to scale on graph paper.**

6 block to each row

2 **Draw the basic block, full-size, on graph paper. Mark each *different* shape and make templates for these shapes only.**

3 **Using the templates, cut fabric shapes, and piece in sequence. When blocks are complete, join according to chosen 'set'.**

Variable Star

Maple Leaf

Card Trick

Robbing Peter to Pay Paul

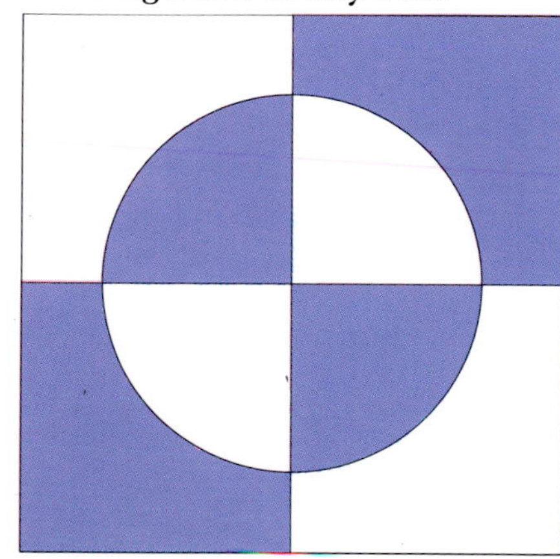

St Louis Star

Dutchman's Puzzle

Northumberland Star

Basket

Grandmother's Fan

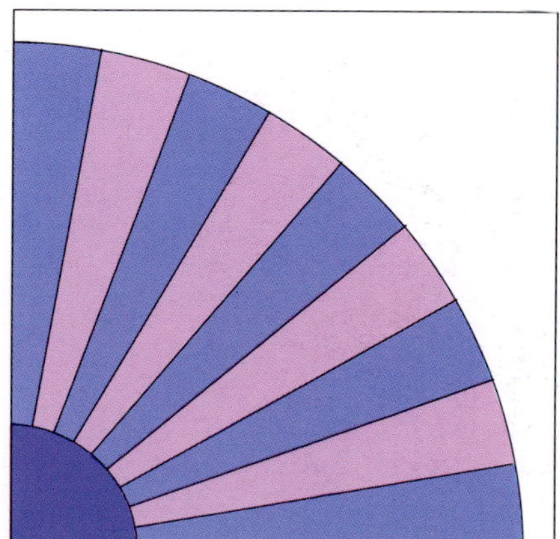

Mosaic patchwork

Intricate patchwork of shapes like hexagons and diamonds is called mosaic patchwork. Since great accuracy is required in piecing, this type of patchwork is usually hand sewn using the backing paper method. Many mosaic patchworks are one-patch designs, in other words they consist of only one geometric shape, but some include more than one shape – octagons with squares and hexagons with diamonds were two popular 19th-century combinations.

Though apparently simple in plan, some thought must be given to the basic units of mosaic patchwork and how they fit together. Plan your design on graph paper using isometric paper for hexagons and the 'tumbling blocks' pattern. Give careful thought to contrasts of colour and of light and shade. You must also consider how to finish the edges of mosaic patchwork. If you wish to have a straight edge to the work you will need to add part shapes into the spaces at the edge.

Tumbling blocks

Octagons and Squares

Hexagons and Stars

Hexagons

Crazy patchwork

Needing no templates and sewn directly to a base fabric, crazy patchwork is simple and speedy. Most fabric types can be used so it is an ideal form of scrap patchwork. Embroidery stitches, hand or machine sewn, are used to seam the patches and form part of the surface decoration. Base fabric should be pre-washed and light in colour – cotton calico (muslin) is ideal. Base units can be any shape, but should be kept to a manageable size. If using crazy patchwork for garments, use the paper pattern pieces for your base units.

There are no rules for the size and shape of crazy patches nor must they have straight edges. Fabrics are chosen at random and shapes scissor cut as required. There are two methods of piecing: either baste the patches in place on a block before stitching; or embroider each patch in place before the next one is applied. If machine stitching, choose a single thread which blends with all fabrics.

1 Cut base units to size (finished block size plus 12mm/½in seam allowance on all sides) and prepare patchwork fabrics. On the right side of the base fabric, mark an outline of the finished block size.

2 Cut the first piece and pin, right side uppermost, to the wrong side of the base in one corner. Cut the second piece, fold over the seam allowance on one edge and lay over the raw edge of the pinned piece. Either baste, or sew into position with hand or machine embroidery stitches.

3 Continue to cover the base fabric with pieces by folding in seam allowances and pinning new patches over ones already applied. Baste in place, or embroider into position. Work across the block so the final pieces are at the edge, not in the middle. If basted, finish with embroidery stitches and remove basting threads. Join the finished blocks, seaming along the marked outline on the reverse.

Log cabin patchwork

A simple and effective form of strip piecing, log cabin patchwork involves sewing strips of two contrasting fabric groups around a geometric shape. Traditionally, the shape is centred in a block, but contemporary interpretations include off-setting the initial shape or placing it in the corner. The size of the initial shape and width of strips can be varied, but a strip width of 2.5cm (1in) plus seam allowances is a popular choice. Contrast is usually achieved by dividing fabrics into light and dark colours, but it is also possible to use fabric prints and 'solids', or two strongly contrasting colours.

Log cabin patchwork can be sewn by machine or by hand (using the running stitch method). Templates are not required and strips need not be cut individually to size before stitching. Two basic methods can be used – stitching to a base fabric or seaming pieces directly together. Instructions are given for piecing a standard log cabin block onto a base; for variations, follow the sequences opposite.

1 **Choose fabrics and divide into two equal contrasting groups. Cut out initial squares (plus 6mm/¼ in seam allowance on all sides) and strips (finished width plus 6mm/¼in seam allowance on both edges). Shapes and strips can be batch cut. Cut base squares (plus 12mm/½in seam allowances on all sides) and mark with diagonal lines for the centre.**

2 **Pin initial square, right side up, to centre of base, aligning corners with diagonal lines. Take strip 1 fabric and lay over one edge of square, right sides together and matching raw edges. Trim away surplus strip at edge of square. Stitch 6mm (¼in) from raw edges. Fold strip to right side and press.**

3 **Turn the block 90 degrees clockwise, take strip 2 fabric (from same group as strip 1), lay over square and strip 1, right sides together and matching raw edges. Trim strip, sew, fold and press as before.**

Standard Log Cabin

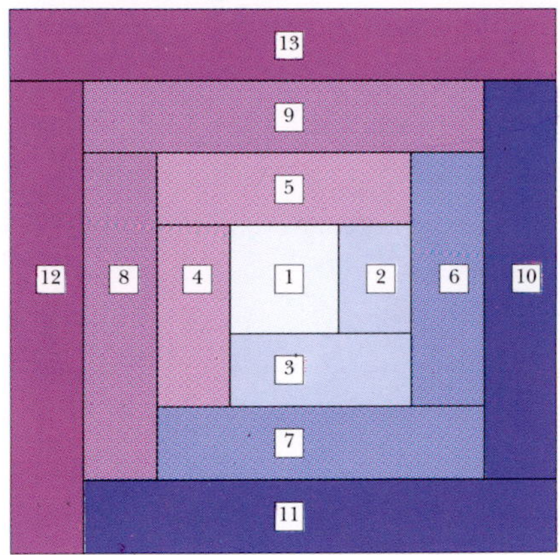

Courthouse Steps variation

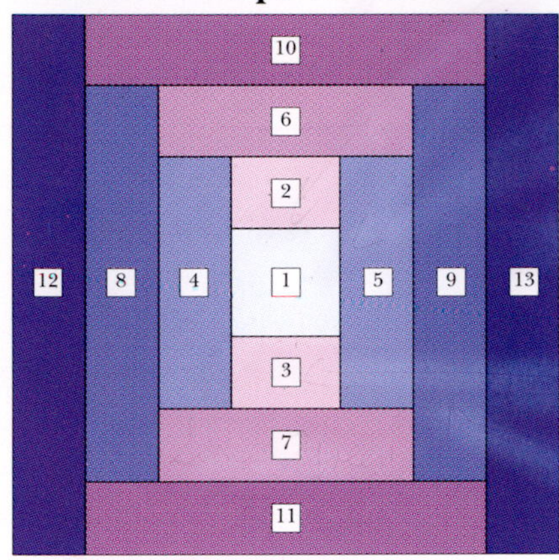

Corner Square variation

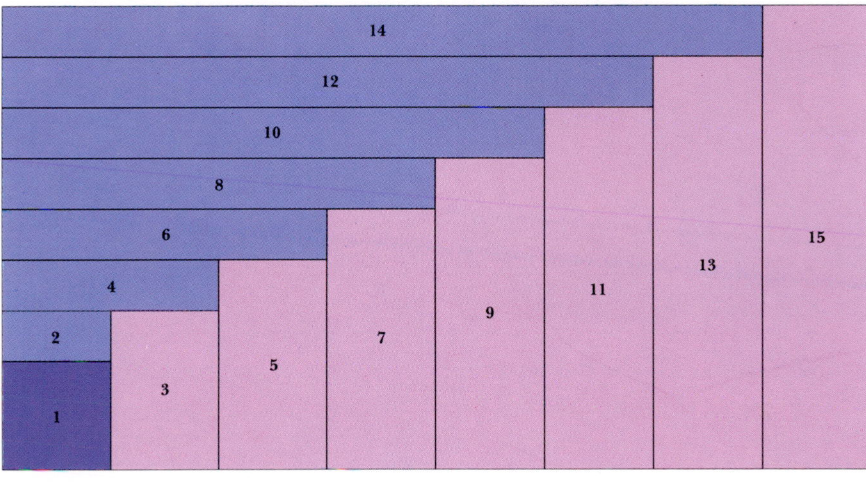

4 Turn block 90 degrees, take strip 3 from contrast group and repeat as for step 3, piecing along the third side of the square and covering the previously sewn strip. Repeat for the fourth side of the square covering, in this case, the previous strip and the first strip. This completes one round of strips. Repeat for all further rounds to complete blocks. Join blocks according to chosen design.

Offcentred Diamond variation

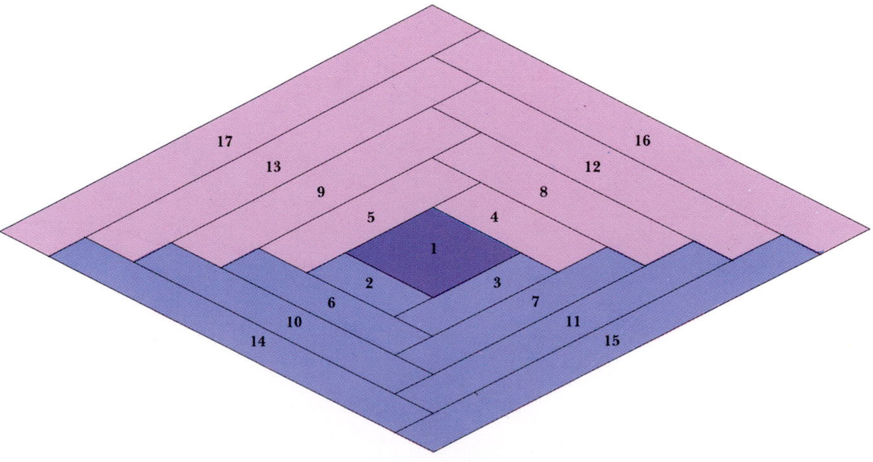

Quick patchwork techniques

Though patchwork can be a time-intensive craft, there are short cuts – particularly for machine piecing. Log cabin patchwork is renowned for its speed, especially when a rotary cutter is used to batch cut strips, but there are other quick piecing techniques for simple shapes. While still maintaining accuracy, it is possible to piece a quilt top in a day, or a cushion cover in about an hour, using speed techniques, though fabric lengths rather than scraps are usually required.

Cutting shapes from pieced strips

Piece strips of fabric by machine. Using large templates (or the lines on a quilters' ruler or cutting mat) and a rotary cutter, cut squares, rectangles, triangles or other shapes as required.

Batch sewing triangles

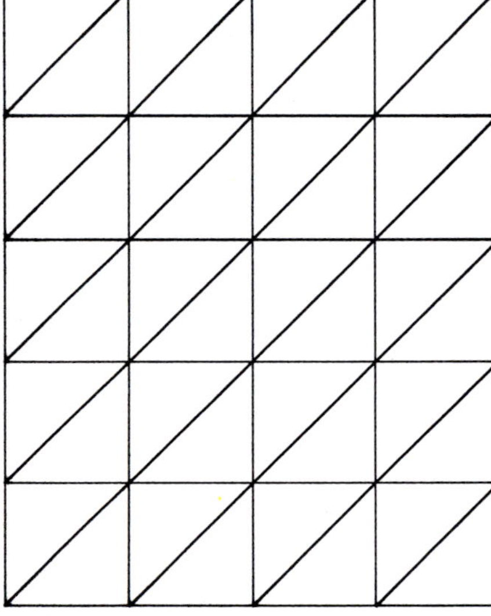

1 **On lightweight paper, make a grid to the size of the required triangles, including seam allowances. Photocopy sheets for the required number of triangles.**

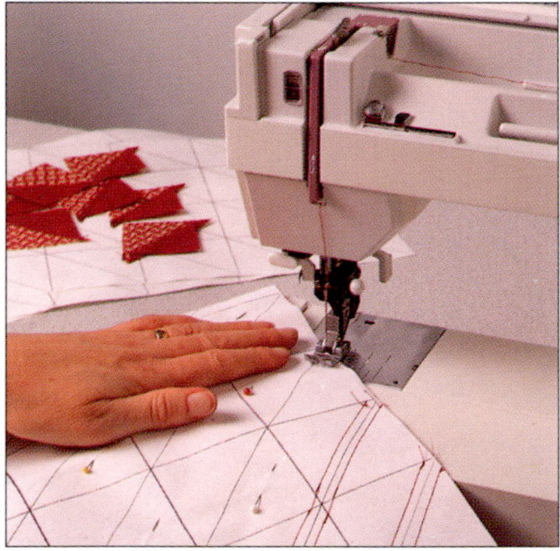

2 **Choose two fabrics. Cut to the size of the paper grids and layer, right sides together. Lay the paper grid on top, pin and stitch seams through all three layers, 6mm (¼in) away from the diagonal lines, backstitching at each horizontal and vertical line. Cut along all the marked lines, tear away paper and press seams.**

Special patchwork effects

As the craft of patchwork has evolved, special techniques for adding another dimension to the fabric surface have developed. Several of these entail folding, others pleat, slash, twist or gather fabric. Some techniques, such as folded star patchwork, have been popular for decades; others, including pleating and twisting, are more recent innovations.

For any of these methods, choose fabrics with particular care. It is often not possible or desirable to quilt patchwork made using these techniques, so the fabric quality and texture is all-important.

Folded star

Folded star patchwork is worked onto a base marked with horizontal, vertical and diagonal guidelines. From chosen fabrics, cut 2:1 rectangles with 6mm (¼in) seam allowance added to the short side, marking the centre point on long edges. On each rectangle, fold in seam allowance along long edge, press, then fold turned edges to centre to form a triangle. Press firmly. Rounds of triangles are placed on the base, and basted in position at the outer edge, in the following sequence – four triangles followed by two rounds of eight, then rounds of 16. Use the guidelines to keep each round in position.

Tucked patchwork

Tucks can be stitched into fabric before shapes are cut. Either pin and stitch tucks in single fabric or cut and insert folded strips. Wide tucks are pressed, or twisted by pressing in alternate directions. Pin tucks can be pressed or left unpressed according to the textural effect required.

Twisted squares

Make up a four-patch block. Around the outer edge divide each square into thirds and chalk mark the edge. Make a fold in top right patch by pinning horizontal seam to second mark on right side edge. Turn block 90 degrees and repeat. Repeat folding twice more. The raised central area of fabric then folds to a square of four triangles. Pin and press. Blind stitch all folds in position.

APPLIQUÉ

Appliqué, in simplest terms, is the stitching of fabrics or other materials to a background in order to create a decorative pattern. There are many traditional styles and methods, and today's embroiderers and appliqué artists adapt these innovatively, combining or modifying existing techniques.

Preparation for appliqué

Careful preparatory work will help to ensure the success of a piece of appliqué. Each technique has its own particular characteristics, making it necessary to use the appropriate method of cutting out and positioning the pieces. In some cases, the whole design is transferred to a backing fabric, or it can be drawn on the background material, with the corresponding appliqué patches stitched in place. For other methods, the cut out shapes may be assembled by eye, either covering a supporting backing or set against a background.

Backing fabrics

Although it is not essential for every type of appliqué, some methods require a backing fabric. This is not the same as a background fabric, because unlike the latter, which is visible, a backing fabric acts as a support, but does not show on the finished work, which is completely covered by the appliqué. Light-weight and stretch background fabrics also need a backing to add firmness and strength, while wallhangings and panels benefit from the extra weight that this treatment gives. The backing fabric, which should be pre-washed, should as far as possible correspond in weight to the background – cotton lawn is suitable for most fine fabrics, calico for other types. The background fabric, which should be at least 10cm (4in) larger than the finished size of the embroidery, to allow for seams, hems or mounting, is basted on top of the framed backing fabric, with the straight grain of both aligned.

Positioning the design

Positioning the design on the background fabric is usually a simple matter, and may be done by eye, but in some cases, such as a centrally placed design, it may be necessary to be more precise.

Positioning the design

1 **To position a design, first find the centre of the design by folding it into quarters and marking two pencil lines along the folds, crossing at the centre. To check that you have the exact centre, either draw a diagonal or simply lay a ruler from corner to corner – the diagonal should run across the meeting point of the horizontal and vertical lines.**

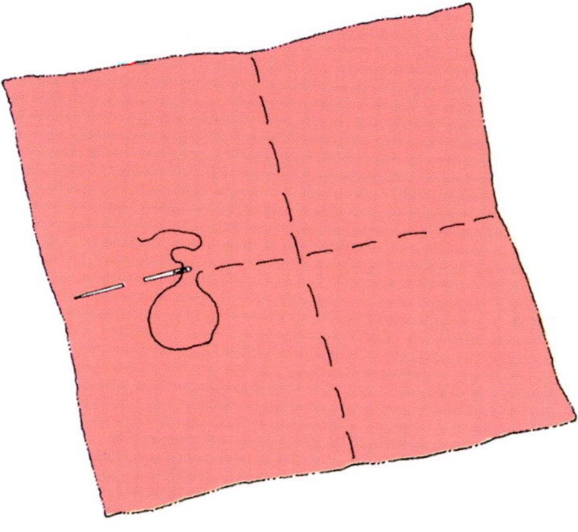

2 **The centre of the fabric can be found by folding this in a similar way and marking the corresponding lines with two rows of basting stitches. When you transfer the design, the two sets of markings can be aligned.**

White diamond, *by Hilary Bower, uses pattern and surface texture to create a feeling of movement and flickering colour. Handmade papers are combined with cotton, silk and satin fabrics. The paper and fabrics were painted, both before and after application, and stitchery has been used in a painterly fashion.*

Transferring the design

The first stage of most appliqué techniques is to make a full-scale drawing of the design. This may be done on tracing paper and should show the outlines only. When you have transferred the design to the paper, enlarging or reducing it as necessary, run over the lines with a black felt-tip pen. Number each separate appliqué shape on the design in order of assembly (see below). This paper design is used to make templates, to transfer the design to the background fabric, and to act as a reference during sewing.

The simplest method of transferring the design to the background fabric is by direct tracing. This is suitable if the background fabric or backing is light in colour and fairly thin. If the outlines do not show through clearly you may be able to see them if you tape the design and then the fabric to a window. Alternatively, try laying them on a glass-topped table, with a lamp underneath. If the fabric is too thick or too dark for this method, use dressmakers' carbon paper. This is used in a similar way to office carbon, which is not suitable, as it is too smudgy and will leave indelible marks. Dressmakers' carbon can be purchased from fabric stores and is available in several colours, so choose the one that is closest in tone to the background fabric. As well as transferring the design to the background fabric, dressmakers' carbon can also be used to mark the outlines of applied shapes and motifs.

Preparing paper templates

Most appliqué consists of precise shapes that correspond to areas of the original drawing, so unless you are using dressmakers' carbon paper, paper patterns or templates must be cut from a tracing. If the design is complex, the pieces can each be marked with a number, indicating the order of application and relating to the numbers on the original design.

Assembling appliqué

If the design has been transferred to the background by direct tracing or dressmakers' carbon paper, the cut-out shapes are positioned over the marked outlines. In some cases, motifs may be assembled by eye, with the pieces moved around until the arrangement is satisfactory. This is particularly appropriate for patchwork appliqué and for some designs in which the basic turned-edge, raw-edge and padded techniques are used. Alternatively, a tracing can be placed over the fabric and the appliqué pieces can then be slipped between the two and moved around until they coincide with the traced shapes.

Transferring the design

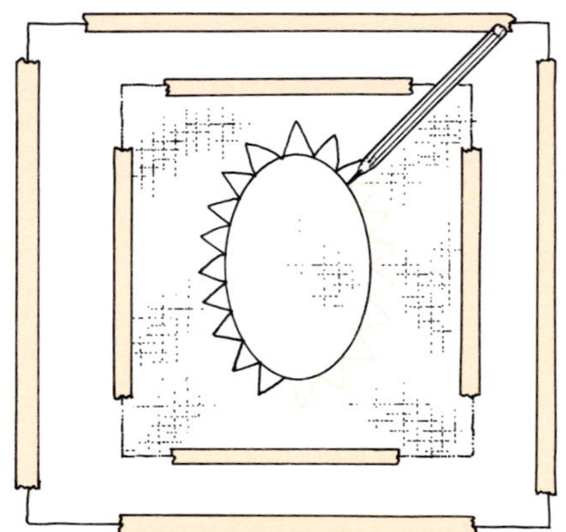

1 **To trace directly onto a fabric, tape the design to a flat surface and place the background fabric over it, right side up. Hold it in place with masking tape. Using a fabric marker, a chalk pencil or a hard pencil, trace around the design outlines. If you cannot see the design through the fabric, either use a light box or tape both the design and the fabric to a window pane (during daylight hours) and trace over the lines.**

This study by Jane Boot uses a sprayed and lino-printed background. Hand stitchery secures the appliqué, and some areas are cut away to reveal contrasting fabrics.

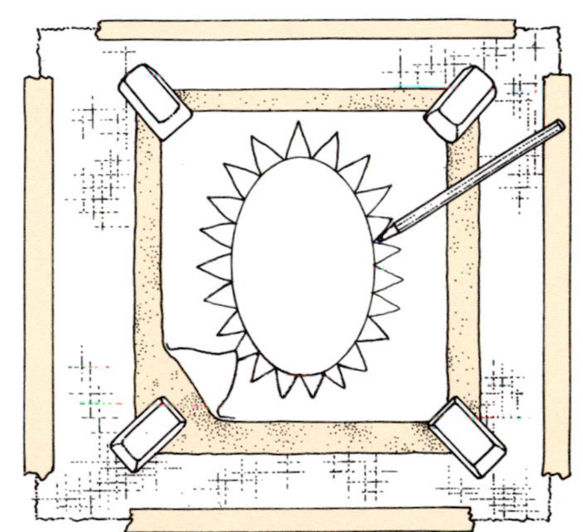

2 **To use dressmakers' carbon, tape the fabric to a flat surface and position the design on top, holding it in place with weights or tape. Slip the dressmakers' carbon paper, coloured (inked) side down between the two. Use an empty ballpoint pen, a blunt-ended knitting needle or a similar blunt tool to trace firmly over the lines of the design.**

Preparing paper templates

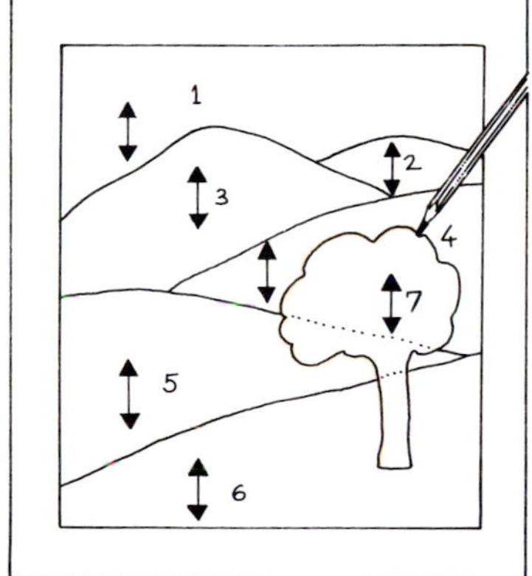

To prepare templates, make a tracing of the design and number each shape, copying the design numbers and indicating the vertical alignment of each piece with an arrow. This will enable you to make sure that you cut out each shape with the grainlines running in the same direction as the background fabric. Cut out each paper pattern and use it according to the appliqué method that you have chosen.

Order of assembly

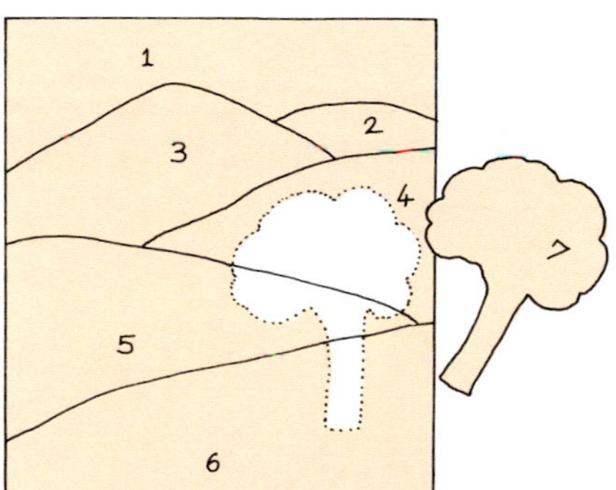

Sections of a design should be applied in a logical order, overlapping as necessary. For example, when assembling a landscape, it is best to start with the pieces in the background and gradually superimpose the separate sections until the foreground is complete. Design sections that will ultimately be overlapped by other pieces may, if this is simpler, be cut out as whole pieces rather than as intricate shapes.

Backing pieces

Traditionally, appliqué pieces were not backed before being applied to the background, and it is by no means necessary always to back pieces. Modern iron-on interfacing and fusible web can, however, be very useful.

Iron-on interfacings

Iron-on interfacing is available in a wide range of thicknesses and qualities. Some interfacings are designed to support jersey and other stretch fabrics and are best used for that purpose, whereas thick craft interfacing could as well be used for a fine cotton as for a heavy wool, provided a stiff, bold piece of appliqué is required. For blind appliqué, iron-on interfacing gives a firm edge over which to fold the allowance. Flimsy fabrics can be given extra 'body', and interfacing also helps to disguise the turned edge of such fabrics from showing through. Fabrics that fray and those that are slippery or difficult to handle can also benefit.

In some cases, interfacing a fabric patch will make it

Iron-on interfacings

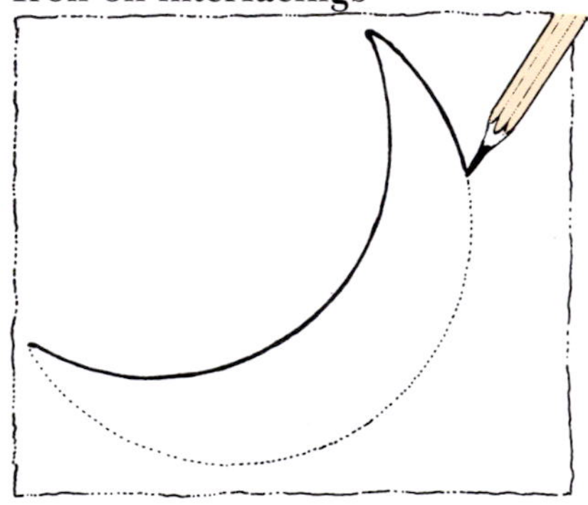

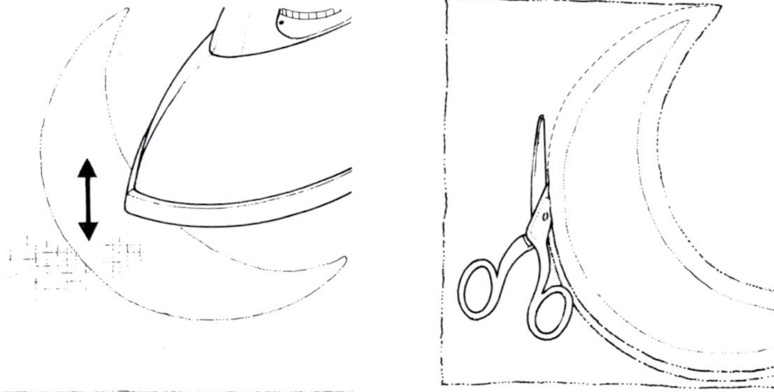

1 **Place the interfacing, shiny (adhesive) side up, over the design and trace, using a hard pencil or a fabric marker. If you are using a template, place this right side up on the shiny side of the interfacing and trace around the shape. Mark the grainline and pattern number on the non-adhesive side.**

2 **Cut out the shape and place it, shiny side down, on the wrong side of the fabric, aligning the grain if necessary. Carefully press with a steam iron, set to the appropriate heat setting.**

3 **Cut out around the perimeter of the shape, leaving a seam allowance of between 6mm and 12mm (¼in and ½in), depending on the size and shape of the piece and the type of fabric. The seam allowance can then be folded over the edge of the interfacing.**

Made with shot silk fabrics, this ivy hanging has appliqué shapes with frayed edges and free-standing padded leaves.

unnecessary to match the straight grain with that of the background. A fabric can therefore be applied at another angle if the design dictates, for example, because a diagonal weave or pattern provides a crucial element. For articles that need to drape, however, the grain of the appliqué must correspond to that of the background.

For machine appliqué, iron the interfacing to the fabric and cut out the motif, without a turning, then apply it with machine zigzag. This method is not suitable for very frayable fabrics.

Fusible web

This paper-backed, double-sided bonding is particularly suitable for the machine appliqué of frayable fabrics. It gives an immaculate result and can bond fabrics together to create free-standing cut-outs. Experiment before embarking on a project – the technique may not be satisfactory if you are applying a fine fabric to a heavily textured background, as the imprint of the latter will be visible. The effect of transparent fabrics will be somewhat altered by the adhesive that shows through.

Using fusible web

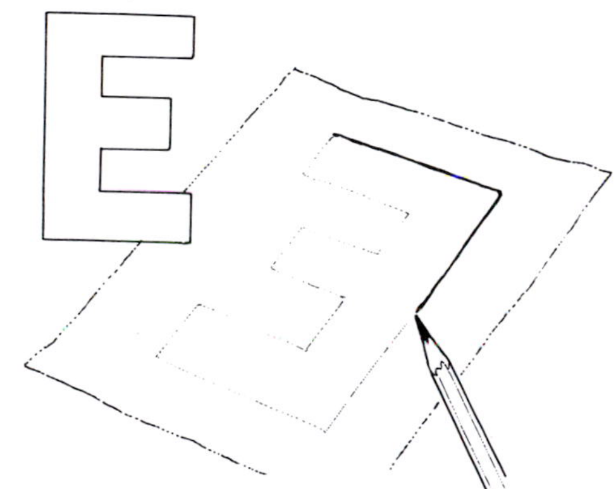

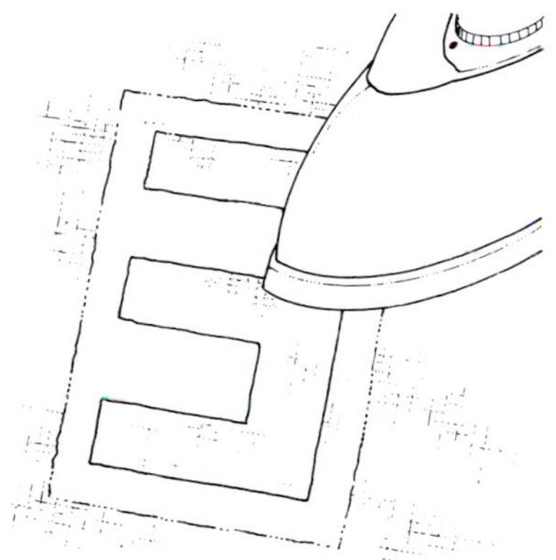

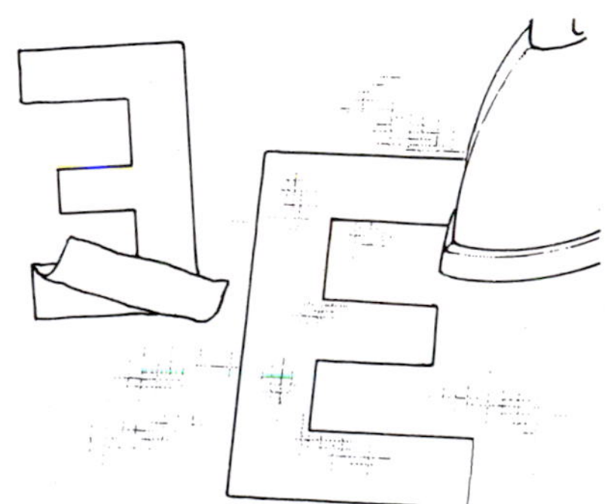

1 **To use fusible web, place it, smooth (non-adhesive) side up, over the reverse side of the design tracing. If you are using a template, place this with the wrong side up over the fusible web, which should be smooth side up. Trace over the outline, to make a mirror (reverse) image of the pattern piece. Mark the grainline and pattern number on the smooth side.**

2 **Cut out the fusible web motif or pattern, allowing a margin all round, and place this rough (adhesive) side down on the wrong side of the fabric, matching grainlines if necessary, and iron.**

3 **When cool, cut out the shape through the backing paper and fabric, cutting along the design outline. Peel off the backing and position the shape on the background fabric and iron firmly.**

Basic hand appliqué

Non-woven fabrics, such as felt, leather, suede and interfacings have many practical advantages for use in appliqué, as they do not fray, stretch or distort; there is no need to turn under the edges of motifs, and consideration need not be given to aligning the straight grain. Although they can, of course, be attached with fusible web, or even with spray adhesive, it is also not usually necessary to interline them, as they are substantial enough in themselves.

Non-woven fabrics, together with net, can all be cut out and applied directly with stab stitch or slip stitch. For these reasons they are often chosen by beginners as the easiest option, but it is advisable that they are selected for their aesthetic qualities rather than their ease of application. The matt surface of brightly coloured felt would, for instance, enhance a simple nursery panel, but could bring an unwanted naivety to a more sophisticated piece.

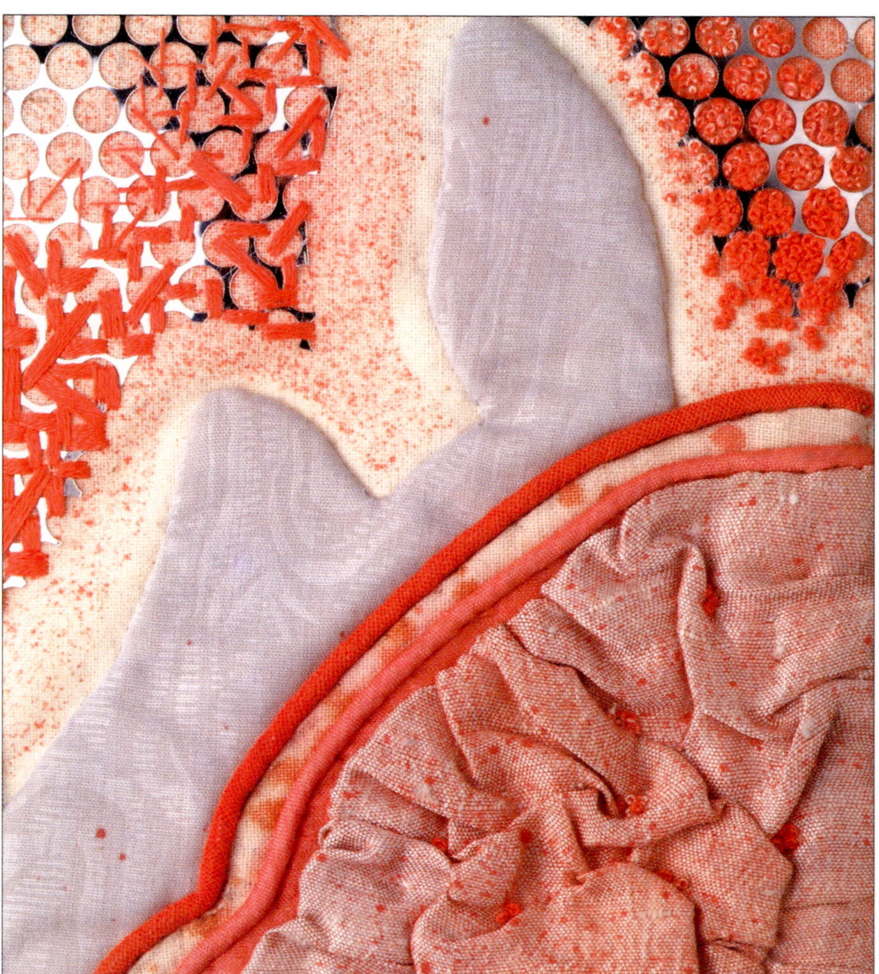

This sample by Prue Dobinson shows variations on the turned-edge method, using a sprayed background, a manipulated fabric section, piping and sequin waste.

Marking and cutting out

1. **If the fabric can be marked directly, place the paper or cardboard template, right side down, on the back of the fabric and draw around it. Cut out the shape along the marked line.**

Applying shapes

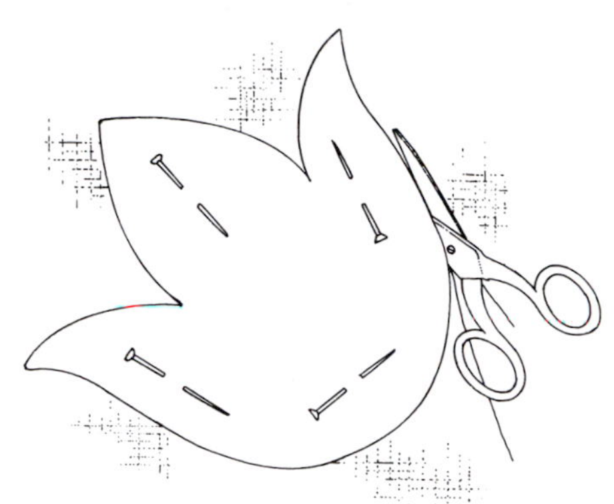

2 **If the fabric cannot easily be marked, pin the paper template, right side down, on the back of the fabric. Cut around the shape without seam allowances.**

1 **Mark the design on the background fabric and either frame it or baste it in position on the framed backing fabric, if you are using one. Pin the cut-out shape in place, fitting it to the design marked on the background. Baste it in place with diagonal stitches, smoothing out any folds or wrinkles as you proceed. Secure the appliqué with your chosen stitch, and remove basting stitches.**

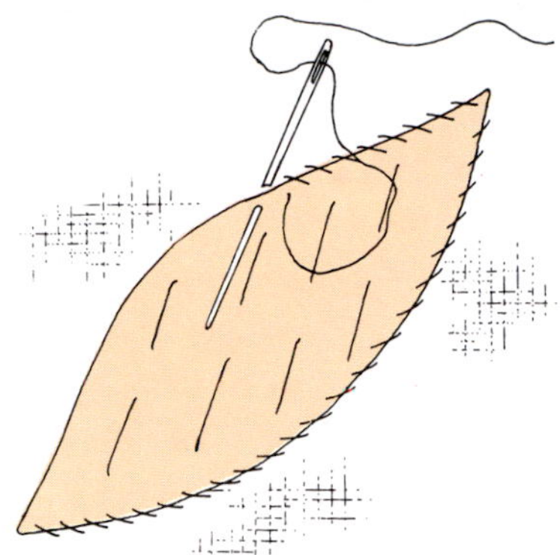

2 **To attach a frayable fabric without seam allowances, cut out the shape and baste it in position on the framed background. Overcast the edges with a thread that matches the colour of the appliqué shape. Conceal the overcasting with a decorative stitch, and remove basting stitches.**

Marking and cutting out

There are several ways of marking and cutting out motifs – much depends on your personal preference, but some methods are more suitable for certain materials than others. For example, it is difficult to make marks on felt, so this is best cut out by pinning a paper pattern to it, whereas suede and leather shapes should be marked on the reverse side with a fabric marker, as it is not possible to use pins. Remember, when marking on the reverse side, to position the template right side down, or the cut shape will be a mirror image, not a copy.

Applying shapes without seam allowances

Shapes cut from non-frayable fabrics can be attached without turnings, but it is also possible to stitch frayable fabrics in position without turning the edges under. It is, however, important to take account of their frayable qualities and to handle the pieces as gently as possible. Fabrics that are difficult to handle may be backed with iron-on interfacing and cut out, omitting seam allowances. Alternatively, fusible web, which gives a flatter effect, can be used to adhere the shape.

Turned-edge (blind) appliqué

Turned-edge appliqué is suitable for fabrics that fray and for those fine enough to allow a hem to be turned under neatly. It is used where a blind edge, without decorative stitching, is required. It is also used for padded appliqué, in which the motif is stitched over felt or batting. Iron-on interfacing, though not essential, can be used as a backing, producing an edge over which the hem may be turned.

Curves, points and corners

To achieve a neat professional finish, in which every detail and subtlety of shape is retained, careful manipulation of the seam

Couching in soft embroidery cotton is used to define the edge of the stones in this sample by Doreen Brewster.

Turned-edge appliqué

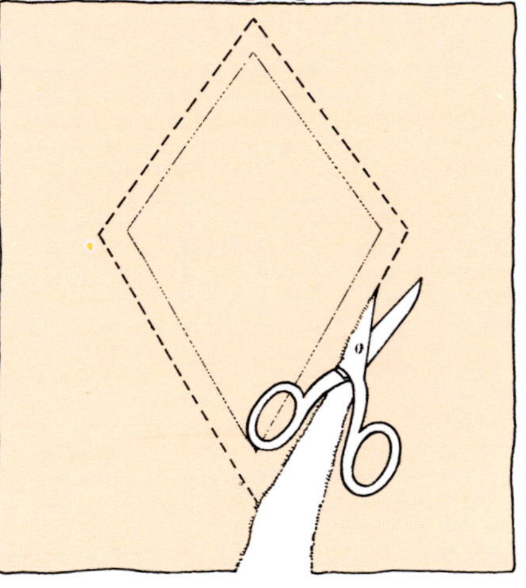

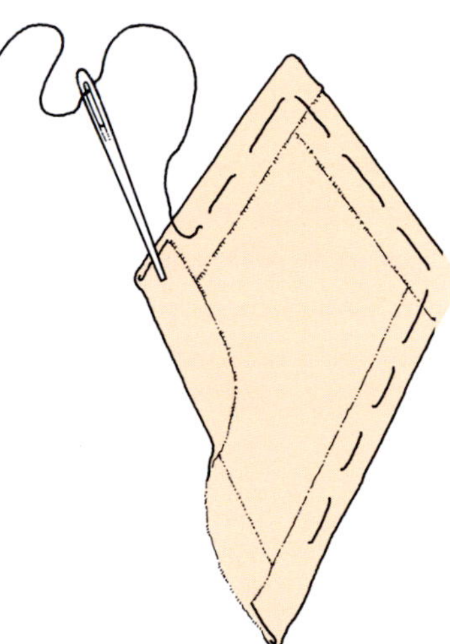

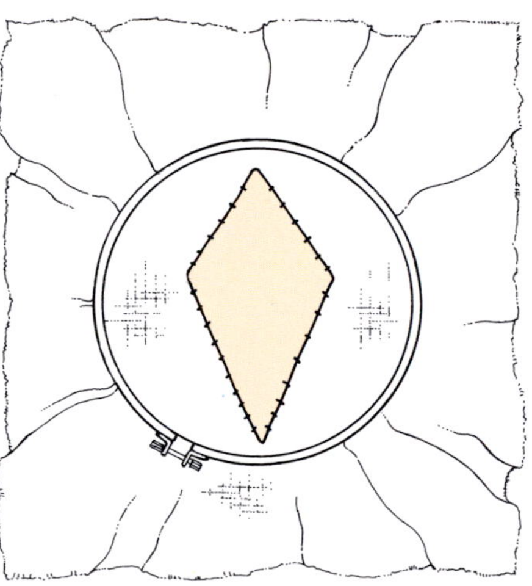

1 **Follow the instructions for marking and cutting out non-woven fabrics, but add a seam allowance all around of between 6mm and 12mm (¼in and ½in), depending on the size, shape and fabric of the piece.**

2 **If you choose, interline the shapes with iron-on interfacing, cut to the size of the finished motif. If not, machine a row of stay-stitching along the marked stitching line. Fold the seam allowance to the wrong side, using the edge of the interfacing or the stay-stitching as a guide. Snip, notch or trim allowances as necessary, and baste them in place, using a fine needle and thread.**

3 **Mark the design on the background fabric and frame it (and backing, if desired). Pin the prepared shape in place and baste with diagonal stitches, smoothing away any folds as you proceed. Secure the appliqué with your chosen stitch and remove basting stitches.**

allowances is essential. Straight edges present few problems, but curves, points and corners must be handled as shown.

Rouleaux strips

For narrow strips of appliqué, for example flower stems, rouleaux strips may be used. To make these, simply cut a bias strip to double the required width, plus a 6mm (¼in) seam allowance on either side. Fold the strip in half lengthwise, with right sides together, and stitch with back stitch or machine stitching. Attach a strong thread to one end of the strip and push the needle, eye forward, through the fold, turning the strip right side out. The strip can then be slipstitched in place, with stitches running along each edge.

Curves, points and corners

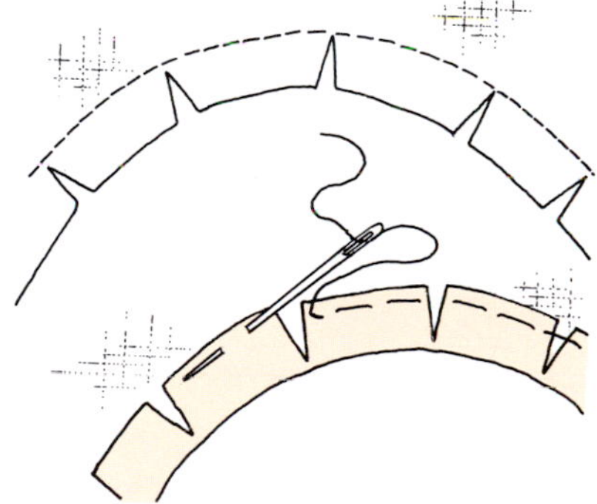

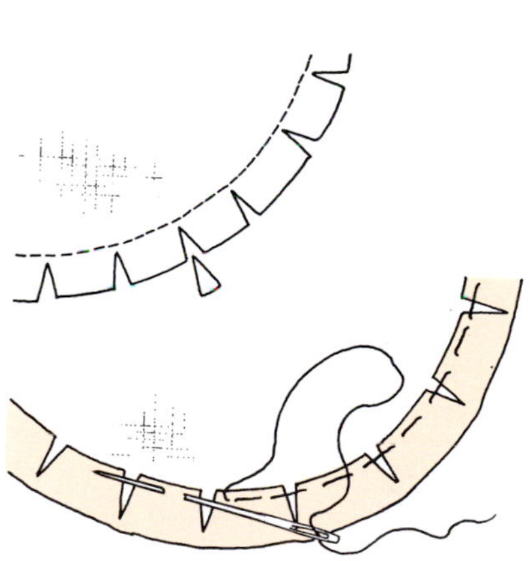

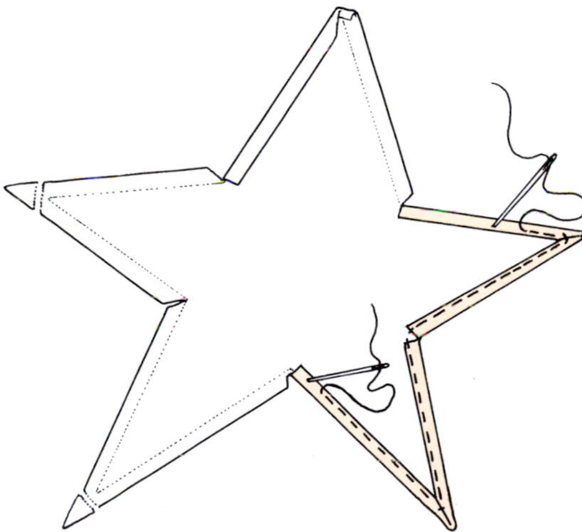

1 **At concave (inward) curves, snip the excess almost up to the stay-stitching (or to within 3mm/⅛in of the interfacing), making cuts at regular intervals. Using a fine needle and thread, fold the allowance over and baste it in place with small stitches.**

2 **At convex (outward) curves, remove small notches of fabric from the seam allowance at regular intervals, in order to reduce the excess bulk that will otherwise show when the fabric is folded. Again, snip to within 3mm (⅛in) of the stay-stitching or interfacing.**

3 **On outer corners and at acute angles, trim the point to reduce bulk. Fold the corner down first, then the two adjacent sides. Baste the seam allowance in place as for curves. On inner corners, slit the fabric up to the stay-stitching or interfacing, in order to turn back the sides.**

Appliqué stitches

A small repertoire of basic stitches for appliqué have traditionally been used to secure the stitches firmly but unobtrusively to the background. Each produces a slightly different effect, and a stitch should be chosen for its suitability in relation to the design and the fabrics being used. Ordinary cotton thread is the usual thread, but pure silk or polyester threads may also be used in combination with fabrics of those fibres.

Stab stitch

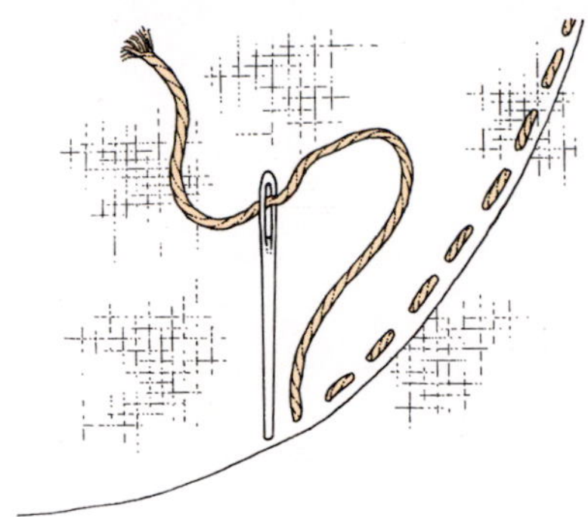

Stab stitch forms a dotted line, with tiny stitches evenly spaced in a line parallel with the edge of the applied shape. It differs from running stitch in that the needle pierces the fabric vertically instead of diagonally. It is suitable for non-fray fabrics and to attach free-standing motifs.

Buttonhole

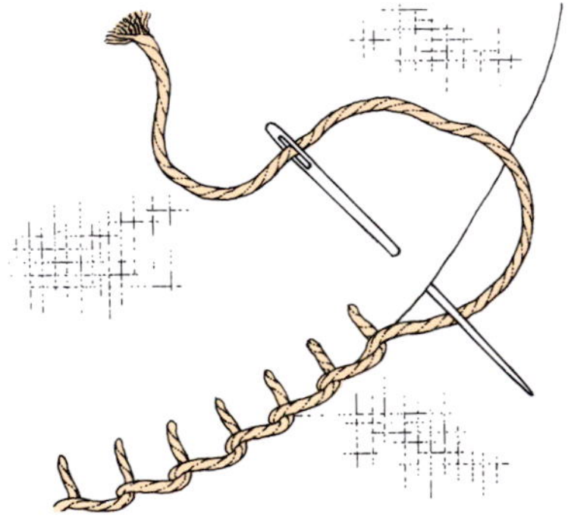

Buttonhole stitch featured a great deal in appliqué work of the past. It should, however, be used with discretion as, although it serves the purpose of securing the fabric in place, it can look primitive and child-like. It should therefore be worked very neatly, with tiny stitches, to create a firm decorative edge that need not impose itself too much on the design.

Couching

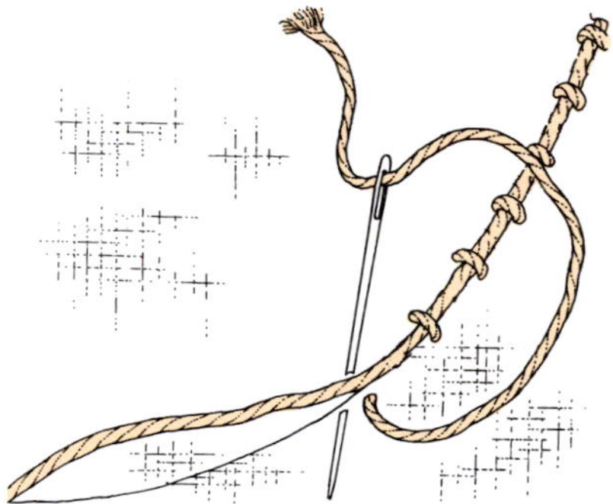

Couching involves the use of two threads – one laid along the edge of the applied motif and another, finer, one fastening it down. When working this stitch, it is essential to mount the fabric in a frame in order to retain the correct tension. This is a useful method, as the laid threads can be discreet if toning colours are used; alternatively, a more defined outline can be created with decorative yarns.

Back stitch

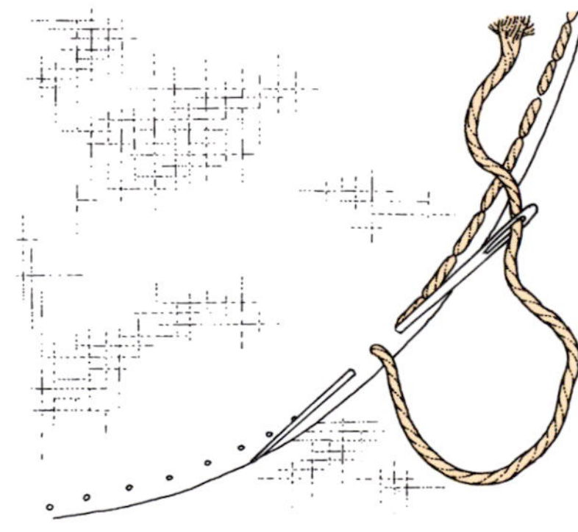

Back stitch produces a continuous line of stitches of even length, similar to machine stitches. It is particularly satisfactory for attaching leather or suede, in which case you should use a leather needle and strong thread. To facilitate stitching thick leather or hide, a preparatory line of holes can be made by using the sewing machine without thread.

Slip stitch

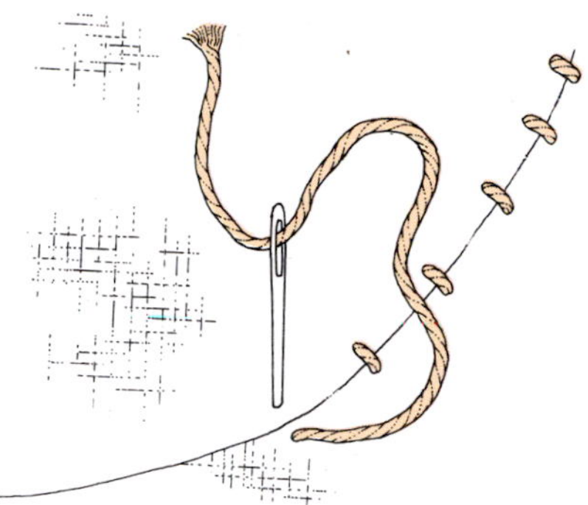

This is mostly used for turned-edge (blind) appliqué and should be worked as unobtrusively as possible. Bring the needle up through the background fabric, close to the edge of the motif, and work a tiny straight stitch into the turned edge. Repeat at regular intervals of about 6mm (¼in).

Basic machine appliqué

The advantage of machine appliqué lies not only in its speed, but also in the firmness and strength of the stitching. The appearance of machine-applied motifs differs from those attached by hand in that they acquire a crispness of definition and, if satin stitch is used, a boldly accentuated outline.

Before embarking on machine appliqué, it is essential to become fully conversant with the working of your machine. Some machines have a special appliqué foot in transparent plastic: this is particularly useful, as it enables the operator to see exactly where the needle will pierce the fabric.

Applying motifs

Two of the most commonly used methods of applying motifs are with fusible web, which will help to adhere intricate raw-edged motifs to a background, thereby creating an immaculate finish, and the stitch-and-cut method. This is suitable for designs that incorporate bold shapes, and it is especially useful for fine fabrics, including any that may fray.

Fusible web

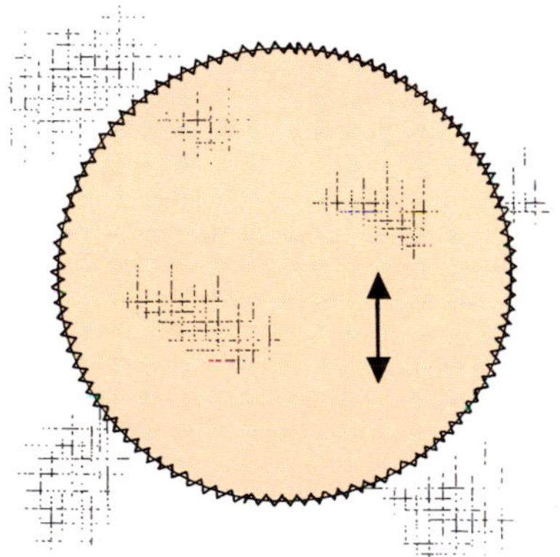

If you are using the fusible web method, bond the motif in place in the normal way, matching the grain with that of the background fabric. Work a line of zigzag stitching to cover the edge, adjusting your machine to a suitable stitch width and length for each motif.

Stitch-and-cut method

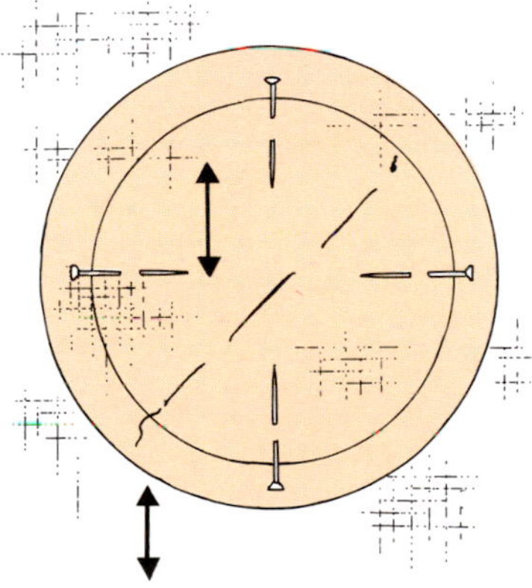

1. For the stitch-and-cut method, first transfer the outline of the appliqué shape to the right side of the fabric and cut it out, leaving a 2cm (¾in) margin all round. Pin the shape to the background fabric, matching grains and with the pins placed at right angles to the marked outline. If necessary, secure with a few diagonal basting stitches.

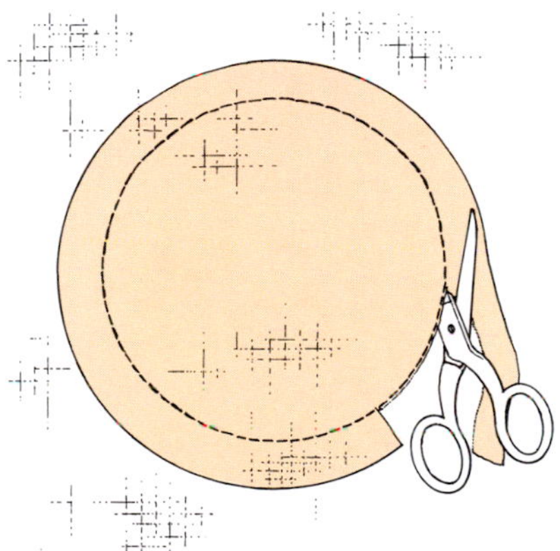

2. Machine with straight stitch on the marked line, working in a clockwise direction. Using small, pointed, embroidery scissors, trim away any excess fabric close to the stitching. If the appliqué is likely to be subjected to hard wear or frequent washing, the single line of machine stitches should be covered with a row of zigzag or close satin stitch, after the fabric has been trimmed.

Stitching

It is not usually necessary to hem the edges of appliqué shapes that are to be machined, unless you are intending to use straight stitching in conjunction with fabrics that may fray. If this is the case, follow the instructions already given for the turned-edge method, replacing the final hand stitching with machine sewing.

Most machine appliqué employs zigzag or satin stitch on raw-edged motifs, this being the method with most strength, although free machining and decorative automatic stitches may also be used. For most purposes, ordinary cotton or polyester thread is suitable, but machine embroidery thread gives a fine, glossy effect that may be appropriate for some designs.

Ordinary straight stitching, in conjunction with either the turned-edge or stitch-and-cut methods, is often used for attaching appliqué shapes to a background. Provided you are fully acquainted with your machine, you will have few problems. It is best to use a short stitch rather than a long one, particularly for attaching intricately shaped motifs.

Zigzag stitching provides a neat but strong method of applying bolder shapes. The width and length of the zigzag can be adjusted in order to create different decorative effects, which can be selected according to the artistic and practical requirements of the design.

Zigzag shaping

Attaching shapes with zigzag or satin stitch is not difficult, but you may need to practise turning at corners, points and tight curves if you are to achieve an immaculate finish. The shapes should either be bonded or pinned and basted in place, and the machine stitching carried out slowly and carefully.

Zigzag shaping

1 **For outside corners, work zigzag or satin stitch to the corner, stopping the machine with the needle to the right. With the needle still in the fabric, pivot the work and continue stitching along the next side.**

Machine zigzag creates a textured pattern of grasses while simultaneously securing pieces of fabric in this panel by Sheila Cahn.

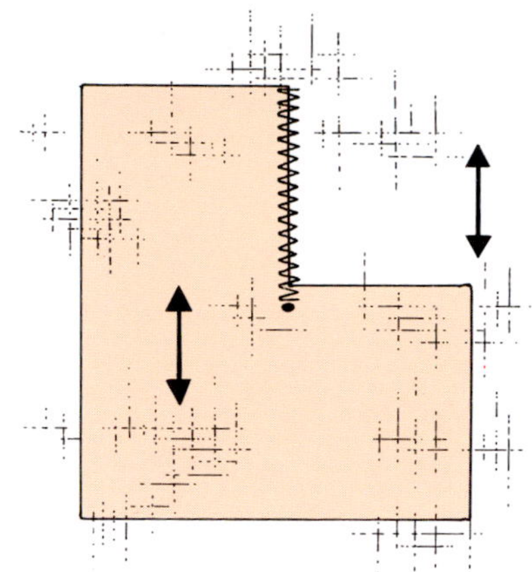

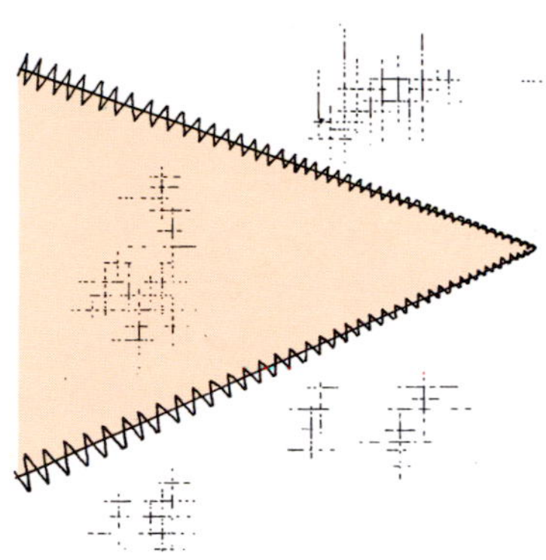

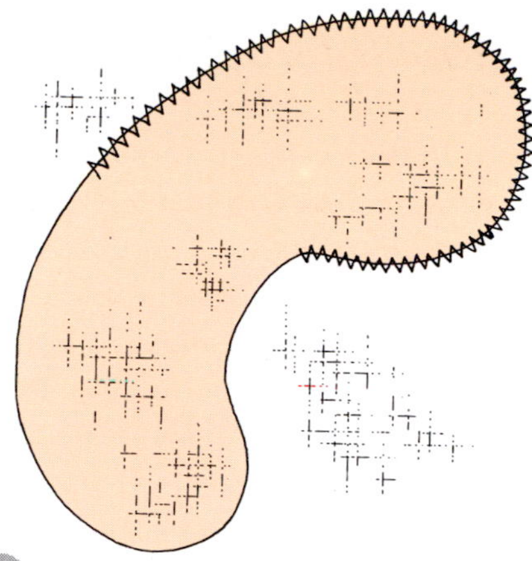

2 Inside corners are worked as for outside corners, but stop the machine with the needle to the left. Pivot as for outside corners and continue stitching.

3 For acute points and inward corners, the zigzag may be tapered by gradually narrowing the stitch width towards the corner. With the needle still in the fabric, pivot the work and stitch down the other side, gradually increasing the stitch width.

4 Shallow curves present no problem and can be stitched as for straight edges. When stitching a zigzag around a tight curve, pivot the work every few stitches, stopping the machine with the needle on the outside of the curves and pivoting the fabric accordingly.

Padded appliqué

In recent years, three-dimensional items have featured prominently in the work of professional textile artists. These include appliqué panels and items such as cushions with free-standing motifs cascading from the surface, as well as completely three-dimensional objects. This type of embroidery is based on padded appliqué techniques that can be adapted or modified to suit the subject. This will add another dimension to the work, either in the form of softly textured areas of focal interest, sculptured motifs of high relief or three-dimensional shapes that project from the background fabric.

The choice of padding depends not only on the raised effect required, but also on the type of fabric used and whether the item to be made is to be washed or dry-cleaned. Synthetic batting, available in several thicknesses, gives a soft squashy effect, while felt tends to be firmer and more solid-looking, and padding with cardboard, balsa wood or craft interlining produces a stiff hard-edged result. All padded appliqué should be worked in a frame.

Padding with felt

Using the paper pattern, mark and cut out a piece of felt the same size and shape as the appliqué motif; then cut several further shapes, each slightly smaller than the previous one (usually, three or four are needed).

Starting with the smallest, pin and stitch it to the centre of the area to be padded, using a stab stitch, worked at right angles to the edge of the felt. Repeat with the next size, stitching it on top of the first, and continue until each piece is attached. Sew the prepared appliqué shape on top, using the turned-edge method.

For an asymmetrical effect, the padding can be varied in depth, with some areas raised higher than others.

Padding with batting

To use batting, prepare the appliqué shape and cut a piece of batting the same size and of the required thickness. Stitch the batting to the background fabric, using loosely tensioned straight stitches, placed at right angles to the edge. Stitch the prepared appliqué shape on top, using the turned-edge method.

To create the comic postcard effect of Cor! What a cheek!, *Margaret Barclay has used card, felt and batting to pad the appliqué pieces.*

Padding with felt

Felt has traditionally been used extensively in ecclesiastical embroidery for padding leather and metal threadwork. It is also a suitable padding for raised areas on pictures and wallhangings, where a firm, slightly domed effect is required. It is normally used in combination with the turned-edge method of appliqué.

Padding with batting

Synthetic batting (polyester wadding), which comes in several weights, is versatile as it can be laundered, which makes it suitable for soft furnishings such as cushions and quilts as well as for decoration on garments. Its applications for wallhangings and appliqué panels include soft sculptural effects of high or low relief. Silk or cotton batting may also be used, but are less readily available.

Padding with cardboard or stiff interfacing

Card is a suitable material for padding areas of appliqué pictures and panels that do not require cleaning. For garments and soft furnishings, stiff craft or pelmet interfacing is an alternative that produces a similar effect and can be drycleaned. The advantage of using this type of padding is the hard-edged effect that it creates, giving sharp definition to designs that include architectural shapes or precise geometric forms. For a hard-edged, but softer, padded effect, batting or felt can be inserted between the fabric and the cardboard. The thickness of the card is dependent upon the weight of the fabric to be applied and the size of the motif. For small and delicate motifs, light cardboard may be used; matt (mounting) board would be a satisfactory choice for a more substantial shape.

For a slightly more raised effect, balsa wood can be shaped and used in the same way as card.

Cut a piece of cardboard or stiff craft interfacing to the size and shape of the finished appliqué motif. Cut out the fabric, making it between 6mm and 12mm (¼in and ½in) larger all around. Centre the cardboard on the wrong side of the fabric and apply fabric glue sparingly around the edge. Fold the fabric edges over to adhere. Curves, points and corners should be snipped, notched or trimmed as for the turned-edge method. Apply the fabric-covered cardboard to the background fabric by working slip stitches around the edge.

In Salad Plate, *by Doris Lopian, padded appliqué is used to produce life-like salad vegetables. The plate and tomatoes are padded with card.*

In this five-panel landscape, Prue Dobinson has created many different effects by ruching, gathering and manipulating fabrics. Cretan stitch secures some areas.

Free-standing motifs

Free-standing motifs, projecting from the surface, can add – quite literally – another dimension to an appliqué design. The shapes may be made with fusible web, or stuffed, with raw edges or with turned edges: the choice depends on the desired end effect. This type of motif is normally attached to the background fabric only at one or two points. The bonding method is most suitable for very intricate shapes (florists' wire is often included inside the shape, which can then be manipulated), while padding – either with polyester or with felt – can add to the three-dimensional appearance.

Fusible web

To make a free-standing motif with fusible web, first adhere two fabrics to each other, with wrong sides together. Mark the design on one side and cut the shape out. The edges will not fray, so they may be left untreated. Details can be embroidered with decorative stitches and the motif can be stiffened, if desired, by spraying it with roller blind stiffener or a weak solution of fabric adhesive. If you want to mould the piece – to create, for example, a curled leaf, you can insert fine florists' wire between the layers before bonding, to make the piece more malleable.

Raw edges

To make a padded motif with a raw edge, first mark the design on the top fabric. Place the top fabric over the bottom fabric, with wrong sides together, and insert a layer of batting between them. (The layer of batting may, of course, be omitted if it is not needed, or felt may be substituted.) Baste the pieces together, then machine stitch along the outline.

Cut out the motif, close to the stitching. Work satin stitch or machine zigzag over the edge, or cover the cut edge with buttonhole stitch.

In this panel by Judy Hope, free-standing organza leaves have been edged with machine stitching, for a delicate effect.

Turned edges

1 Mark the design on the wrong side of the top fabric. Place the top and bottom fabrics right sides together, with the batting underneath them. Baste them together, then straightstitch by machine along the outline, leaving an opening through which to turn the work.

Remove basting switches and cut out the motif. Remember to allow for the turning, but trim excess fabric as necessary. Trim the batting close to the stitching line.

2 Turn the motif to the right side, turning through the opening. Press the seam lightly, and slipstitch the opening. The edge may be finished with an additional row of machine stitching or a decorative edge, sewn by hand.

Reverse appliqué

The Cuña Indians of the San Blas islands off the coast of Panama are famous for this technique, which they use to create lively designs of brightly-coloured cotton, depicting legends and scenes of daily life. These *molas* are nowadays much sought after, though the modern versions do not have the same quality as those of the past. A similar technique is used by the hill tribes in Thailand, but there the work has a much more delicate and refined character.

To stitch reverse appliqué in the traditional manner requires a certain dexterity, but once mastered, the technique produces an effect that cannot be achieved in any other way. The basic method is for several pieces of fabric to be laid one on top of the other and for the layers gradually to be cut away to reveal those beneath. Fabrics should be fine and non-slip: cotton lawn is ideal. Plain contrasting colours produce the most satisfactory effects, though small prints can be used with discretion, provided the tonal value and the scale permits. Dark colours should be placed on top of light, so that the turnings do not show through, and laundering qualities should be considered if you are making garments or soft furnishings.

If you are new to this technique, choose a design that is bold and simple, making sure that the enclosed motifs have straight or shallow curved edges. It is best to avoid narrow shapes and acute angles.

Machine method

As with the hand method, choose a bold design that can easily be manoeuvred on the sewing machine. Non-fray fabrics may be stitched with straight stitch, but a close zigzag or satin stitch would be more appropriate for other types of material. The stitch width should be adjusted to relate to the scale of the areas to be cut away.

The layers of fabric are prepared in the same way as for the hand method, with two rows of additional basting both ways across the centre of the design to hold the fabrics firm. Stitch around the shape to be removed, then cut away the top layer, close to the stitching, to reveal the fabric below. Continue within this motif, alternately stitching and cutting away, to reveal selected areas of the underlying fabrics.

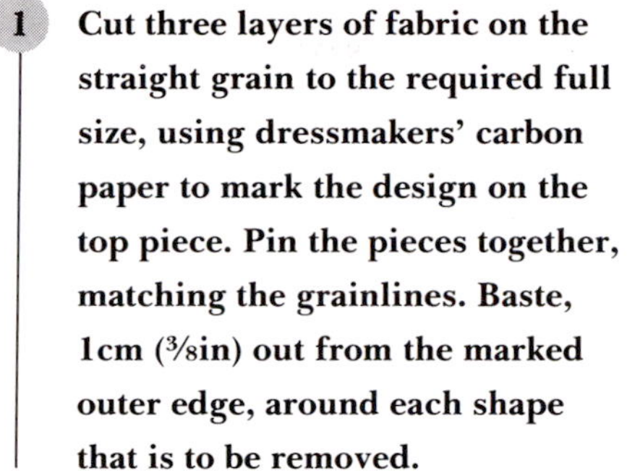

1 **Cut three layers of fabric on the straight grain to the required full size, using dressmakers' carbon paper to mark the design on the top piece. Pin the pieces together, matching the grainlines. Baste, 1cm (3/8in) out from the marked outer edge, around each shape that is to be removed.**

2 **With small sharp embroidery scissors, start to cut away the top layer of fabric, cutting 6mm (1/4in) inside the marked outline.**

3 **Turn this raw edge under and, using thread that matches the upper fabric, slipstitch in place through all layers, snipping curves as necessary. Continue cutting away, turning under and stitching until the shape is completed. Repeat steps 1 and 2, cutting through the second layer to reveal the third. Additional shapes may be applied within the cut-away area, using the turned-edge method.**

This section of a quilt made by Elspeth Kemp shows a combination of reverse appliqué with turned-edge shapes, attached both by hand and machine.

Inlay

Inlay is not a technique that is often used, but it has the advantage of producing a smooth effect that is unobtainable with other types of appliqué, and in addition it can be made reversible if the pieces are not stitched on a backing.

The easiest fabrics to work with are those, such as felt, closely woven wool and painted or dyed interfacing, that do not fray. The type of design best suited to the technique is one containing bold shapes and without narrow strips, as the pieces of appliqué fit together like a jigsaw puzzle with the edges abutting one another. Although the finished appliqué was traditionally unmounted, a simpler way to work is to mount a backing in a frame, place the main background fabric on this and stitch the inlay pieces into the appropriate spaces.

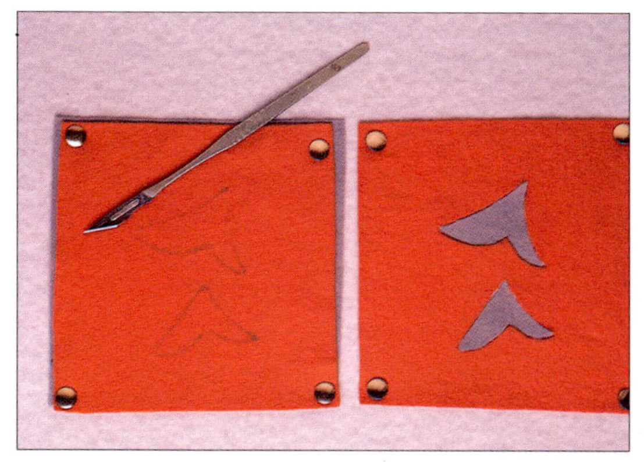

1 **Mark your design on the right side of the main (background) fabric, using dressmakers' carbon paper or drawing around a template. Lay this on top of the fabric to be inlaid. Place the two fabrics on a cutting board and pin them both to the board to hold them firm. Using a sharp scalpel or craft knife, cut through both layers of fabric, following the marked outline. This will produce two sets of shapes which can be inlaid, one in the other.**

2 **Traditionally, inlaid appliqué has no permanent backing, and the work can therefore be reversible. Pin and baste the pieces of fabric – main fabric and inlaid piece(s) to a temporary backing of brown paper (originally, parchment was used). The raw edges may be joined either by sewing the join with couched cord or thread, or by working a row of buttonhole stitch on both raw edges, interlocking the second row with the first. The stitching should not pierce the brown paper.**

3 **A modern method is to mount a backing of firm fabric in a frame, and then pin and baste the appliqué pieces in position. Either work feather stitching along the joins, catching in both edges and the backing, or replace the handstitching with machine zigzag. In this case, the finished appliqué has a backing and is therefore not reversible.**

Shadow appliqué

Shadow appliqué uses a variation of the stitch-and-cut method (see page 175) but in this case the fabric to be applied is placed beneath the transparent background fabric and the excess cut away. This method produces a very delicate impression, due to its use of transparent fabrics such as organdie, organza, voile, nylon or net. As the appliqué is stitched to the underside of the sheer fabric the result is mainly of muted tones.

Traditionally, only white fabrics have been employed, but more exciting effects can be achieved by using materials of different colours. This will produce alterations of hue; for example, a yellow cotton placed beneath a red organza will appear to be orange. As with most types of appliqué, designs for this method should be fairly bold in concept. Unless there is going to be some additional decorative stitching, it is necessary to divide the design into sections, rather like a stencil, with each area separated from its neighbour by a space. Originally a hand sewing method, sewn with pin stitch, shadow appliqué can also be made by machine, using a narrow close zigzag.

The same design shown in the steps has here been stitched by machine.

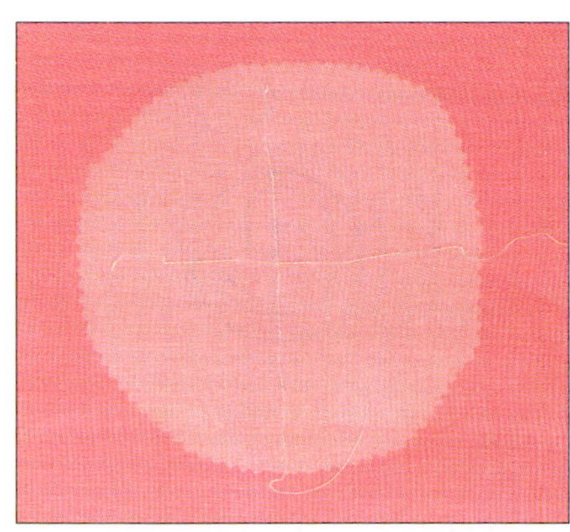

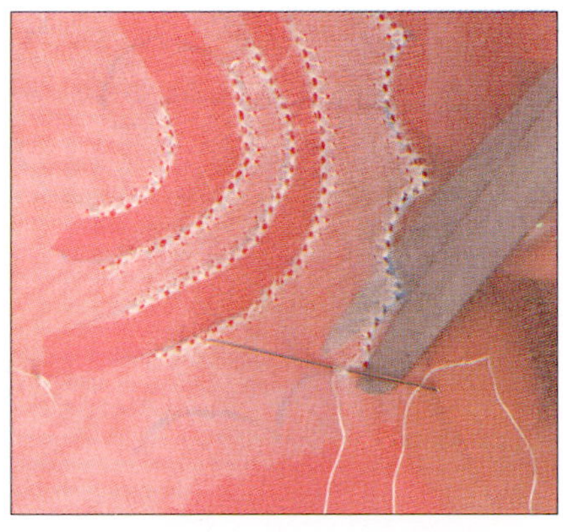

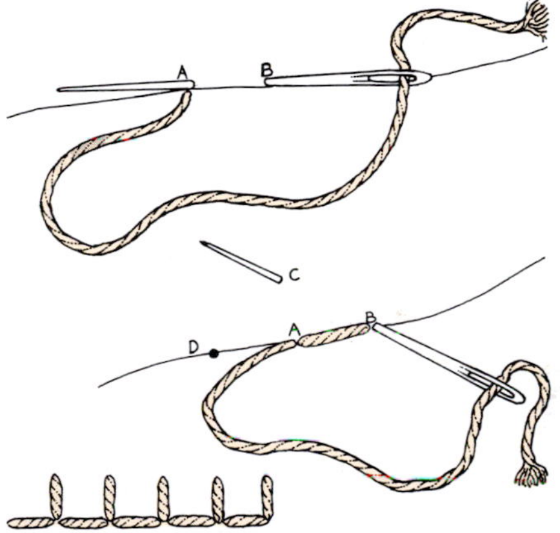

1 **Transfer the design to the top, transparent fabric with a water-soluble fabric marker or dressmakers' chalk, using the direct tracing method. Mark very lightly.**

Mount this fabric in a frame, then cut enough of the appliqué fabric to cover the design area completely and baste it in place underneath, making sure that the straight grains of the two pieces are aligned.

2 **From the top, work pin stitch in fine thread, stitching through both layers and along the marked outlines around each shape. Remove from the frame and carefully cut away the excess fabric from the wrong side.**

If you are using a machine, baste the traced design over the two layers of fabric. Work narrow satin stitch or close zigzag through all three, then tear the paper and trim the excess fabric.

3 **To work pin stitch, make a back stitch from A to B and bring the needle up again at A. Repeat the back stitch, this time bringing the needle up at C. Take the needle down at A and bring it up at D. Repeat the stitch, pulling the thread fairly tightly to form small holes.**

QUILTING

Quilting is a centuries-old form of stitchery that has been newly invigorated and rejuvenated by its acceptance as a textile art form. Exciting and challenging, contemporary quilts, whether stitched by hand or machine, now complement the enduring traditional designs and techniques that have evolved over the years.

Designing to scale

The planning stage of a quilting design usually begins on paper. This gives you the opportunity to work out:

- how to divide the quilt surface into design spaces for patterns
- how to fit patterns accurately into spaces
- how to balance pattern elements
- the relationship between positive and negative areas
- the type of symmetry of the design
- the nature and importance of spaces between patterns.

1 **Using a large sheet of plain paper, make a scale drawing of your cover design and then colour it in with pencil, paint or cut fabric shapes and glue them in position.**

2 **Using tracing paper, pencil and ruler, draw your quilting design to scale. Scaled-down pattern templates will help you to draft some motifs; a rolling ruler is useful for drawing certain filling patterns.**

3 **Place your quilting design over the cover design in order to gain a visual impression of what the two designs will look like when combined.**

Setting your designs on paper also allows you to develop them, and to experiment with pattern and space. Like any form of experimentation, mistakes will be made – but mistakes on paper are cheaper and easier to rectify! Choose a scale that has a simple numerical relationship to the size of the finished quilt – quarter, fifth or eighth scale, for example – so that any measurements can easily be translated from one scale to the other.

Enlarging scale designs

When you have drawn a design to scale, you may wish to enlarge it in order to trace either the full design or some of the pattern elements on the quilt top. The simplest way to do this is to use an enlarging photocopier to increase the design to the required size.

Your scale design can usually be increased in size by 50 per cent or by any percentage in between. Each enlargement can also be further enlarged. The thicker, bolder lines of the final enlargement are ideal for tracing on fabric.

This technique of scale-drawing and then enlarging is particularly useful for geometric designs and patterns based on circles. It is much easier to draw to scale using compasses than to draw large circles by whatever means are to hand.

1 **Draft the design on plain white paper, using a pencil, a ruler, and compasses, if required. Go over the pencil lines with a black pen, making them either solid or broken, and then enlarge the design in sections.**

2 **Using your initial design, make photocopy enlargements of sections until you have a complete set of the required size.**

3 **The final enlarged design can be used either in a cut and taped form or it can be traced onto another large sheet of paper.**

Drafting a full-scale design

You may wish to draft quilting design ideas to the precise size of your intended quilt rather than to scale. You may even decide to do this after preparing a scale design. There are advantages; it gives the clearest possible two-dimensional impression of how the completed design will look on the quilt surface; it allows you to use full-size templates when planning; it gives you a chance to work out how the patterns fit together, and, finally, it provides a completed design which can then be traced on to a quilt top.

You will, however, need table space and large sheets of paper, such as lining paper, if a big quilt is planned. If necessary, piece paper sheets together with masking tape. Remember, though, that if you plan a symmetrical design, only a part of it will need to be fully drafted. For quilts with a four-fold symmetry, only a quarter of the full-scale design is required. If your quilt outline is *square*, the quarter-design can be turned to fit into any of the quarters. For a *rectangular* quilt, however, use either tracing paper or thin paper through which the lines are visible on the reverse. On a rectangle, you will need to turn the quarter-design over to produce a mirror image on adjacent quarters.

Draw out your full-scale design with a hard, sharp, lead pencil, a quilters' ruler and whatever other marking tools are required. Use Blu-tak to anchor your paper to the table top and keep a large eraser close by for the inevitable errors.

If you wish to mark out the quilt top on a light box or glass table, using the pencil-drawn design as a tracing pattern, thicken the pencil lines with a black drawing pen to make them more clearly visible.

A quilters' ruler is an invaluable tool when marking straight-line filler patterns either, as here, on a full-scale design or directly on the fabric.

Transferring designs to fabric

More discussion takes place among quilters about the best way in which to transfer quilting designs to fabric than about almost any other stage in quiltmaking. There are two problems to resolve: how to draft the design onto fabric, and which marker to use for the drafting. To transfer a design to fabric, you can either draw it or trace it – or use a combination of the two, choosing whichever is the appropriate method for each element of the pattern.

Preparation

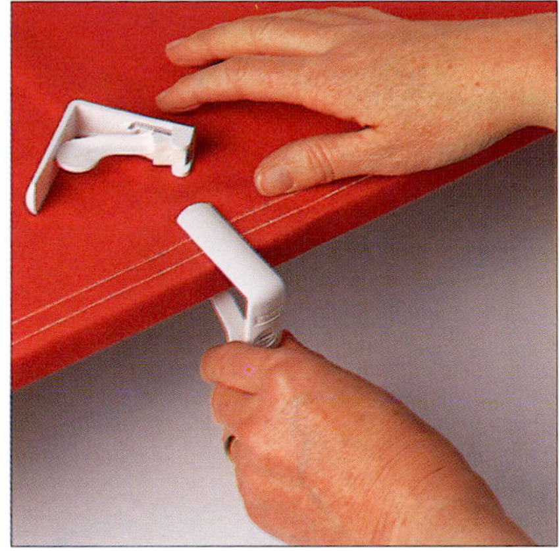

1 **Press the quilt top carefully, with all seams open. Set it, right side up, on a table positioned in good light (preferably daylight). Place the table so that you can work all around it; this will minimize the extent to which you will need to move the quilt top as you mark. Have marking tools and pattern templates close to hand, but not on the marking table – a small trolley alongside is useful for this.**

Mark the outer edge of the quilt with either a single or double line – this will not represent the absolute edge of the finished quilt, but the line to which the quilting design will extend. On most quilt designs these outer containing lines are quilted.

2 **Before marking any patterns, mark the important design areas of the quilt, for example border divisions, the quilt centre, and lines dividing the quilt into quarters. If these points and divisions are also lines within the design, use your marking tool to draw them. If not, use basting thread or an easily erasable marker, so that these guidelines can be removed when the design is fully drawn.**

3 **Anchor the fabric to the table top. If the quilt top is smaller than the table, tape the corners to keep the top in position. If the quilt top is larger, then use clips – for example, table cloth clips – to hold the area you are marking. Fabric is much easier to mark if it is held taut.**

Drawing on fabric

Using whatever combination of templates, freehand drawing and line drawing is appropriate for your design, draw directly on the fabric with a marker. To ensure accuracy, check measurements constantly with your paper design as you mark.

An alternative method is to place the templates or design on a light box, with the fabric on top, and trace over the lines with a marker.

These pattern outlines are skilfully produced on tracing paper, but not all commercially-available patterns are of this quality. If you are buying patterns, look closely at the way in which lines have been drawn.

Order of drawing

1 **Draw motif and border patterns first. To maintain the symmetry of the design, border patterns should be drawn from the centre of the border out towards the corners.**

2 **Once the motifs and borders have been completed, draw the filling patterns. Maintain the accuracy of line width and intersecting angles by constantly checking with a ruler and set square or protractor – most errors are made in marking out filling patterns.**

Popular and widely available from specialist suppliers, stencil templates of traditional and other simple stylized patterns are easy to use.

Strip designs

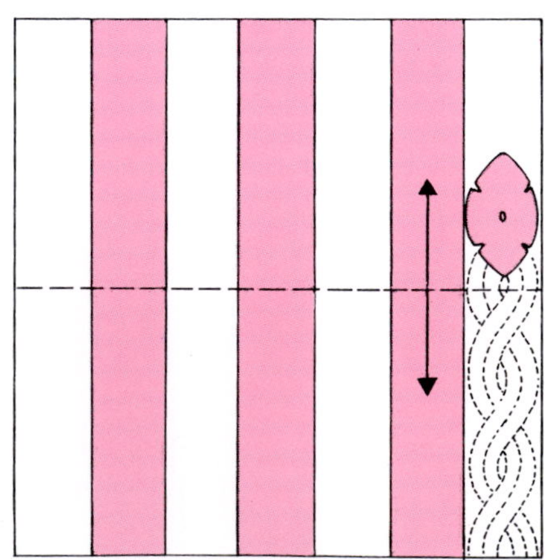

For strip designs which run vertically down the quilt, mark a central *horizontal* line across (with basting stitches or an erasable marker), and mark your patterns to top and bottom from this horizontal. They should then fit symmetrically into the strip length. Strip designs based on horizontal divisions are similarly marked, but from a central *vertical* line.

Templates

For some motifs, border and filling patterns you will require templates, especially if the patterns are to be repeated in a design. The templates are used either as an aid to drawing patterns directly on the quilt surface or when drafting a full-scale design on paper. (Reduced-scale templates are also a useful tool when you wish to map out a design on a small scale during the planning stages.)

Templates should be of stiff paper, cardboard or plastic. You can buy them ready for use, but many are simple to make. Template plastic, or mylar, from specialist suppliers is easy to cut with scissors, and the ability to make your own templates will give you greater flexibility of size and pattern.

Outline templates

With these, only the pattern outlines can be drawn; internal details will need to be filled in by hand. This is not the disadvantage it may seem. If you use an outline template, you are free to fill the shape in a variety of ways, according to choice, and the need to draw internal lines both encourages and sharpens your drawing skills.

Outline templates can be home-made, though useful sheets of paper outlines of many traditional patterns are commercially available; for practical purposes, these should be cut out and mounted on cardboard or plastic.

Stencil templates

Plastic stencil templates have the internal pattern lines cut away in the form of long dashes, so they act as guides for both external and internal lines. This is quick, convenient and produces identically-detailed repeats. The danger, though, is that this perfection tends to result in patterns that are mechanical and lifeless elements within a design as a whole, lacking the rhythmic quality that may come from hand-drawn work.

Stencil templates can be made at home: all you will require is card or template plastic and suitable equipment for cutting internal lines. Popular traditional patterns can also be bought in stencil form from specialist suppliers.

Making templates

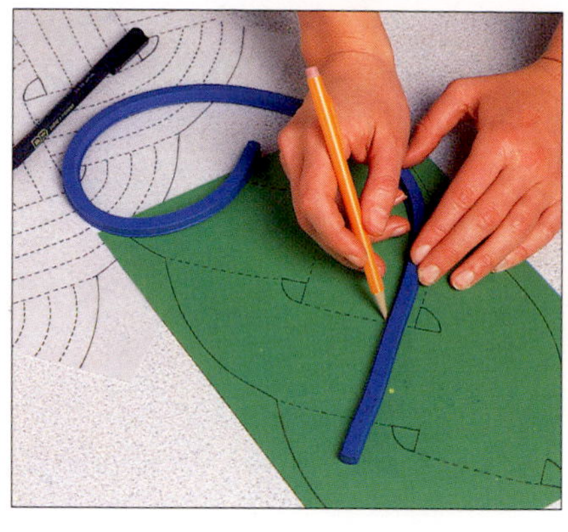

1 Draw the pattern, in detail, on matt board or tracing paper. If you are making templates from bought patterns, cut roughly around the shapes, leaving a margin of paper.

2 Glue the pattern to cardboard or template plastic and cut around it to produce an outline template. Use scissors (curved ones for tight corners and curves), or a cutting mat and craft knife or rotary cutter.

3 To make the outline into a stencil template, cut dashed lines along the internal lines of the pattern, using a craft knife and cutting mat.

The planned asymmetry of Celtic I, *by Linda Maltman, has been developed from a single filling pattern and celtic knot border patterns. This wholecloth quilt in grey cotton is designed as a panel decoration for a door. Size: 76cm × 198cm (36in × 78in)*

Circular templates

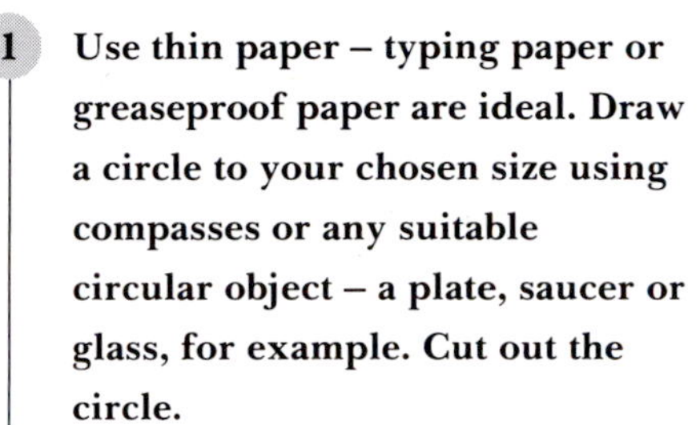

1. Use thin paper – typing paper or greaseproof paper are ideal. Draw a circle to your chosen size using compasses or any suitable circular object – a plate, saucer or glass, for example. Cut out the circle.

2. To create symmetrically shaped edges, fold the circle three times, producing a wedge-shaped segment. Three folds will produce a pattern with an eight-fold symmetry, such as an eight-pointed star; for a 16-edged pattern, fold once more.

3. At the curved edge of the segment, draw cutting lines according to the pattern required: a single scallop for a rose; an inverted 'V' for a star, or a pointed arch for a daisy, sunflower or composite heart. Cut the folded paper along the drawn line. These paper patterns can be made into outline or stencil templates as previously described.

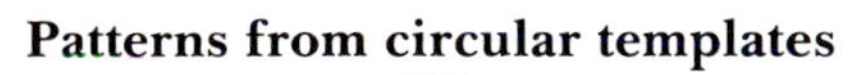

Patterns from circular templates

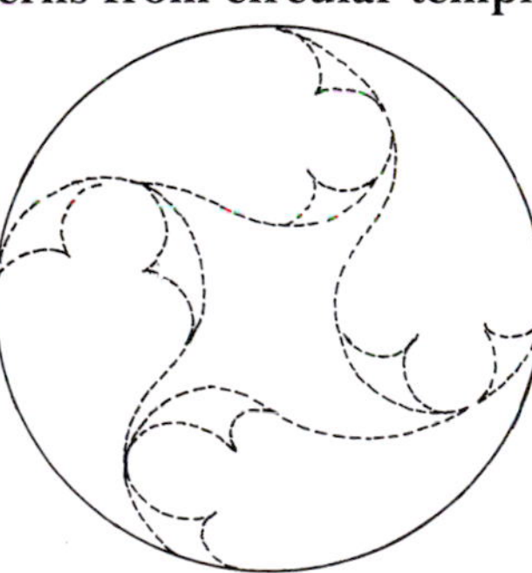

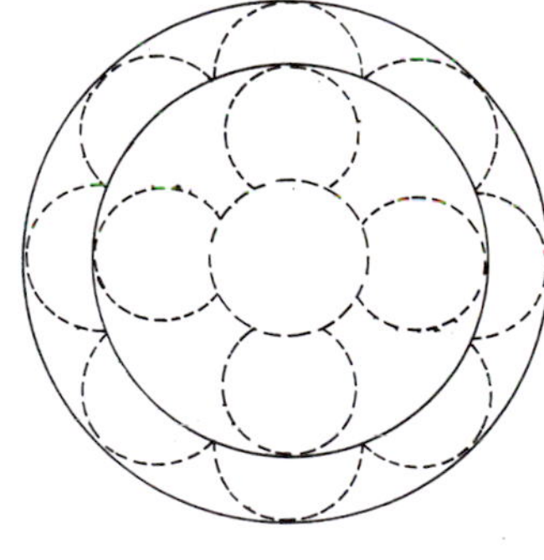

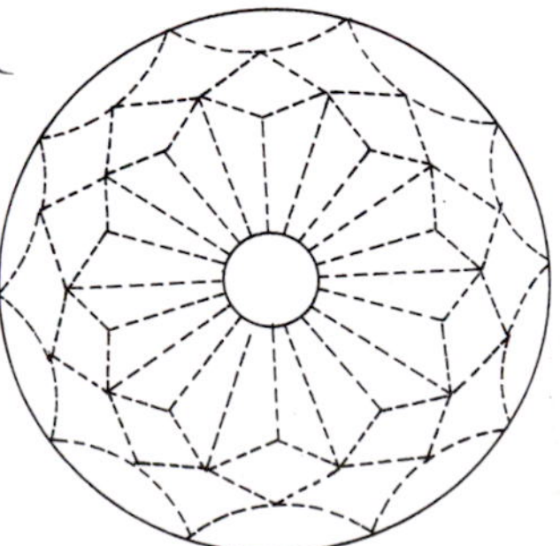

Preparing for quilting

A quilt is, basically, a textile sandwich with a fabric cover on the top and bottom and the batting inside. Quilts can be reversible, with both covers intended for use and show, but more usually one side is the decorative quilt top and the reverse is a backing fabric.

Careful preparation is needed to prevent the quilt layers moving and puckering during stitching. The precise method of preparation depends on whether you intend to quilt by hand or machine and, if hand quilting, whether you will use a large frame, a hoop or a tube frame.

Note, however, that the quilting design should always be marked on the quilt top (or top cover) before this preparation stage.

Layering

When hand quilting is held in a hoop or tube frame, or when you are machine quilting, the fabrics for the quilt sandwich need to be smoothed out, layered together and secured, either with basting stitches or safety pins. (Only use safety pins if you can be sure that they will not leave pin marks in your fabric.)

The fabric layers must first be cut to size – with an allowance on all sides for finishing, and for the small reduction in size that will take place during quilting – and then carefully pressed.

Large quilts

1 **Mark the centre and the mid-point of the four edges on all layers. Centre the bottom layer on a large table, wrong side up, securing the surplus with clips.**

Small quilts

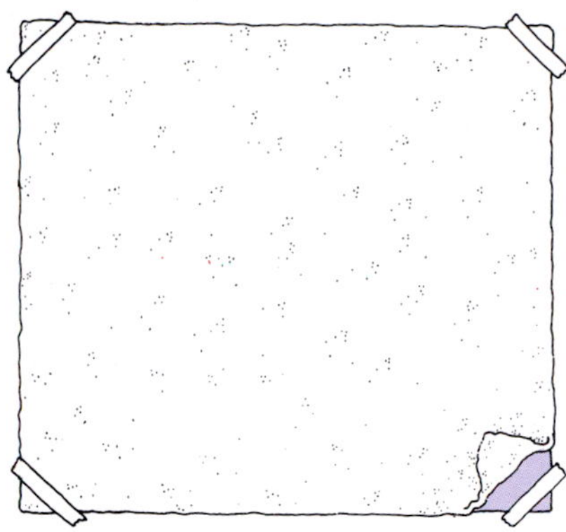

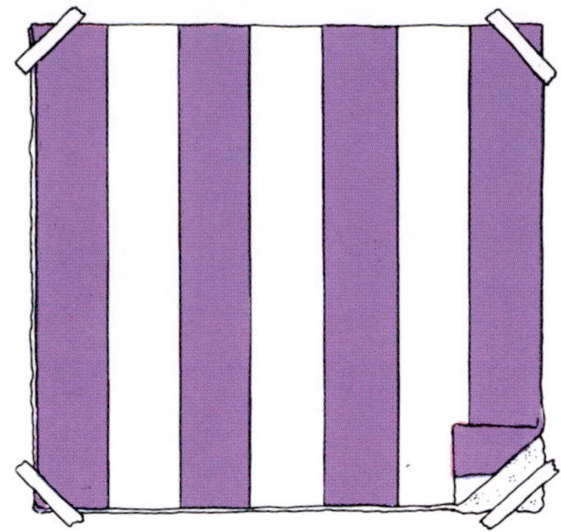

1 Lay the unmarked (or backing) fabric, wrong side up, on a hard, flat surface such as a table or the floor; smooth it carefully, and secure it at the corners with tape.

2 Lay the batting over the bottom fabric, smoothing and securing it with tape, as for the backing fabric.

3 Smooth the top over the batting. Tape corners, then pin layers together, from the centre towards the corners and edges. Secure with lines of basting, as described opposite for a large quilt.

2 Fold the batting into quarters. Match the corners of the batting to the centre point and edges of one quarter of the bottom layer, and then open out the batting in place over the bottom layer. Without stretching the batting, smooth it gently outwards.

3 Fold the top into quarters, with the right side in. Matching the centre point and centre edges with those on the batting, open it out, and smooth and pin it in position. Once you have pinned the area on the table surface, smooth the three layers of the outer areas of the quilt in turn, and pin them in position.

4 Secure the layers together with lines of basting stitches 10–15cm (4–6in) apart, both across and down the quilt. Always baste from the centre outwards, beginning with a long length of thread and leaving half of it at the centre, to be rethreaded for the other half of the line. Basting stitches are removed after quilting. For machine quilting, safety pins can be used in place of basting threads.

Setting in a large frame

When it is worked in a large frame, a quilt does *not* need to be basted together. Following this time-honoured method of setting, the quilt layers stay firmly tensioned and in position.

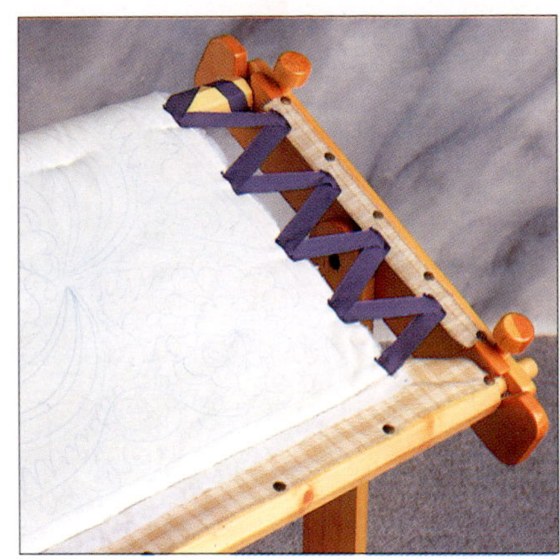

1 **Mark the centre point of the webbing on each rail and of the top and bottom fabric edges. Baste the (unmarked) backing fabric, wrong side up, to the webbing fixed to each rail, matching centre points. Roll the fabric on to the far rail until about 45cm (18in) is left, then fix the rails and stretchers in position, with the fabric flat but not too taut.**

2 **Lay the batting over the bottom layer, edge to edge. Smooth carefully, allowing any surplus to hang over the far rail. Lay the quilt top over the batting, marked side up and edge to edge, and smooth it out. Next, baste the batting and quilt top to the webbing along the near rail. At the far rail, pin through all three layers, using fine pins or size 10 quilting needles. Fold up the quilt top and batting where they hang over the far rail, to prevent them touching the floor.**

3 **Tension the two side edges of the quilt with a 2.5cm (1in) wide tape, looped over the stretchers or pinned to the side webbing, then pinned in position through the quilt layers. Leave some flexibility in the tensioned layers for ease of stitching – enough to take several running stitches at a time.**

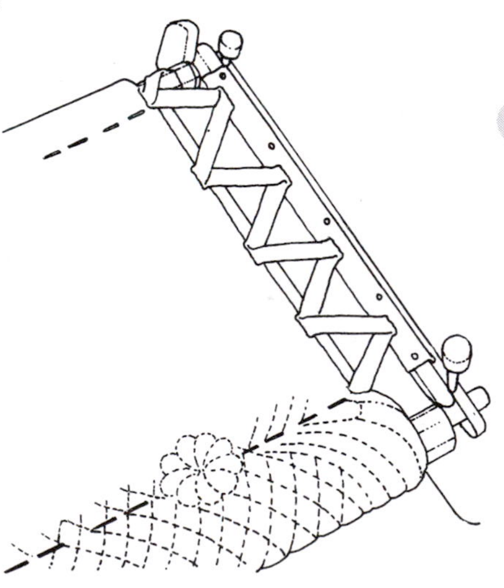

4 **Quilt progressively across the top to the far rail. Remove pins and tapes; loosen the rails and stretchers to roll the completed section on to the near rail, and unroll a new part of the bottom layer. Smooth the batting and quilt top over this as before, then re-pin and re-tape, ready to quilt. Repeat until quilting is completed.**

Quilting hoops

Smooth out the layers and place the inner ring of the hoop under the working area. Unscrew the clamp, and lay the outer hoop on the quilt and over the inner hoop. Ensure that the layers are evenly stretched and are not puckered at the front or back. Tighten the clamp, but leave enough flexibility to allow several stitches to be taken with ease.

Tube frames

To set the assembled layers in a tube frame, smooth them out, and then lay the tube part of the frame under the quilt. Secure the quilt to the frame by fixing the 'grips' over the quilt on all four sides of the frame. Adjust to a flexible tension by sliding the grips on the frame.

Hand quilting

Hand quilting is still the preferred option for many quilters, and to understand why such a time-intensive method remains so popular, we need to consider the differences between the nature of hand-sewn quilting stitches and a machine-sewn straight stitch. Because it interlocks two threads, the machine produces a flat, continuous line stitch.

A hand-sewn running stitch, on the other hand, produces a line of quite different appearance. The quilted line appears as a series of sunken stitches and raised spaces in which the filling lofts up between the stitches. It is this broken, almost puckered line, with its contrasts of light and depth, which gives hand quilting its particular character and a subtlety of line that cannot be reproduced by machine.

Basic skills

The basic techniques of hand quilting are very simple. The aim is to produce even, straight stitches, and the way to do this is to practise until you develop a relaxed, steady rhythm. Thimbles and finger protectors may feel clumsy at first, but it is worth persevering with them. You will find that it also helps to keep several needles in play at the same time, so that you maintain the flow of continuous lines across the work.

The number of stitches taken to a given measurement will vary with the individual and with the thickness of the batting. If this is very thick, it will be impossible to take as many stitches as it would with a very fine batting. What is more important is that the stitches should be of much the same length and evenly spaced throughout.

Starting a thread

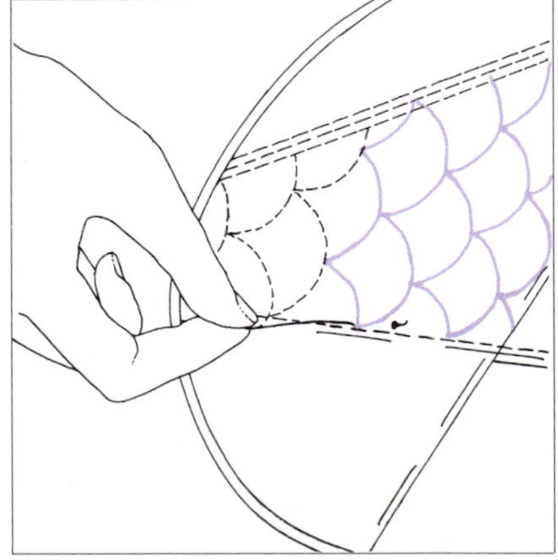

Take a thread about 45cm (18in) long, preferably waxed, with a single knot at the end. Push the needle into the quilt top, about 2cm (¾in) from the line that you intend to quilt, and bring the needle up on the line, without going through the back cover. Pull the thread through until the knot is at the quilt top, then gently pull it through the fabric to bury it in the filling.

The running stitch

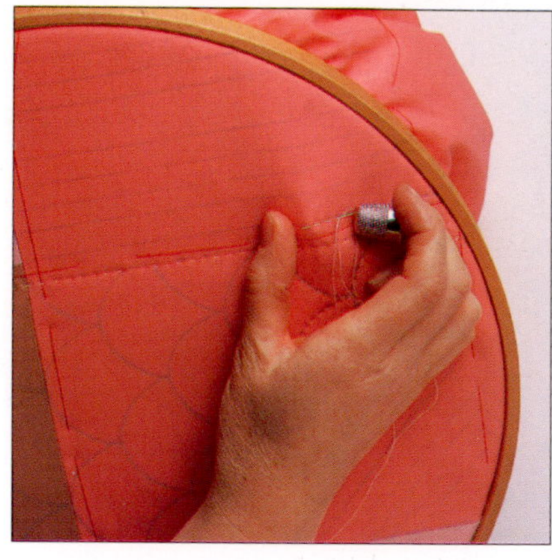

Push the needle tip through the quilt layers until, with the hand below the work, you can draw the needle out through the bottom layer, then guide it back up to the top. Pull the thread through firmly, to make two stitches – one above and one below. With practice, you will be able to take several stitches together by using the thimble on the middle finger of your (top) quilting hand to rock the needle up and down before pulling the thread through. Use the thumb of your quilting hand to press down the fabric ahead of the stitches.

Moving

If you have reached the end of a pattern line but still have sufficient thread to continue, move the needle through the filling to another pattern line. In practice, this can only be done if the line is less than a needle-length away.

Travelling

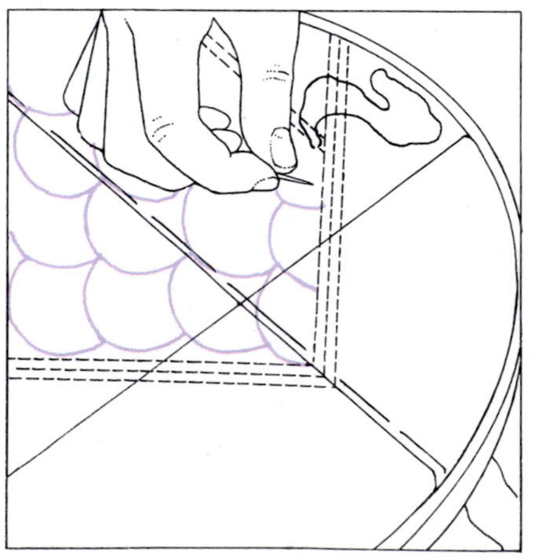

To cover a wider gap, travel the needle to the next quilting line: push the needle through the filling as far as possible in the direction of the new line and through to the quilt top. Pull the needle part way through, then swivel it around and push it, eye first, in the required direction. Push the needle eye part way up through the top, swivel, and repeat until you have reached the next pattern line.

Quilt designs from Allendale and Weardale, two of the most northerly English dales, reached their peak in the late 19th and early 20th centuries. Working in the same style, Lilian Hedley has designed an elegant sateen wholecloth quilt, Echoes of the Past. *Size: 224cm × 224cm (90in × 90in)*

Finishing

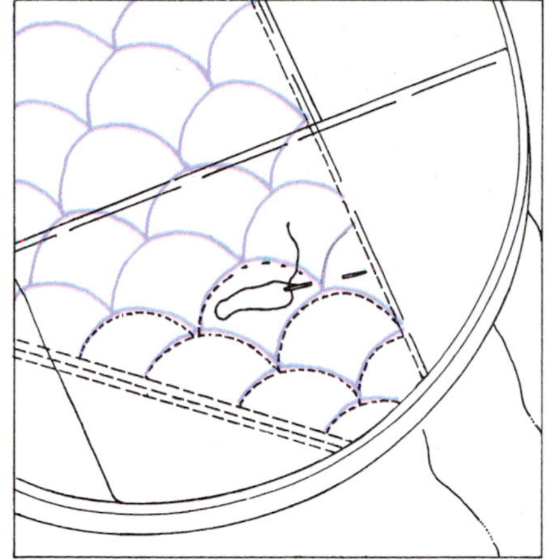

1 When finishing a thread part way along a line, make a back stitch, then run the thread through the filling, taking a few tiny stitches, about 2cm (¾in) apart, along the unstitched line. Run the thread through the filling again, then cut it off. The tiny stitches will be anchored by succeeding stitches along the line.

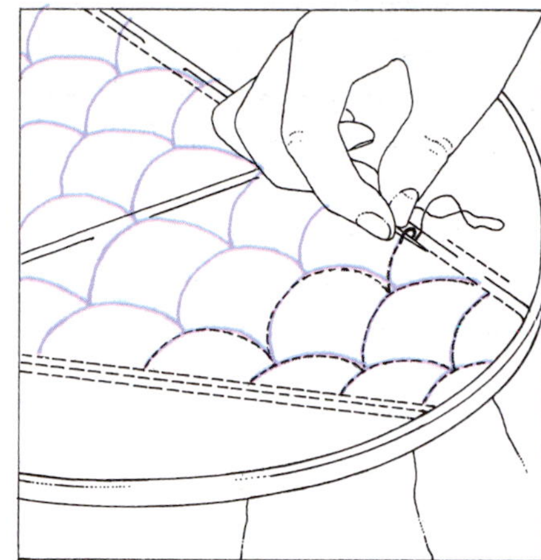

2 At the end of a pattern line, backstitch, bringing the needle up through the hole at the end of the stitch, leaving a small loop. Push the needle through the loop, taking it back down the same hole and through, to anchor in the filling. Run the thread as far as possible through the filling before coming up. Cut the end on the quilt surface.

Quilting curves

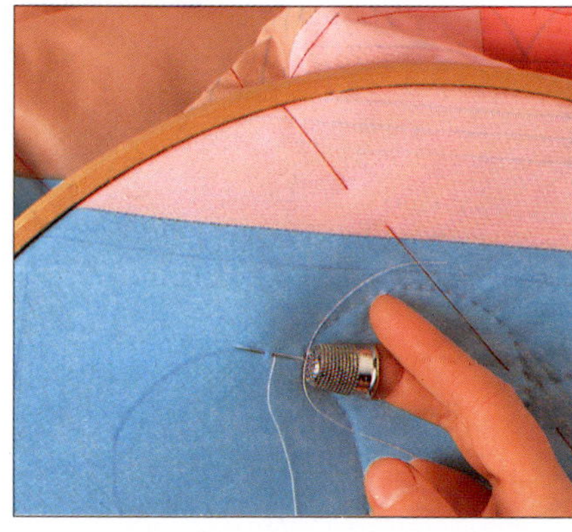

On tightly curved lines, it may be necessary to take only one stitch at a time. When a curve forms both the outline and the inner detail of a pattern – for example, rose petals – quilt it as one line to prevent an angular join where the outer and inner lines meet.

Automatic machining

It goes without saying that quilting by machine is quicker than hand stitching, but it must be stressed that it is essentially different to hand quilting. Whatever stitches and threads are used, the machined line is continuous and flat, in contrast to the broken, lofted line of hand quilting. Because this continuous line depresses the filling more, there is less loft between the stitched lines of machine quilting and none at all between the stitches. If that sounds a bit technical, think of it this way – there are no 'bumps' along a machine-stitched line, only stitches.

With automatic machining, the feed dogs that feed the fabric through the machine are up and functioning. Feed dogs, however, only work on the lowest layer of fabric and, with the three layers of a batted quilt, this results in some differential in the movement of the layers. A means of pushing the top and bottom layers together must be found. This can be achieved in two ways – either by using a machine equipped with a dual

Setting up

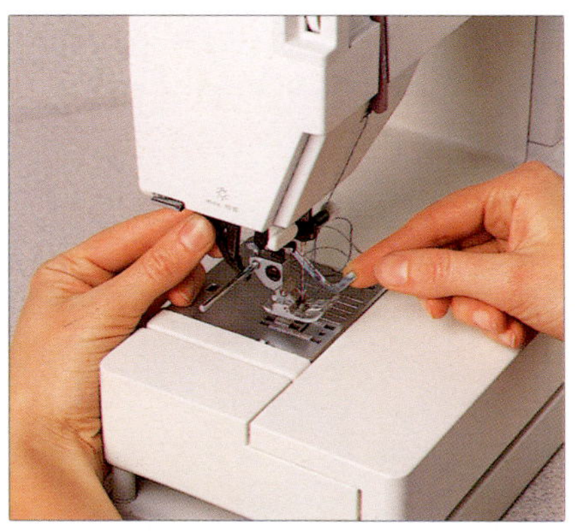

Set your machine for dual feed or fit a walking foot. Choose your stitch and set the machine accordingly; check the tension. For straight stitching, choose a stitch length of approximately eight stitches to every 2.5cm (1in). For grid quilting, fit a quilting bar.

Starting and stopping

1 **For straight stitch, bring both threads to the top surface, to prevent snarling of the bobbin thread, by taking a single stitch manually. Begin forward stitching with the stitch length set at zero and gradually increase over the first 1cm (3/8in) to the required length. To finish a line, reduce the stitch length over the last 1cm (3/8in) down to zero at the end of the line. Snip threads above and below.**

2 **For decorative stitches, again bring both threads to the top surface. Begin and end with a forward stitch, leaving about 15cm (5in) of thread at the top and bottom; the threads can be secured with a needle on the reverse of the quilt when machining is completed.**

This completed sample was first quilted with straight-line quilting, using a quilting bar as the line guide. After this, torn strips were overlaid and stitched, using an automatic decorative stitch and shiny rayon thread.

Turning angles

Slow the speed of stitching as you come close to the angled turn and stop, with the needle down, at the apex. Lift the presser foot and reposition the quilt, ensuring that no sections are dragging against the needle. Continue forward stitching.

feed mechanism, or by fitting an attachment known as a walking foot.

Automatic machining with a straight stitch is suitable for 'quilt-in-the-ditch' patterns, for patterns formed by straight lines and sharp angles, or even for large-scale curved patterns. It is much more difficult, however, to use automatic stitching to quilt curved patterns that require constant movement and changes of direction.

In addition to quilting with a straight stitch, bear in mind that decorative machine stitches can create a variety of textures and original effects on your work.

Free machining

With free machining (see also pages 124–145), the fabric layers are not fed automatically through the machine but are moved by hand. This allows the fabric to move in any direction and at any speed. Free machining is the best way to straight stitch small-scale curvilinear patterns or meander lines, though zigzag stitching can also be worked with this technique.

Successful free machining is an acquired skill. You will require some practice before you are able to follow a line and at the same time maintain an even stitch length, using just your hands to work the fabric through the machine, but it is worth persevering with the techniques. Once mastered, free machining opens up a whole world of decorative machine stitching – as well as enabling you to quilt around curves!

In order to prevent the fabric from being fed through automatically, it is necessary to disengage the feed dogs. The feed dogs can be lowered on most machines, but in some cases there is a plate attachment that can be used to cover the feed dogs so that they do not touch the fabric.

Setting up

Lower or cover the feed dogs; disengage any dual feed mechanism, and fit a darning foot. Check the tension, then set the stitch length to zero to prevent any movement of the feed dogs snagging the lowest layer.

Stitching

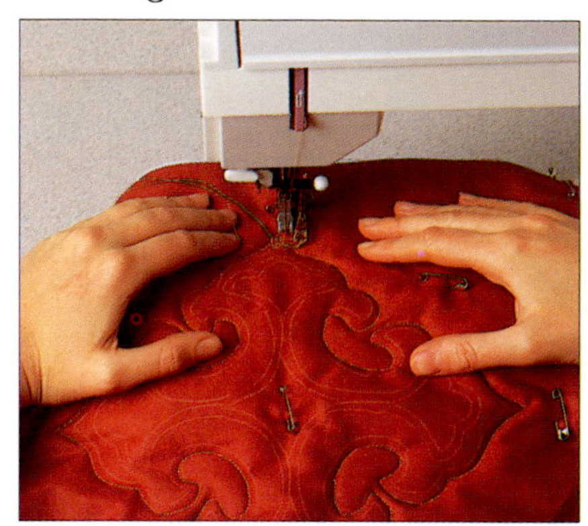

Bring both threads to the top surface. Take several tiny stitches by moving the fabric gently to and fro, to lock the threads. With fingers slightly extended and hands either side of the needle, stitch along the pattern lines, controlling the stitch length by the speed with which you push the fabric. Maintain a steady, fairly high running speed and do not rotate the fabric. Finish with several tiny stitches and trim loose threads.

The oriental feel of Barbara Howell's Hashed *quilt has been created by assembling pieced blocks of multicoloured cotton and polycotton fabrics. These were quilted with automatic and free machine stitches onto a thin polyester batting and a cotton backing. Size: 122cm × 198cm (48in × 78in)*

Quilt-as-you-go

The technique known as quilt-as-you-go is an ideal way to overcome the problem of manipulating a large quilt around the machine. The quilt is broken down into smaller sections of any size or shape; these are quilted individually before being joined together. Quilt-as-you-go is also a popular technique for hand quilting in a hoop or small frame, especially if the work is to be portable, or if the bulk and weight of a large quilt would prove a problem during stitching.

A variety of quilt types – traditional quilts of square or rectangular blocks, strip quilts – can be quilted in this way, especially if the quilt is composed of units within which the patterns are contained. Unless you have had a lot of experience, it is not easy to match up quilting lines from one unit to the next, especially if they are closely spaced. For this reason, finely worked wholecloth quilts cannot be successfully quilted in this way.

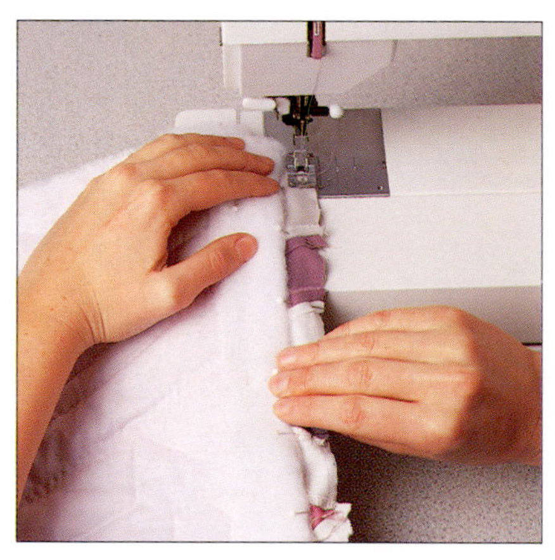

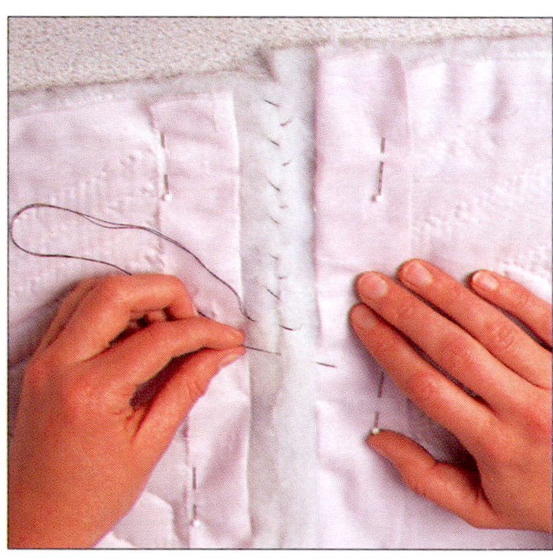

1 **Mark the quilt design and layer each quilt unit in the usual way. Allow *at least* 1cm (3/8in) on each side of the unit for seams. Quilt units separately, by hand or machine, keeping free of the seam allowance. Lay them out on a flat surface in their correct position. Work out a practical joining sequence. Take adjoining units, fold back the batting and bottom layer and, with right sides together, seam the quilt top only. Neaten and press seams.**

2 **Open out the quilt and trim away surplus batting until the batting edges butt against each other. Stitch these together, using a ladder or herringbone stitch. Use a light-coloured thread, though in the quilt illustrated a dark thread has been used for clarity.**

3 **Finally, fold one edge of the unattached bottom layer over the unfolded edge of the adjacent unit and hand sew into position, using either a blind stitch or decorative feather stitch. Add borders and edge the quilt as required.**

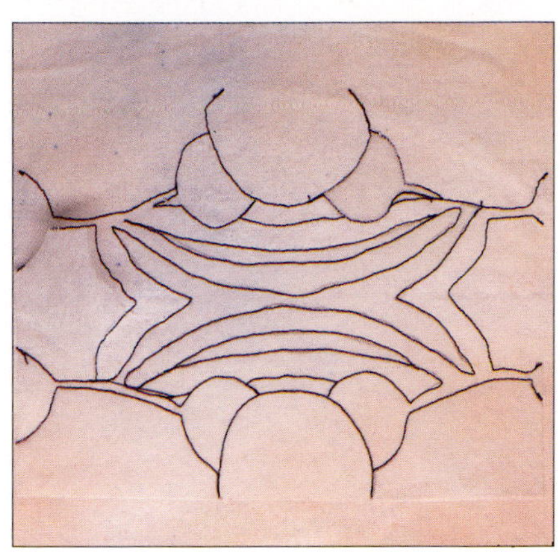

2 With the general sewing foot on, stitch around the design, using straight running stitch. Use normal or slightly shorter than normal stitch length. Free machining may be used, if desired.

stitch, piercing the paper and fabrics. This will transfer the design to the fabrics. After all design lines have been stitched, tear away the paper.

Turn the fabrics to the right side and cut away any excess fabric around the appliqué design. Finish the appliqué from the front (right) side, using free machine or automatic stitches.

Backlit design transfer

Draw the design in very dark felt-tip pen or pencil on lightweight paper, then position the fabric over the paper and shine light through both.

Unless you have a lightbox, the window is likely to be the most convenient light source. Simply tape the design to the window; position the fabric over the design, and tape it to the window. The design may then be clearly seen through the fabric, allowing it to be traced with a tailors' marking pencil or a very hard drawing pencil. If, however, the lines are likely to show through the finished stitching, use dotted lines to reduce the amount of visible pencil.

Photocopy transfers

The development of the modern photocopier has provided embroiderers with yet another method of producing transferable designs and patterns. To transfer a design from the copy paper, make a solvent of one part water to one part white spirit (paint thinner). Add about a teaspoon of liquid detergent.

Protect your working surface with several layers of fabric. Lay the photocopy, print side up, on the surface. With a large watercolour brush, quickly paint the solvent over the surface of the photocopy – a light coating will be sufficient.

Position the fabric (light cotton works best) over the photocopy. Apply a light coat of solvent over the transfer fabric until it adheres to the copy. Do not apply too much solvent – the material must not be sopping wet. Place a few layers of fabric or paper over the transfer fabric, and press with a dry iron set to the hottest temperature. Do not let the hot iron come into contact with any solvent. This method is best used to provide an outline pattern over which dyeing or embroidery techniques can be applied. The transfers are not washable, because the inks are not fast and will run.

Greenhouse, *by Jane Boot, shows a contemporary approach to appliqué, using many different fabrics and other elements, such as paper and photographs, together with machine embroidery.*

INDEX

ACKNOWLEDGEMENTS

Thanks are due to Madeira Threads (UK) Ltd, for generous supplies of hand and machine embroidery threads and soluble fabrics to Julia Barton, Gail Harker, Dorothy Osler and Pauline Brown. Mulberry Silks of Chipping Norton contributed silk threads to Peggy Field and June Linsley, who also received samples of canvas from the Chipping Campden Needlework Centre and Nairn of Salisbury. Freudenberg Nonwovens Ltd (The Vilene Organization), UK, supplied interfacings.

Dorothy Osler also received materials and equipment from Crimple Craft of Harrogate, threads and equipment from Quilt Basics of Cheshunt, fabrics from Liberty, Regent Street, a quilt frame from Philippa Abrahams, a tube frame from R&R Enterprises of Malvern, and fabrics from Piecemakers, Epsom, Surrey.

Pfaff (Britain) Ltd loaned sewing machines, needles and accessories used in the sections on Machine Embroidery and Quilting. Elna Sewing Machines (G.B.) Ltd, Frisster and Rossman Sewing Machines Ltd and Bernina Sewing Machines also loaned machines.

A. West & Partners Ltd contributed Pebeo fabric paints and dyes to Gail Harker.

Finally, the authors would like to thank all those embroiderers and textile artists who have kindly allowed examples of their work to be shown in this book.